# FROM THE ENDS
# OF THE EARTH

Essays in Honor of Joseph Tong & Melvin Loucks on
Theology, Mission and Leadership

**Enoch Wan, Editor**

A Publication to Celebrate the 40th Anniversary of
**INTERNATIONAL THEOLOGICAL SEMINARY**
www.itsla.edu

Western Academic
Publishers

Edited by Enoch Wan

# FROM THE ENDS
# OF THE
# EARTH

Essays in Honor of Joseph Tong & Melvin
Loucks on Theology, Mission, and Leadership

**From the Ends of the Earth: Essays in Honor of Joseph Tong & Melvin Loucks on Theology, Mission and Leadership**

Copyright © 2023 by Enoch Wan and ITS

Published by Western Academic Publishers

**ISBN: 978-1-954692-21-3**

Printed in the United States of America

# Table of
# CONTENTS

## Introduction

## Part I Theology

## Part II Mission

## Part III Leadership

# CONTENTS

## Part IV Interviews of Honorees

## Part V Tributes to Honorees

## Part VI History of ITS

# FOREWORD

International Theological Seminary (ITS) celebrated its 40th anniversary in 2022. As we remembered this significant milestone of the seminary, it was important and meaningful for us to recognize two long-time professors and former presidents, Joseph Tong and Melvin Loucks, who dedicated their lives to teaching and mentoring students at ITS. Hence, we decided to publish this book in honor of our two esteemed colleagues.

Joseph Tong was born in 1941 in Xiamen, China. His father Tong Pai Hu was a businessman whose family was highly regarded by the Qing government, and his mother was Tan Tjien Nio (Indonesian: Dorcas Tanjowati). He is the seventh of ten children. His father passed away when he was very young. Dr. Tong's mother fostered their brothers and sister alone. In 1949, Joseph Tong, with his mother and siblings, migrated to Surabaya, Indonesia, to find a safe and better place during the Chinese Communist Revolution. His mother was a devoted Christian, a woman of prayer. According to Stephen Tong, Joseph's elder brother, "When I was small, the first words I'd hear in the morning were those of my mother while she prayed. She prayed for each of us children by name and asked God to guide us." Thanks to her prayers, all her children went into Christian ministry when they grew up. Many of her sons became pastors. Solomon Tong was the conductor of the Surabaya Symphony Orchestra. Stephen Tong is a pastor and evangelist well-known throughout Southeast Asia and China.

Tong obtained his B.A. in Philosophy B.D. and Th. M. at Calvin College and Seminary; Ph.D. (Educational Psychology) at USC; and MBA (Church Administration) at Graduate Theological Foundation, Indiana. He was involved in Theological Education for over 40 years. He began serving as President of ITS in 1995 and stepped down from the Presidency in 2008. He also served as President of Bandung Theological Seminary, Indonesia. Later, he was elected Chairman of the Board of Trustees of ITS (2010-2012) and took the office of Chancellor of ABDI Allah Seminary in Indonesia and China Aletheia Theological Seminary. Even after he left these positions, he never stopped teaching and preaching. He continues to teach at ITS and preaches at local churches. Until recently, he was a frequent speaker at conferences and seminars in various countries and served as visiting professor at various seminaries and universities in the United States, China, Brazil, and Indonesia.

Tong has written many articles and books, among others: Basic Christian Beliefs; A Reflection and Rebuilding of Christian Beliefs; On Being a Servant without Shame; Collection of Theological Treatises; Philosophical and Ethical Contemplations, Theological Contemplations, A Study of the First Born Rights, and hundreds of articles and treatises. Mostly in Chinese and Indonesian, they may be downloaded from most public websites: like www.google.com.

Melvin Loucks was born in the modern Democratic Republic of Congo to missionary parents. Due to instabilities in the country, his family returned to the US, but his passion in life remained the world mission.

He began his academic career at Westmont College, where he completed his Bachelor of Arts in History. During his time on campus, he remained very active, participating in the Student Government Body and in the Volunteer Ministry organization.

Upon graduation, Loucks went on to complete his Master of Divinity at Trinity Evangelical Divinity School, Master of Theology in Historical Theology, and Ph.D. in Systematic Theology at Fuller Theological Seminary. Loucks' career has been divided between his work in academia and his service within his church. Loucks has over 40 years of experience working in education and has been working as a professor teaching theological studies. Loucks has worked at International Theological Seminary since 1982. That is for 39 years—one year after the seminary was founded! He has served ITS longer than any faculty and staff. ITS owes greatly to his lifetime dedication and service. He was the president of ITS from 2010-2013. Before then, he served as the academic dean. Although he retired a few years ago, he never stopped teaching. As Professor Emeritus of Systematic Theology, he continues to teach and mentors our students.

When not teaching at the seminary, he served as an associate pastor with the Emmanuel Evangelical Free Church and on the Board of Directors of the nonprofit organization called "Global Teaching Network," which he founded in 1996. Throughout his career, Loucks traveled the world, giving seminars, lectures, and training, and helped those entering into ministry in the areas of leadership, conflict management, and ministerial development.

Festschrift literally means celebration writing in German. In academia, a **Festschrift** is a book honoring a respected person, primarily an academic, and presented during their lifetime. It generally takes the form of an edited volume containing contributions from the honoree's colleagues, former pupils, and friends.

Our Festschrift Committee decided to title this book "From the Ends of the Earth" because while the ends of the earth are the destination of mission and evangelism, they are where Christianity is now growing rapidly and is becoming a fertile ground for new ways of theologizing and doing ministry. Intense contextualization is taking place where the Gospel reaches and where the Word of God meets cultures. Each essay in this volume is a thoughtful reflection on theology, mission, and leadership born out of each author's own ministry and teaching experience, and research. Loucks and Tong have dedicated their lives to teaching and raising leaders from the majority world for the global church. I hope this volume is a fitting tribute to their lifelong legacy of ministry around the world.

This book approaches the topics of theology, mission, and leadership from a global perspective. It consists of essays contributed by scholars and practitioners who minister and teach in a majority-world context or are familiar with that perspective. The essays will include ministry trends, leadership, missiological models, and theological viewpoints that emerge from the majority world context.

I would like to thank the Festschrift Committee members, Priscilla Adoyo, Ei Meren Gusto, Susan Liu, Patrick Nasongo, Joseph Shao, and Enoch Wan, for the gracious offering of their time and service to serve on the Committee and for making the publication of the book possible. Especially, I thank Enoch Wan, who undertook the editing of the book and guided us through the publication process. I am deeply grateful to all the contributors of the chapters. They've considered it a great joy to contribute their scholarly work to this volume despite their busy schedule. It has been my great privilege to work with the great scholars, teachers, and pastors. Our collective work exemplifies excellence in theological scholarship, and it will serve as a valuable resource for many ministry practitioners and academicians.

I thank the ITS Board for their enthusiastic support of this project and many friends of ITS who believe in our mission and have given so generously to ITS and for this project.

ITS graduates are the fruit and result of the seminary's ministry, written not with ink but with the Spirit of the living God, not on tablets of stone but on tablets of human hearts (2 Cor 3:2-3). We give all the glory and honor to God for the transformative ministry ITS has been able to carry on through its alumni/ae for forty years.

Dallas, August 22, 2023                                James S. Lee

# CONTRIBUTORS

### Lami Rikwe Ibrahim Bakari
Dr. Bakari graduated from ITS with a ThM degree and received her PhD degree in Intercultural Studies from Trinity International University. She is currently the head of the Department of Mission at the ECWA Theological Seminary in Jos, Nigeria. Dr. Bakari and her husband have fostered many children, and five of them are married and have become parents.

### Patrick Nasongo
Dr. Nasongo is an Associate Professor at Virginia Christian College. He is an ITS alumnus and earned his PhD degree in Biblical Studies from Piedmont International University in Winston-Salem, North Carolina. Dr. Nasongo is married to his wife Sylvia and blessed with two children.

### Joseph Too Shao
Dr. Shao is a President Emeritus of the Biblical Seminary of the Philippines. He received his PhD degree in Hebraic and Cognate Studies from Hebrew Union College in Cincinnati Ohio. Dr. Shao and his wife Dr. Rosa Shao have three grown children.

### Enoch Wan
Dr. Wan is the Professor of Intercultural Studies, Director of three doctoral programs at Western Seminary in Portland, Oregon: PhD, EdD and DIS (Doctor of Intercultural Studies). He received his PhD degree in Anthropology at the State University of New York at Stony Brook. He was past president of EMS (Evangelical Missiological Society: two terms) and founder of the multi-lingual e-Journal www.GlobalMissiology.

### David McKinley
Dr. McKinley is an Associate Professor of Practical Theology at ITS. He is a Canadian who has earned a ThD degree from the University of Santo Tomas in the Philippines. Dr. McKinley lives in Monterey Park, CA with his lovely wife Laura.

### James S. Lee

Dr. Lee has been the President of ITS since 2014. He is also an Associate professor of Old Testament at ITS. Dr. Lee earned his PhD degree in Old Testament from Union Presbyterian Seminary. He and his wife Dr. Charlene Jin Lee have three children, and they currently reside in Dallas, Texas.

### Michael Woodcock

Dr. Woodcock is the Professor of Hebrew and Old Testament at ITS as well as a Pastor at the First Baptist Church North Hollywood. He received his DPhil degree from Fuller Theological Seminary. Dr. Woodcock and his wife Kathy have been living in Southern California and have recently become grandparents.

### Finney Premkumar

Finney is a Lecturer of Apologetics at ITS and the President of Truth Matters International. He is an active speaker at many prestigious universities around the world and has made a great impact by spreading the gospel truth and responding to voices and theories that challenge Christianity. Finney currently resides in Monrovia, CA.

### Jae-Suk Lee

Dr. Jae-Suk Lee is an Assistant Professor of Bible and Mission and the Director of Graduate Studies at ITS. He received his PhD degree from Fuller Theological Seminary. Dr. Jae-Suk Lee and his wife Eun Sook Han live in Los Angeles, CA. They have two sons.

## Other writers and translators:

### Ei Meren Gusto

Ei Meren is the Communication Director and Assistant to the President at ITS. She received her BA degree in Biblical Studies from Biola University. Ei Meren is married to Josh Gusto, and they currently live in Norwalk, CA.

**Mya Mansoor**

Mya Mansoor is a Freelance Copywriter at Mya Mansoor Copywriting. She received her BA degree in English from Biola University. In her free time, she enjoys exploring the beauty of the United States in a cozy van alongside her husband, Shelby Hands, a well-regarded travel photographer. They currently reside in Austin, TX.

**Li Hua Gu**

Dr. Gu is the Dean of Chinese Program at ITS and received her DMin degree from ITS in 2023. Dr. Gu currently lives in Irvine, CA with her husband Shouming Zhang, who is the Director of Church and Community Engagement at ITS.

**Susan Liu**

Susan is the Librarian and Director of International Student Services at ITS. She earned her MA degree in Library and Information Studies from the University of Wisconsin-Madison. Susan lives in Arcadia, CA with her father Wing Kan Liu, who worked as a translator at the Hong Kong Government Secretariat for 27 years and kindly offers help to this project.

# PART I

# THEOLOGY

# CHAPTER 1

# THEOLOGICAL EDUCATION AS MISSION

by Joseph Shao, PhD

## Introduction

Rev. Dr. Joseph Tong is my good mentor and respectable friend. I have had the privilege of knowing him for more than 40 years. Upon learning about service in my honor to celebrate and commemorate my work at the Biblical Seminary of the Philippines (BSOP) for more than 30 years, he made sure to fly in to attend the event on May 30, 2019. It was indeed a sweet surptwo childrenrise to have him with us as my wife Rosa and I officially retired from the seminary that we loved and served. We treasure his guidance and friendship.

As my mentor, I learned from him how to be a pastor-scholar in any setting, whether serving in a church or at a seminary. As a scholar-pastor, we need to prepare ourselves at work and at play. Since God is the giver of wisdom, we are but the instruments of his grace and mercy. We need to be his channels of blessings through our life and profession. Upon his invitation, I have often taught at the International Theological Seminary (ITS) as a visiting professor. Dr. Tong in turn has come to our seminary to teach for our students at BSOP. He too has a lot of ministries in his home country in Indonesia. He also invited me to serve at the Bandung Theological Seminary, where he has served for many years as her President. As I rubbed shoulders with him, I have learned a lot from him through his lectures in a classroom and his authentic action outside the classroom. Because of his constant mentorship, I have been invited by many seminaries to serve as a visiting professor. His passion to inspire others, to read, and to think through tough questions, is something I untiringly have learned from him.

As a friend, Dr. Tong has inspired me with his enormous vision and gigantic heart. As the president of ITS, already an accredited member of the Association of Theological Schools in the United States and Canada (ATS), he even applied for accredited membership in the Asia Theological Association (ATA). This shows his awareness and advancement in his thinking that Asia, as the Global South, is the place where theological education started (specifically in West Asia) through the teaching of Jesus to his disciples. Theological Education is a mission and needs to be re-emphasized again. If theological seminaries are strong in the training of pastors and educators, churches surely will have healthy and vibrant pastors and educators. With his commitment, he has equipped lots of senior and younger leaders in the big country in East Asia.

As a theological educator serving in California, he is instrumental in assisting and helping other Asian seminaries in California to become better educational institutions. Indeed Dr. Tong is a global leader, and a godly exemplary servant of the Lord!

With his theological and educational background, he is one of the leaders who has helped set up the way how pastors can be educated, either by coming to ITS, or being educated right in their context. His love for the students from the Majority World resulted in raising many key leaders in Asia and Africa. They have become strategic theological educators in Asia and Africa as the president and dean of important seminaries. This article is dedicated to Rev. Dr. Joseph Tong for his service. I thank God for his contribution to the Kingdom of God through ITS and beyond ITS.

## The Purposeful Aspect of Theological Education

The word "theology" comes from two Greek words, *theos* ("God") and *logos* ("word"). The study of theology is to know God and make him known holistically. In seminary, we have at least four areas that a student needs to study. Biblical studies focus on the interpretation of scriptures. Church history studies the history of Christianity and the way the Christian Church has developed since its inception. Systematic theology addresses issues in an orderly manner and formulates the doctrines of Christian faith. Practical theology is a study of theology in a way that is intended to make it useful and applicable. Nonetheless, the most important theological education is not the area of studies, but the focus to know God and let him be known!

"Theological Education" is a noun, but the purpose of education is to introduce to the theological community the great Almighty God as revealed in the Bible. Moreover, it is to edify the learner about how he and she can experience the Almighty God, our Lord, in an accurate, coherent, and relevant way. I would like to propose the following themes and related theology that we need to emphasize in theological education.

## The Greatness of God and the Theology of Glory

The Torah, the Pentateuch, starts with a marvelous revelation on the greatness of God. "In the beginning, God created the heavens and the earth" (Gen. 1:1). The introductory and declarative phrase, "in the beginning," is not the beginning of God but the beginning of everything related to creation. The concise statement identifies the Creator-God and his creation. It also declares who is in-charge of the origin of the world. The Creator-God is the one who creates the heavens and the earth! The verb "create" (*bara'*) never occurs in a context in which materials are mentioned. This implies that our Almighty God creates the world out of nothing. Theology proper should start with the greatness of God.

Compared with the Ancient Near Eastern myth such as *Enuma Elish*, known as "the Babylonian Genesis," Genesis 1:1 portrays, along with other Old Testament texts,[1] that there is only one God who is the Lord of heaven and earth. *Enuma Elish* describes the victory of Marduk, the god of Babylon over Apsu and Tiamat. Because of this victory, Marduk is installed as king among the gods. In contrast with the Babylonian creation account, Genesis 1:1 presents the greatness of God. He is the Creator-God of the universe. He does not need to fight with other gods. He is the only God! The two creation accounts display God's grace. In the first account (Gen. 1:1-2:3), he gives the "world" to human beings after he finishes his creation by dividing the waters and furnishing its resources. As he finishes his creation, God creates man and woman in his image and likeness. He gives human beings their cultural mandate to be his representative on earth, and to be his steward taking good care of the environment (Gen. 1:28). In the second creation account (Gen. 2:4-25), he forms human beings from the ground. With his breath

---

[1] The worldview of Old Testament differs from the Ancient Near Eastern myths. Instead of portraying God's initial victory in a cosmic pre-creation battle, the Almighty God has ongoing power over creation and presence in the world (Ps. 74:12-17; 93:1-4; Isa. 51:9-10).

he gives human beings a life to live. He gives human beings freedom to choose (Gen 2:15), and a spouse to enjoy life together (Gen. 2:20-25).

Indeed, the psalmist contemplates with awe the majesty of God through God's creation, "The heavens declare the glory of God, and the sky above proclaims his handiwork" (Ps. 19:1). The peculiar revelation of God's glory in nature testifies to his greatness. The heavens and sky above communicate knowledge about God, especially his glory and his creative ability. It is not a natural theology, trying to argue from nature to God. The declaration is a statement seeing the gloriousness of God through the eyes of faith as the psalmist encounters his Creator-God.

In the Global South, there is no need to learn apologetics on how to prove the existence of God because ordinary people may believe in many different gods. Asians would never doubt the existence of powerful gods. Sometimes they may think that there are many gods for them to fear. But there is a great need to learn how to introduce, believe and experience the biblical God. Theology in the Global South should start with the greatness of God, presenting the gloriousness of God. He is the one who gives honor and an important role to human beings. As the Creator-God, he not only owns his creation and creatures, but also takes good care of them (Ps. 104). No gods can be compared with the biblical God of creation (Isa. 40:12-20). Instead of fear, the greatness of the Almighty God brings us to worship him in spirit and truth (John 4:23).

## The Creation of Man and Woman and the Theology of Walking

The high point of God's creative activity is the creation of man and woman, in Genesis 1:26-27, in God's image and likeness. While these terms "image" and "likeness" are interchangeable in the OT, they provide slightly different nuances. "Image" refers primarily to a concrete image, a definite shape. "Likeness" is more abstract — a resemblance, or a likeness. The image of God sets human beings apart from other creatures. Because of this image and likeness, God can have closer relationship with human beings than with animals.

In the second creation account, it flashes back to the sixth day of creation and focuses on how God the potter, molds Adam from the ground and makes him different from the animals in materials with his spiritual breath from God (Gen. 2:7). In contrast to the first account of creation, the second account describes in detail, how God gives man a delightful garden of Eden full of fruit trees, rivers, gold and gemstones. God also carefully designs a woman, a suitable helper for man. He presents her to the man as his partner.

Theology of walking can be seen with God's noteworthy action at the garden of Eden. After the creation of man and woman, God walks in the garden (Gen. 3:8). The "walking" portrays his divine action wanting to have fellowship with human beings. The verb used here describes his walking back and forth, iterative action.[2] As a response to God's love, Enoch "walked with God" (Gen. 5:22, 24). The repetitive phrase describing Enoch's action of walking with God is the reason why he did not die. It also expresses "a life of faithfulness and obedience to God."[3] Likewise, Noah "walked with God" (Gen. 6:9). "When Abram was ninety-nine years old, the LORD appeared to him and said, "I am God Almighty; walk[4] before me faithfully and be blameless" (Gen. 17:1). The command from the Lord is for Abraham to faithfully follow him. Indeed, both Abraham and Isaac are God's faithful servants walking with him (Gen. 24:40; 48:15).

The verb "walk" (*halak*) is a very common verb in the Hebrew Bible. It appears more than 1500x to express an act or process of living. It describes men and women living out their days in obedience to the divine principles. In the early days of Solomon, he "showed his love for the Lord by walking (*hlk*) according to the statues of his father David..." (1 Kgs. 3:3). Likewise, The Chroniclers present the life of Jehoshaphat as walking in God's command (2 Chron. 7:14).

Among the blessings for those who obey the Lord are his gifts of rain and good harvest (Lev. 26:4-5), and the gift of peace with no defeats or famine (Lev. 25:6-10). The gift of his presence is listed as he lives among them and makes his dwelling with them (Lev. 26:11) including his action of "walking" (Lev 26:12).[5] This action of

---

[2] The Hebrew verb is hithpael.

[3] John Sailhamer, "Genesis" in *Expositor's Bible Commentary.* Revised Edition (Gen Ed. Temper Longman III and David E. Garland; Grand Rapids, MI: Zondervan, 2008), 108.

[4] Just as Genesis 3:8 is hithpael, the verb in Genesis 17:1 is hithpael, wanting Abram to continue iteratively walk before the Lord.

[5] The Hebrew verb is hithpael. It shows the iterative active of God caring for his people who obeys him!

walking iteratively means that he will continually show his presence through walking with those who obey him. The action of "walking" of the Lord includes his protection as the people respond to his desire of holiness (Deut. 23:14).

In the Global South, the population is growing at a fast pace. With the virtual environment happening in every continent, the importance of human beings could become an issue. God's creation of man and woman in his image and likeness should be at the forefront of our discussion. Moreover, the theology of God's initiative of wanting to have a fellowship with human beings through "walking" to show his very presence, emphasizes his purpose in the creation of man and woman. He could be disappointed with Adam and Eve. But as Enoch, along with the patriarchs and other Old Testament respond to his love, they walk with him. The Lord, in turn, continues to walk with his people as they follow him. Walking could be a very common action in our communities today, but it is a healthy action. Walking as partners requires a common goal with similar spirit and goal (cf. Amos 3:3). God is not only the creator, but through his very presence of walking, he provides and protects!

## The Call of Servant and the Theology of Deliverance

The call of Moses from the burning bush is an important biblical story and very important for those who have a desire to serve the Lord. This call narrative shows God's concern with his suffering people. It seems God is silent for a long span of time. But he is always there and is very much concerned about their suffering (Exod. 2:23-25). The call narrative starts with God initiating the call, "Moses, Moses!" (Exod. 3:3). The name of Moses is repeated twice to show the urgency of the message (cf. 1 Sam. 3:10). With this call, the Lord would like to show his plan of deliverance. He would like Moses to be the messenger of his word of hope to his people.

The Lord expresses the reason why he is calling Moses. The encounter of Moses with God happens in a mountain in the wilderness. The dialogue between God and Moses focuses first on who God is. He is "the God of Abraham, the God of Isaac, and the God of Jacob" (Exod. 3:6). He has seen the misery and is very passionate about the suffering of his people. He has heard the crying of the people, and he knows what his people are enduring in Egypt. He would like to intervene and deliver them (Exod. 3:7-8). The need for deliverance and God's solution is to commission Moses and send him to Pharoah to be an emissary to bring Israel out of Egypt (Exod. 3:9-10).

Who is delivering? God or Moses? Moses is an instrument in and through whom, to redeem God's people. God waits for Moses to obey him. Between Exodus 3:4 to 4:17, God speaks to Moses thirteen times. Although Almighty God certainly can overpower Moses, he still waits for Moses to obey.[6] God takes initiative, and he uses his servant to accomplish his purpose. Moses is called to be God's servant (`ebed, Exod. 14:31; Num. 12:7; Deut. 34:5; Josh. 1:3, 7; 9:24) who accomplishes God's purpose of redemption. It is an honorific title describing Moses' relationship with God.

Theology of deliverance is very much needed in today's world. The year 2022 is known to be "a year of suffering" with war, Covid-19, climate change and economic crisis. The United Nations projects that it would need "$51.5 billion to help 230 million of the world's most vulnerable people in nearly 70 countries in 2023."[7] The omnipresent God sees the misery of the people, and he hears their cries, and he knows their needs. With the suffering of the people, we need many "Moses" to deliver them out of bondage. The theology of God's deliverance starts with his call. He wants to deliver his people out of suffering. Just like the commissioning of Moses, God waits for his servants to respond and to join the mission to serve him. We need God's servants in the public square to serve him. We need pastors to faithfully shepherd his flock. But as we answer his call, we know that God's redemptive plan will work through each of his servants. Just like Moses of the Old Testament, each one of us will carry his message to the world.

## The need of Nurturing and the Theology of God's People

Moses hears the call of God at Mount Sinai, and now he brings the people to Mount Sinai. This fulfills what God has promised in Exodus 3:12, that is for the people to worship him. They arrive three

---

[6] Terence E. Fretheim, *Exodus*. Interpretation (Louisville: Westminster John Knox Press, 2010), 67.

[7] https://gazettengr.com/2022-year-of-suffering-solidarity-expected-in-2023-un-official/. Cited on June 20, 2023.

months after they left Egypt (Exod. 19:1). They leave this area "on the twentieth day of the second month of the second year" (Num. 10:11). In one year's time, fifty-nine chapters of Scripture are given to his people (Exod. 19-40; Lev. 1-27; Num. 1-10). Why use so many chapters to record the lives of the Israelites in their route to the land of promise? The essential reason is to nurture their faith in God. As the people of God came out of Egypt, with so many gods, they needed to receive wholesome training at Mount Sinai.

On one hand, reaching Mount Sinai is important to prove that God has indeed sent Moses. As his people, they are beneficiaries of God's activity in Egypt, carrying upon the eagles' wings (Exod. 19:4). On the other hand, it is for the people to receive instructions from the Lord. It is for them to know their important roles as God's treasured possession, a kingdom of priests and a holy nation (Exod. 19:5). This is the message of God to his people. As God's "treasured possession" (Deut. 7:6; 14:2; 26:18), they are God's valuable property and distinct treasure set aside with a distinct purpose. As "a kingdom of priests," the people are set apart for service with free access to God's presence. They are to act as God's representative. They are to live out the teachings of God's Word, with real life application matching their faith with action. The original purpose of the priestly role is delayed until in New Testament times when all believers are called to this role (1 Pet. 2:9; Rev 1:6; 5:10; 20:6). The "holy nation" designates Israel as people set apart from other nations to belong to God. It is a time of nurturing of their faith in God.

The theology of people is a theology that emphasizes the role of God's people in God's kingdom. God's people should have God's character in the world. We live in the world, but we do not belong to this world. Deliverance originates from God's grace; obedience and faithfulness should be the people's response of gratitude. As God's chosen people, royal priesthood and holy nation, a people belonging to God, we become a blessing undertaking this role.

## The Missional Aspect of Theological Education

Theological Education is not an end in and of itself. It is an integral part of the wider ministry of the church. At times, students think that after their first degree, they should continue to study till they reach the most advanced degrees. The outcome of equipping in a theological institution has its missional aspect. I would like to use God's covenant with his people in the Old Testament to present the missional aspect of theological education.

## Channeling God's Blessings and Abrahamic Covenant: from Enjoying to Teaching.

When God calls Abraham (Abram, as he was originally known) out of Ur to the land of promise, he makes a covenant with Abraham providing him with many blessings such as the promised land, the promise of descendants, and the promise of blessing and redemption. In Genesis 12:1-3, it is recorded:

> 1 The LORD had said to Abram, "Go from your country, your people and your father's household to the land I will show you. 2 I will make you into a great nation, and I will bless you; I will make your name great, and you will be a blessing. 3 I will bless those who bless you, and whoever curses you I will curse.

The unconditional nature of the covenant is recorded in Genesis 15. God binds the covenant to himself by moving between halves of the animals. The rite of circumcision for Abraham's male descendants is a sign and seal of God's promise (Gen. 17:9-14). The promises of Abrahamic covenant are given again to Isaac (Gen. 26:2-5), and Jacob (Gen. 28:13-15). Abraham's descendants enjoy God's blessings.

The Abrahamic covenant is not only a blessing to his descendants to become a great nation, but it is also a blessing to others. The passive verb of "be blessed" of Genesis 12:3 (see also Gen. 18:18; 28:14) is explained by the New Testament writers to show that the covenant is a blessing to others (Acts 3:25; Gal. 3:8). Aside from being a man of faith, exchanging the unknown for the known path that God wants Abraham to follow, the channeling of blessings is an important spiritual aspect of the Abrahamic covenant. God's purpose of blessing Abraham is to bless the families of the world.

The missional goal of theological education is to be God's channel of blessings. It is not just an ordinary blessing for us to enjoy, but a blessing to create a community that is morally and socially distinctive, committed to righteousness and justice. [8] Abraham set as a good example in praying for Lot who lives in a corrupt world of Sodom and Gomorrah (Gen. 18:20-22). The reason for calling Abraham and using him as a blessing, is for him to "direct his children and his household after him to keep the way of the Lord by doing what is right and just" (Gen. 18:19). Notice right here that it is directed internally ("keep the way of the Lord"), with an end view that Abraham and his household will do "what is right and just." The teaching purpose is an expansion of God's desire in Abrahamic narratives, wanting him to "walk before me and be blameless" (Gen. 17:1). Abraham's walking with God sets a good example for him to teach his household. The fulfillment of God's purpose in Abraham as a blessing to the world is for him to first manage his own household. He is called not only to teach about God, but to instruct the people about the ethical character of God.[9]

Theological education, therefore, is missionally focused on ethical teaching. As our students are enjoying their studies, faculty and students ought to focus on the missional aspect of teaching. As our students are equipped with knowledge and living out their learning, Abraham with his covenant is a good reminder to be God's channel of blessings. The transformational teaching mandate starts with our own life practicing righteousness and justice before our God! In the chaotic post-truth era, as God's redeemed leaders of the church, our lives before him should be a good teaching model. We need to intentionally teach to our own household and descendants, as we channel out to the greater community.

### Affirming God's steadfast love and the Davidic Covenant: from Longing to Affirming.

The Davidic covenant in 2 Samuel 7 emphasizes the Lord's faithfulness to David's descendants in showing his steadfast love to them even when they are unfaithful. This seems to be a tension between a call to obedience of the book of Deuteronomy and the unconditional nature of the Davidic covenant. If Israel breaks the

---

[8] Christopher J. H.. Wright, "Theological Education as Mission," in *"Be Focused...Use Common Sense...Overcome Excuses and Stupidity...:Essays on Holistic Biblical Ministries,"* Festschrift in Honor of Dr. Manfred Waldemar Kohl (Bonn: Culture and Science Publ. 2022), 154.

[9] Ibid. 155.

covenant, the Lord may punish her rebelliousness, but the covenant is never annulled. Compared with what is recorded in Leviticus 26 and Deuteronomy 27 and 28, 2 Samuel 7 presents the unbounding grace of God, the long-term commitment of God to David and his household. Although the word "covenant" (*berit*) cannot be found in Nathan's utterance to David, it is used later as God's commitment to David and his descendants (2 Sam. 23:5; 1 Kgs. 8:33; Pss. 89:3, 28, 34; 132:12; Jer. 33:21). It is God's steadfast love to David and his descendants.

David as a candidate to become a king of Israel is presented as "a man after his (the Lord's) own heart" (1 Sam. 13:14). The discussion between David, Nathan and the Lord about a house (*bayit*) is the reason for the giving of the Davidic covenant. In this covenant, the Lord gives a series of promises (2 Sam. 7:8-17). Firstly, God promises the preeminence of David's power and fame (2 Sam. 7:8-9). Secondly, rest will be given as they have a land that is no longer under pressure from others (2 Sam 7:10-11a). Thirdly, God will "establish a house" (*bayit*), a permanent reign of David's descendants (2 Sam. 7:11b-13). The Lord has made an unconditional promise. Fourthly, a promise of father-son relationship for his descendants means that God may punish him for wrongdoing, but he will never, never be rejected. The Lord's steadfast love (*hesed*) "will never be taken away" (2 Sam. 7:14-17). Solomon acknowledges God's steadfast love to his father David as he starts his reign (1 Kgs. 3:6). Indeed, God has shown his "faithful love" to David and it is the reason why all who are thirsty can come and seek him (Isa. 55:3).

In the heartfelt response of David to the covenant is his prayer. It consists of his gratitude to God's favor (2 Sam. 7:18-21), his doxology on what God has done (2 Sam 7:22-24) and his prayer for fulfillment of God's promise (2 Sam. 7:24-29). In David's prayer, he asks whether this is "the usual way of dealing with man" (2 Sam. 7:19; literally, "the law for man" [*torat ha'adam*]).

The significant reason for the Davidic covenant is David's initial passion to build a "house" (*bayit*; 2 Sam. 7:1) for the Lord. But the Lord in turn would like to build his "family," literally his "house" (*bayit*; 2 Sam. 7:11, 16). David is thankful to God that he will build his "family," Seven times in his prayer (2 Sam. 7:18, 19, 25, 26, 27, 29 [2X]). David is confident that his "family" will be great in the future as God promises. David is affirming God's steadfast love for his family.

The Lord has promised the "forever" (2 Sam. 7:13, 16) nature of David's descendants. As we study the Old Testament history, David's descendants sat on the throne despite their sins and wrongdoings. The Lord has given two tribes to the Judahite kings. The missional goal of theological education is not only to long for God's steadfast love, affirming what he has done to David's family, it is also to see and affirm how God's steadfast love continues to manifest in the lives of those who are serving his "house." This paradigm of God's caring for his servants' "family" is an encouragement for those who are and will be serving the Lord.

The missional goal of theological education is to emphasize the privilege of serving the Lord. In David's prayer, it really shows the greatness of God and the insignificance of David. The Lord has honored his servant beyond measure. Aside from emphasizing the biblical text in theological education, testaments of how God uses and blesses modern servants of the Lord in the churches and seminaries should be shared and declared.[10]

## Contemplating on God's Work and the New Covenant: from Arrogance to Submissiveness

The prophecy of the new covenant of Jeremiah (Jer. 31:31-34) is unique in the Old Testament. It is the deepest insight of God's desire for his people. The making of the new covenant does not imply that the previous covenant is already annulled. But that the Lord through the prophet recognizes the necessity to re-new the relationship with his people, so that his people continue to keep their side of the relationship with him. The new covenant is written into the wills of God's people.

The old covenant that God establishes with his people at Sinai requires the people of God to recognize the Lord as the sovereign God (Exod. 19:1-24:11), and to obey to the stipulations of the covenant (Jer. 11:1-11). Failure results in judgment, whereas obedience brings blessings. The Lord God desires to have this type of relationship with his people (Exod. 6:7; Jer. 7:23; 11:4; 24:7). The

---

[10] The reason for this Festschrift is not only to celebrate the accomplishments of Rev. Dr. Joseph Tong, it is also to testify how the Lord has used him in his kingdom. It is a way to glorify the Lord through the life of Dr. Tong.

Lord needs to write the teaching of Moses into the mind of the people, circumcise their hearts, or give them a new mind (Deut. 30:6; Ezek. 36:26). He will bring about the necessary changes in people's inner nature (Jer. 31:33). The beauty of the new covenant is to restore their relationship with the Lord as their God and their position as his people. The beauty of the new covenant is that the Lord "will forgive their wickedness and will remember their sins no more" (Jer. 31:34).

The promise of the new covenant finds partial fulfillment in the Second Temple community with their commitment to the Lord. Before the exile, Old Testament prophets keep reminding the people to keep their commitment to the Lord and put aside worship of other gods. After the exile, during the time of Ezra and Nehemiah, they live more consistently with their faith. But once a spiritual leader is not in their midst, they need renewal of their mind (Neh. 13).

Jesus fulfills the promise of the new covenant in the renewal of heart, mind and will of the people (Luke 22:20; 1 Cor. 11:25; Heb. 8:8-9:28).

The missional role of theological education in the 21st century is to proclaim the good news of our Lord Jesus Christ. Whereas the old covenant was written in stones (Exod. 31:18; 34:28-29; Deut. 4:13; 5:22), or in a book (Exod. 24:7), but the new covenant is written on hearts. People will obey not by compulsion, but by choice. They will submit to the Lordship of Jesus! With the submissiveness of his servants, God's work will be done according to his plans and for his glory!

## Conclusion

The world is constantly changing. Theological Education is especially needed in our post-truth era. As Jesus reminded his Jewish believers to hold on to his teaching, and to be his disciples, he calls us to the same. Truth shall set us free (John 8:32). The more we focus on the deeds and works of our Almighty God on his greatness, creation of man and woman, call and nurturing at Mt Sinai, with practical and life application of training as we teach, we shall be excited to be in the field of theological education.

Theological Education has a missional role to play. We are to channel God's blessings, affirm his steadfast love and contemplate on his works!

# Bibliography

Fretheim, Terence E. *Exodus*. Interpretation. Louisville: Westminster John Knox Press, 2010.

Sailhamer, John. "Genesis" In *Expositor's Bible Commentary.* Revised Edition. Gen Ed. Temper Longman III and David E. Garland. Grand Rapids, MI: Zondervan, 2008.

Wright, Christopher J. H. "Theological Education as Mission," In *"Be Focused...Use Common Sense...Overcome Excuses and Stupidity...: Essays on Holistic Biblical Ministries."* 151-162. Festschrift in Honor of Dr. Manfred Waldemar Kohl. Bonn: Culture and Science Publ. 2022.

# CHAPTER 2

# A MISSIONAL READING OF THE EPISTLE TO THE GALATIANS

by Jae Suk Lee, PhD

## Introduction

The purpose of this study is to read Galatians from a missional perspective. Paul was an apostle and missionary sent to the Gentiles. He preached the gospel in Galatia and established a church.[1] However, by "some who were disturbing" (Gal 1:6), the Galatian church believers came to accept "another gospel" (1:7). In response, Paul defends his gospel and urges them to live by keeping the gospel he preached. This study aims to examine how Paul is teaching various themes as a missionary to the Gentiles. For this, I suggest reading Galatians from the perspective of God's mission. Paul explains his gospel through the story of God sending the Son, the Holy Spirit, and the apostles (4:4, 6, 2:7, 9). It is the story of God's mission. This study will look into the missional themes through a missiological-exegetical approach.

## God's Mission Story: God's Sending Story

Galatians tells a variety of stories.[2] It is the story of Paul himself and the story of Jesus and Abraham. The stories are linked together in an overarching story. It is the story of God's mission (*missio Dei*). His mission is marked by the story of the Father sending his Son,

---

[1] This study supports the Southern Galatian theory. See F. F. Bruce, *The Epistle to the Galatians. A Commentary on the Greek Text* (NIGTC, Grand Rapids, MI: Eerdmans, 1982), 5-18, 23-32; R. N. Longenecker, *Galatians* (WBC 41; Dallas: Word, 1990), lxiii-lxviii, lxxxviii-c.

[2] Richard Hays argues that what forms Paul's theological framework is not a system of doctrine or religious experience, but a narrative structure as "one sacred story" (Richard. B. Hays, *The Faith of Jesus Christ: The Narrative Substructure of Galatians 3:1–4:11* [Grand Rapids, MI: Eerdmans. 2002], 6). For another study of Paul's stories, see A. Andrew Das, *Paul and the Stories of Israel: Grand Thematic Narratives in Galatians* (Minneapolis: Fortress, 2016), 1-2, 24.

the Holy Spirit, and the apostles "to deliver us from this evil age" (1:4, 2:7, 9, 4:4, 6).[3] Paul provides a perspective on the story of God's mission through the sending formula (4:4, 6 "God sent the Son or the Holy Spirit"). Scholars have debated whether Paul coined this formula in his missionary context or whether it was cited as a pre-Pauline formulation.[4] Although we cannot clearly decide which is right, one thing is clear: Paul sees the sending of the Son of God as the fulfillment of God's plan. The phrase "when the fullness of time had come" (4:4) refers to a point in God's salvific history. God sends his son to fulfill his plan to enable his children to receive their inheritance according to the promise he made to Abraham (cf. 3:24-25).[5] Paul's phrase "according to the will of our God and Father" (1:4b) refers primarily to Jesus's "faithful obedience to God." However, it implies that the works accomplished through Jesus Christ are fulfilling His plan.[6] God makes the new age suppress the old age through Christ (cf. Col 1:13).[7] This plan was written in the Bible as a promise (cf. Rom 1:2, "through his prophets in the holy Scriptures"; 1 Cor 15:3, 4, "in accordance with the scriptures"). He

---

[3] For a narrative reading of Paul's thought in the substructure of his letter, N. T. Wright, *The New Testament and the People of God* (Minneapolis: Fortress, 1992), 405; Hays, *The Faith of Jesus Christ* (2002 [1983]); Bruce W. Longenecker, "Narrative Interest in the Study of Paul: Retrospective and Prospective," in *Narrative Dynamics in Paul: A Critical Assessment*, ed. Bruce W. Longenecker (Louisville: Westminster John Knox, 2002), 3. For a "grand thematic narrative" methodology to observe the narratives that Paul alludes or echoes the Old Testament story in Galatians, see Das, *Paul and the Stories of Israel*, 1-2, 13-31.

[4] Douglas J. Moo claims that Paul borrowed the idea of "God 'sending' his Son" from early Christian tradition (Jn 3:16, 1 Jn 4:9) (*A Theology of Paul and His Letters: The Gift of the New Realm in Christ* [Grand Rapids, MI: Zondervan, 2021], 75). Hays also sees that Paul is describing the story of sending the Son of God according to the confession of the early church (Hays, *The Faith of Jesus Christ*, 111 n. 82). On the other hand, regarding the suggestion that the "sending" formula from the tradition of Mark 12:6-7 can be linked to Galatians *4:4-5* (James D. G. Dunn, *Christology in the Making: A New Testament Inquiry into the Doctrine of the Incarnation* [Grand Rapids, MI: Eerdmans, 1989], 39–42). Regarding the connection between the sending of the Son and the sending of wisdom (Wis 9:10, "Send her forth from the holy heavens, and from the throne of your glory send her"), see Seyoon Kim, *The Origin of Paul's Gospel* (WUNT 2.4; Tübingen: Mohr Siebeck, 1984), 111–36 (cf. Das, *Paul and the Stories of Israel*, 38-39).

[5] Bruce, *Galatians*, 239.

[6] J. L. Martyn, *Galatians: a New Translation with Introduction and Commentary* (Vol. 33A; London: Yale University Press, 2008), 91.

[7] Bruce, *Galatians*, 77.

claims that God sent Jesus to this earth to die according to God's promise. And Paul is delivering the story of the sending of the Son of God to the Galatian saints through the story of "the gospel."

The purpose of God's mission is to "redeem" sinners from their sins/"the curse of the law"/"under the law" through the Son (1:4, ἐξαιρέομαι, 3:13, 4:5, ἐξαγοράζομαι) so that he gives them the Holy Spirit.[8] The act of sending the Holy Spirit of God also forms an important axis of his great mission story. This story is the fulfillment of the promise given through the story of Abraham, and ultimately reveals that God becomes the subject of the fulfillment of the promise as the subject of the act of sending. And God sends the apostles to the Jews and gentiles to preach the "truth of the gospel," just as he served as a missionary to tell Abraham "the gospel beforehand" (3:8, προευηγγελίσατο τῷ Ἀβραὰμ) (2:5, 7). This is an important basis for declaring that Paul himself is a missionary sent by God and that the gospel he preaches is given from God (1:11-12).[9]

## The 'Sent' Paul of God and His Mission

Paul's sentness to the gentiles purported to preach the gospel (1:1, 16, 2:2, 7-9). In Galatians 1:11-24, he tells how he became a missionary to preach Christ Jesus among the Gentiles ("the gentiles" or "the uncircumcised" 2:2, 7, 8 [τὰ ἔθνη], 2:9 [ἡμεῖς εἰς τὰ ἔθνη]). He was originally zealous for Judaism and the traditions of his ancestors (1:13-14).[10] He did not even tolerate Jewish Christians who believed in Jesus (1:13, 23). However, as he received "the revelation of Jesus," he had a paradigm shift in missionary work in which he preached the gospel to the Gentiles through faith, not by the works of the law, from the Judaism-centered perspective ("[Jesus] also worked through me," 2:8). He became the one who preached to the Gentiles "his faith," which was the reason he

---

[8] Hays, *Faith of Jesus Christ*, 98-99, 101.

[9] Longenecker, *Galatians*, 171; Mika Hietanen, *Paul's Argumentation in Galatians: A Pragma-Dialectical Analysis* (London: T&T Clark, 2007), 79.

[10] Most interpreters think that Paul was "'an ardent observer of the Torah', where ζηλωτὴς is understood to function as an objective meaning 'zealous for, zealously devoted to'" (Jeff Hubing, *Crucifixion and New Creation: the Strategic Purpose of Galatians 6.11-17* [London: T & T Clark, 2015], 130-31).

persecuted Christians (1:23). We will examine his understanding of mission through several controversial themes in his letters.

### Paul and Some who Preached "Another Gospel"

Paul's gospel to the gentiles is that "through the faith of Jesus Christ," both Jews and Greeks are redeemed from sin, become God's children, and receive the Holy Spirit (3:1-2). However, "some people" (1:7) came into the church in Galatia and preached a different message from Paul. Paul calls it "another gospel" (ἕτερον εὐαγγέλιον, 1:6). He harshly criticized them. Because they distort Paul's "true gospel" (1:6-7) or "truth of the gospel" (2:5, 14).[11] Some scholars claim that the core of another gospel of "some" was undoubtedly circumcision. A. Andrew Das observes that the third-person groups ("some") in Paul's statement (1:7, 5:12, 6:13) are connected with "the rite of circumcision; 'they' are advocating the circumcision of the Galatians" (5:2, 6:12-13).[12] Das' observation about the term ταράσσοντες clarifies Paul's connection of circumcision with the instruction of his opponents throughout his epistle. In-Gyu Hong highlights the subject-matter of circumcision as a main issue between Paul and his opponents in Galatians, by categorizing Galatians logically into the following structure:[13]

---

[11] Bruce W. Longenecker, *The Triumph of Abraham's God* (Edinburgh: T & T Clark, 1998), 25.

[12] A. Andrew Das, *Paul and the Jews,* edited by Stanley E. Porter (Peabody, Mass.: Hendrickson, 2003), 18-19; "Another Look at ἐὰν μὴ in Galatians 2:16," 536 no. 29.

[13] Hong, Hong, In-Gyu. *The Law in Galatians,* edited by Stanley E. Porter (Sheffield: Sheffield Academic Press, 1993), 100-101.

| | |
|---|---|
| 1:6-10 | The gospel of the opponents versus the gospel<br>of Christ |
| 3:1-14; cf. 2:15-17 | Justification by the works of the law versus<br>justification by faith of Christ |
| 3:23-4:7 | Slavery under the law versus sonship in Christ |
| 4.21-31; cf. 2:18-21; 5:1-12 | Circumcision versus faith |
| 5:13-6:10 | The flesh versus the Spirit |
| 6:12-16 | Circumcision versus the cross of Christ |

This structural analysis indicates that Paul deals with "the gospel of the opponents versus the gospel of Christ" as the propositional antithesis of the whole argument regarding Galatians. Given that Paul deals primarily with circumcision as "works of the law" (2:3, 5:2, 3, 6:12, 13) in the debate about the righteousness of the law, the central message of the "some" is circumcision. However, the function of circumcision as a work of the law is still debated. On the one hand, some scholars have seen circumcision as one of the 'works of the law' as a marker for maintaining ethnic distinctions and their covenant identity. E. P. Sanders postulates that the 'works of the Law' in Galatians is the mark of the membership of God's community for the maintenance of the status ("staying in"), but not the requirement for salvation ("getting in").[14] James D. G. Dunn develops Sanders' idea, the so-called "nationalistic and racial concept of the covenant and the law or law-keeping in General."[15] The works of the law were not the whole of the Law but some of the laws like Circumcision, Food laws and Sabbath. Dunn's idea is contrary to the traditional idea that circumcision is representative of the Mosaic Law, the so-called works of the law that contrasts with faith in Christ through which the Galatian Christians
are justified for salvation (2:16).

---

[14] E. P. Sanders, *Paul, the Law, and the Jewish People* (Philadelphia: Fortress, 1983), 19.

[15] James D. G. Dunn, "Works of the Law and the Curse of the Law," *New Testament Studies* 31 (1985): 523-92; Dunn, *Galatians*, 127-29; Longenecker, *Abraham's God*, 27.

N. T. Wright supports both Sanders's and Dunn's ideas by stating, "*torah* provided three badges in particular which marked the Jew out from the pagan: circumcision, Sabbath, and the kosher laws, which regulated what food could be eaten, how it was to be killed and cooked, and with whom one might share it. In and through all this ran them of Jewish 'separateness'." [16] Wright's argument is based on the interpretation of MMT ( **מְקָצָת מַעֲשֵׂי הַתּוֹרָה** [*Miqṣat Maʿaśey Ha-Torah*, 4QMMT, C27]) which is translated "some of the works of the law."[17] He thinks that MMT plays a role in segregating the Jews and the Gentiles or the devout Jews and the Jews who disobey the laws within the boundary of the covenant people of God regardless of the requirements of one's entry into the community of God.[18] In Wright's hypothesis, "some men" miscomprehend Paul's elimination the boundary between covenant people and sinners by uniting all the people in faith, and interprets the words of Jesus who fulfilled the promise of Deuteronomy 30:1-2 and 31:29 and inaugurated the new eschatological and covenantal people.[19] As a result, "some men" strived to discriminate between the Jews and the Gentiles by depending upon the content of the form of MMT.[20] Accordingly, "some who were disturbing" in Galatians 1:7 should be called missionaries who understand the nationalistic separation between the Jews and the Gentiles by way of these markers. The *different*

---

[16] Wright, *New Testament*, 237. Wright presumes that the "agitators" in Galatians pertained to the mainstream Judaism (N. T. Wright, "4QMMT and Paul: Justification, 'Works,' and Eschatology," in *History and Exegesis,* ed. Sang-Won Son (New York, London: T & T Clark, 2006, 130).

[17] Wright, "4QMMT," 122; See Dunn, "Echoes of Intra-Jewish Polemic in Paul's Letter to the Galatians." *Journal of Biblical Literature* 112 (1993): 466-68, 471.

[18] Wright, "4QMMT," 122.

[19] Wright, "4QMMT," 125. Wright argues that Paul utilizes the structure and form of MMT through the key line C 31 of MMT emerging from Deuteronomy 30:1-2 and 31:29 regarding Israel's returning to God in terms of a true recovery event from exile. Subsequently, the paradigm shift of Paul is to redefine the new eschatological and covenantal people of God, by substituting "some of the works of the laws" of MMT for "by the faith of Jesus" (Ibid., 112 no. 20). Faith is the marker of the new covenantal people during life as well as the token of God's vindication at the last judgment (Ibid., 114).

[20] Ibid., 109, 129.

*gospel* of the agitators is that 'faith in Christ' must be accompanied by the Jewish laws and customs.[21]

However, on the other hand, some scholars object to limiting Galatians' use of "the works of the law" as merely a marker of national distinctions. William D. Barrick argues that Paul uses "salvific language, the language of entrance into salvation," by contrasting "works of the law" with faith in Galatians 3:2.[22] The phrase ἔργων νόμου ("works of the law") that occurs in Romans 3:20, 28 and Galatians 2:16 (*3); 3:2, 5, 10 denotes legalism for justification.[23] There are the interpretations of τοῦ νόμου in largely two ways: as an objective genitive ("works that fulfill the Law") and as a subjective genitive ("the works that the Law requires").[24] Galatians 2:16 contains the phrases, ἔργων νόμου and πίστεως Χριστοῦ, in the genitive construction. Moses Silva demonstrates that these phrases should be translated in a literary and historical context.[25] He goes on to assert that ἔργων νόμου should be understood as "law-works" on the basis of the historical event of Antioch (Gal 2:11-14).[26] Paul L. Owen proposes that the phrase ἔργων νόμου means "the efficacy of the Law," so that the phrase is

---

[21] William D. Barrick, "The New Perspective and 'Works of the Law'," *The Master's Seminary Journal* 16 (Fall 2005): 278.

[22] Ibid., 286.

[23] Bruce, *Galatians*, 137; Burton, *Galatians*, 120.

[24] For a discussion on the subjective genitive, see Douglas J. Moo, *The Epistle to the Romans,* ed. Gordon D. Fee (NICNT; Grand Rapids, MI: Eerdmans, 1996), 209 no. 61; C. E. B. Crandfield, "'The Works of the Law' in the Epistle to the Romans," *JSNT* 43 (1991): 100; Daniel Wallace, *Greek Grammar Beyond the Basics* (Grand Rapids, MI: Zondervan, 1996), 113; Dunn, *Galatians*, 139; "Once More, PIXTIX CRIXTOU," *Pauline Theology: Looking Back, Pressing On,* vol. IV of *Pauline Theology: Looking Back, Pressing On*; ed. E. E. Johnson and D. M. Hay (Atlanta: Scholars Press, 1997), 61-81. By contrast, for a discussion on the objective genitive, see Hans D. Betz, *Galatians: A Commentary on Paul's Letter to the Churches in Galatia* (Philadelphia: Fortress, 1979), 117-18; David M. Hay, "*Pistis* as 'Ground for Faith' in Hellenized Judaism and Paul," *JBL* 108 (1989): 461-76.

[25] Moses Silva, "Faith versus Works of Law in Galatians," in *Justification and Variegated Nomism: the Paradoxes of Paul.* Vol. 2 of *Justification and Variegated Nomism: the Paradoxes of Paul,* eds. D. A. Carson, Peter T. O'Brien, and Mark Seifrid, 246-47 (Grand Rapids: Baker, 2004), 220.

[26] See B. W. Longenecker, "Defining the Faithful Character of the Covenant community: Galatians 2:15-21 and Beyond," n.p. (England, 1995), 4 no. 14; Wallace, *Greek Grammar,* 116.

"best translated 'righteous works produced by the Law'."[27] In other words, "the works produced by the Law cannot justify any person (Gal 3:11; cf. Paul's quotation, Deut. 27:26), but the faith (fullness) of Jesus Christ can justify any person (Gal 3:16)."[28]

In my view, Schreiner and Barrack appropriately argue that Wright's argument includes a critical weakness. 4QMMT is not restricted to the nationalistic markers, but to the entire law and the biblical *Halakhah*. Schreiner argues that *Ma'aśey Ha-Torah* ("works of the law," 4QFlor 1:7; cf. 1QS 5:8, 21; 6:18) indicate the whole law because, when the phrase is used in the parallel expression, it does not mean a part of the law in the contextual view, but contains the whole law of Moses (cf. 1 QpHab 7:11; 8:1; 12:4-5; 11 QTemple 56:3-4; 4QMMT). [29] Similarly, Barrick argues that Paul's use of "works of the law" presupposes the observance of the entire Mosaic law on the grounds of the interpretation of the curse of disobedience to the law (Deut 28:58, Josh 1:7 and Neh 9:34; cf. Deut 29:29 [Heb 29:28]; 31:12; 32:46; Neh 22:5; 23:6; 2 Chr 14:3; 33:8).[30] Through strong evidence of the interpretation of the same source (4QMMT), Schreiner and Barrick directly reject the foundation of Wright's assertion that MMT should be interpreted as the nationalistic or covenantal markers.[31]

Likewise, according to Schliesser, 4QMMT C30 testifies that "understanding and doing the 'works of the law' leads to eternal salvation." He continues to object to Dunn's theory as follows: "a restricted understanding of 'work of the law' in terms of boundary markers, as well as a proposal of a 'pattern of religion' in terms of 'covenantal nomism' do not seem to do full justice to the textual evidence of 4QMMT."[32] But Dunn's proposal lost the basis of the

---

[27] Owen, Paul L. "The 'Works of the Law' in Romans and Galatians: A New Defense of the Subjective Genitive." *Journal of Biblical Literature* 126 (2007): 562-63.

[28] Ibid., 563.

[29] Thomas R. Schreiner, *Romans* (Grand Rapids: Baker, 2004), 173.

[30] Barrick, "New Perspective," 278.

[31] cf. Robert H. Gundry, "The Nonimputation of Christ's Righteousness," *Justification: What's at Stake in the Current Debates,* eds. Mark Husbands and Daniel J. Treire (Downers Grove, Ill.: InterVarsity, 2004), 21. One of them is "4QMMT 117 (= 4Q398 I II, 4, and 2 II,7): 'it will be counted for you as righteousness when you do what is upright and good before him'."

[32] See Benjamin Schliesser, *Abraham's Faith in Romans 4* (WUNT 2; Tübingen: J. C. B. Mohr, 2007), 200 no. 282.

background of Judaism because of Silva's study: Sir 3:30, "As water extinguishes a blazing fire, so almsgiving atones for sin" (NASB), denotes "good deeds," giving Jewish people with the requirement of salvation. [33] Fitzmyer points out that *Miqṣat* in 4QMMT means "uprightness," and that this phrase occurs in the story of Gen 15:6 (εἰς δικαιοσύνην, [LXX]) and is cited by Paul in Galatians 3:6 (εἰς δικαιοσύνην, [NBT]). [34] The usage of the phrase in Gen 15:6 was general in Jewish society. According to Fitzmyer, the broad usage of δικαιοσύνη ("justification or righteousness") in Paul's day substantiates not only that *Miqṣat Ma'aśey Ha-Torah* ("some of the works of the law," [4QMMT]) is not restricted to circumcision, Sabbath, and food observance in a context, but also that Paul clearly made sense of the meaning of the contemporary usage in the Judaism of his time. [35]

In two ways, I support Galatians' circumcision as a "work of the law" linked to the issue of compliance with the whole law. First, in Paul's stories, the "works of the law" does not mean only as a marker for national division, but refers to the entire law.

1) 2:16, 19, 21, not even "one person" or "all flesh" representing mankind is justified by the works of the law (ἔργων νόμου). Since it should be seen that all flesh includes Jews, it seems unreasonable to limit circumcision to an act of the law that serves as a marker for national distinction.

2) 3:2, 5, Paul asks the Galatian Christians if they received the Holy Spirit through ἔργων νόμου. This is linked to 3:10. There is a parallel between "Cursed are those who are under the works of the law" and "Cursed is he who does not always do all things as written in the book of the law." The works of the law mean "all the things" shown in the book of the law, and those who do not do them can be read as being under the curse of the law. Especially in 3:13, the expression of the curse of the law does not limit the law to merely

---

[33] Silva, "Faith," 246-47.

[34] Joseph A. Fitzmyer, *Romans: A New Translation with Introduction and Commentary* (Anchor Bible 33; New York: Doubleday, 1993), 338.

[35] Ibid., 339. cf. Ben Witherington and Darlene Hyatt, *Paul's Letter to the Romans* (Grand Rapids, MI: Eerdmans, 2004), 103. Ben Witherington observes that in 4 Ezra, and 2 Enoch, righteousness is based on law-observance, and rewards and judgments result from individual deeds. In addition to this, God's righteousness is realized when He judges and rules according to justice, but not according to His covenantal faithfulness.

some acts of the law. In the same context, "the Scripture puts all men under sin" (3:22) and "the law holds all men captive" (3:23) can be read interchangeably. If so, it could be said that the Scripture means the law.

3) 4:4-5 (4:21), the Son of God was born "under the law" and redeemed "those under the law." If we understand circumcision and some legal works as national markers, we will read that the Son of God is born of the Jews and redeems them. Then, in 4:6 ("because you are sons"), a discrepancy arises with the content of the redemption of Gentile Christians. This problem is also an issue that can arise in the logical flow of chapters 2 and 3. If the works of the law would be markers for the distinction between Jews and Gentiles, the expressions like "Paul himself died to the law (2:19)" or "redeemed us from the curse of the law" (3:13) will have questions. He is a Jew who, unlike "the heathen sinners," has fully carried out the mark of national distinction (2:15; "excessive faith [in Judaism]," 1:14). Therefore, to say that he was under a curse for the works of the law as a national mark is to deny his own confession (1:13-14). But Paul declares that all are under the curse of the law. It may be assumed that he refers to the works of the law as those required by the whole law (5:3). Moreover, in the contrast between justification by law and justification by faith, the law is synthetic (2:16). When Paul speaks of the cross of Christ, he declares that he has been crucified with Christ (2:20). In the flow of Paul's story, Christ's crucifixion was "the curse of the law" for "us." If so, it means that Paul, who was crucified with Christ, was under the curse of the law along with Christ. As a result, Paul became a righteous man. Therefore, if Paul proclaims the cross of Christ as the truth of the gospel, naturally, the center of his gospel must include the correlation between sinners who die under the curse of the law and justification (3:24). Above all, the important theme of Paul's gospel is the Holy Spirit. The gospel, which was preached to Abraham beforehand, will be blessed through him by all gentiles (3:8). The result given by this blessing in Jesus Christ from the gentiles is to receive the promise of the Holy Spirit (3:14). Paul's gospel presents the sending of the Son of God, putting him to death on the cross, bringing sinners out of the curse of the law by dying with him by faith, being justified, and living by the Holy Spirit.

4) 5:3, Paul declares that all "those who are circumcised" must keep "the whole law" (cf. 5:14). This argument suggests why Paul

made circumcision a central issue in his debates with other preachers of the gospel. The Jews require Galatian Gentile Christians to be circumcised so that they may become law-keepers (6:13; cf. cf. Acts 15:5b, "It is necessary to circumcise them and to order them to keep the law of Moses").

Considering these four literary-contextual usages, it can be assumed                                                                that for Paul, circumcision was an act that presupposed obedience to the entire law.

Second, compared to Acts, circumcision is related to the observance of the Mosaic Law. I presume that Paul's use of ταράσσοντες ("some men who were disturbing," Gal 1:7) is based on the incident of Antioch (Acts 15). "Some" from the Jerusalem church asked the Antioch church members to be circumcised in order to be saved (15:1, 24). J. Louis Martyn offers an insightful work in which he found the use of the term not only in Luke's works (ἐταράχθη, Lk 1:12; τεταραγμένοι, Lk 24:37-38), but especially in Acts (ἐτάραξαν, 15:24). The subject of the verb (15:24) is "some" (τινες) and appears in Acts 15:1 again. [36] These two groups of "some" are obviously the same people who incited the church members of Antioch to deviate from Paul's teachings by saying: Ἐὰν μὴ περιτμηθῆτε τῷ ἔθει τῷ Μωϋσέως, οὐ δύνασθε σωθῆναι ("Unless you are circumcised according to the custom of Moses, you cannot be saved," 15:1). This fact enables us to connect "ταράσσοντες" of Galatians 1:7 with "some men" of Antioch (Gal 2:1-10; Acts 15:1, 24).[37] I accept Hans Dieter Betz's opinion that the

---

[36] Martyn, *Galatians*, 112.

[37] In Galatians, Paul applies another term ψευδαδέλφους ("*false brothers*," Gal 2:4) to his opponents, while remembering the incident of Antioch (2:1-21; cf. Acts 15:1). This term occurs in Paul's epistles twice (Gal. 2:4, 2 Cor 11:26)(Victor Paul Furnish, *2 Corinthians* [AB 32; New York: Doubleday, 1984], 518; William F. Arndt and F. Wilbur Glngrich, *A Greek-English Lexicon of the New Testament and Other Early Christian Literature* [Chicago: The University of Chicago Press, 1971], 899). Victor Paul Furnish presumes that Paul coined this specific designation because the expression is found nowhere in the NT except for Galatians 4:16 and 2 Corinthians 11:26. According to Furnish, Paul used his own term in order to attack those who entice members of the congregation from the church into a *different gospel*, by challenging Paul's apostleship (10:7-18) and his gospel (11:2-4, 20)( Furnish, *2 Corinthians*, 510). Furnish provides this study for the contextual

incident at Antioch (Gal 2:1-10) took place after the Jerusalem Council (Acts 15) because of Ὅτε (indeterminate conjunction subordinating, Gal 2:11; cf 1:15, 2:11, 12, 14, 4:3, 4) in the statement of Paul.[38] If those who entered the Galatian churches held the same views as the "some people" referred to at the Jerusalem Council, it is likely that their other major themes of the gospel were those of the Mosaic Law and salvation. Therefore, those who were sent by the leaders of the Jerusalem Church came to Galatia and then began to compel the Galatians to be circumcised on the basis of their soteriology that no one can be saved without Judaism or without observance of the Mosaic Law.[39]

I presume that Paul continued to adhere to the teachings of Galatians during his missionary years. As a result, among Jewish Christians and Jews, Paul was recognized as a traitor or slanderer of the Mosaic law. It might be known to Jewish Christians that, in Acts 21:21, Paul taught all Jews in the Gentile world not to circumcise and not to observe their customs. They regarded Paul's teachings as a betrayal of Moses. To disprove this assertion,

---

similarity between 2 Corinthians and Galatians. That is to say, Paul insists on the same topics in two epistles: he is the servant of Christ (2 Cor 11:23, Gal 1:10) and his gospel came from God (2 Cor 11:7, Gal 1:3-4; cf. Gal 1:11-24) and that his gospel is that people can be righteous and saved only through faith (2 Cor 4:13-14; cf. 1 Cor 1:17-18) and the grace of Christ (2 Cor 5:16-21), but not by works of the law (2 Cor 4:12) like circumcision (Gal 1:6, 2:14). Dunn does not object to the relationship between 2 Corinthians and Galatians; rather, he positively advocates the similarity of false brothers in two provinces by stating that "some men" at Galatia were those who asked the Corinthians to be circumcised (5:2-12, 6:12-13). For these reasons, the ψευδαδέλφους appearing in the setting of Galatians 2:4 and the designation ("false brothers") is used by Paul according to his particular intention to earnestly attack his opponents who repudiate his gospel and teach the "*different gospel*" to enslave (καταδουλοῖ, 2 Cor 11:20, Gal 2:1) the gentile believers. Moreover, it is right that circumcision is not merely an additional gospel of Paul's opponents, but is the *different gospel* in opposition to Paul's gospel that people can be saved by Jesus's grace and faith. In this respect, Bruce rightly observes that the reason why Paul calls them *false brothers* is that they tried to destroy the freedom of the true gospel of Paul (Bruce, *Galatians*, 112; Ben Witherington, *Grace in Galatia* [New York: T & T Clark, 2004], 25).

[38] See Betz, *Galatians*, 117-18; David B. Capes, Rodney Reeves and E. Randolph Richards, *Rediscovering Paul* (Naperville, Ill.: InterVarsity, 2007), 99 no. 31. On the opposite theory, see F. F. Bruce, *The Book of the Acts* (NICNT; Grand Rapids, MI: Eerdmans, 1988), 283-84.

[39] Michal Goulder, *St. Paul versus St. Peter* (Louisville, Ky.: Westminster John Knox, 1994), 1-2.

Jerusalem church leaders demand that Paul could prove himself to be a law-keeper (21:24). This is proof that Jewish Christians were considering circumcision and keeping the law as the same thing. On the other hand, in 21:28, Jewish non-Christians also understand Paul as a slanderer of the Jews, the law and the temple. So, when they arrested Paul in the temple, they said, "This man taught everyone everywhere against our people, against the law, and against this place" (21:28). To them Paul was branded as a slanderer of the law.

If both of the "some" in Acts and the "some" in Galatians have the same idea, then they could be seen as requiring gentile Christians to follow the laws of the Jews. Paul, in Galatians, points out that they required gentiles to live like Jews. F. F. Bruce argues that Paul intended to apply the term Ἰουδαϊσμῷ (1:13, 14), so-called Judaizers ('lived like a Jew,' 2:14), to his opponents, by using the word that occurs in the NT two times and means Jewish faith and life (cf. 2 Macc 2:21, 8:1, 14:38, 4 Macc. 4:26).[40] "Some" who preached the *different gospel* were identified as Jewish Christian Judaizers who force the Galatian believers to keep the law in the same way as the Jews. They understood the Judaism-centric gospel and taught it to the Gentiles. On the other hand, as a Gentile missionary, Paul understands the gospel from the perspective of God's universal mission to all nations, not a Judaism-centered understanding of the gospel (3:2-3). His mission is to preach the cross of Jesus Christ and to make all Jews and Gentiles children of God to receive the Holy Spirit (3:1–4:7). In the Gentile world, his gospel does not merely speak of a marker for "maintenance" of national identities, but begins with announcing how those who were once sinners will become children of God. The premise of his gospel is that everyone is "under the curse of the law"/"under sin" (3:13, 22). The way for them to be redeemed is not by the works of the law, but "through the faith of Jesus Christ." His gospel tells of the death and resurrection of Jesus who was sent, and that all nations under the law are saved from sin/redemption from the curse of the law through faith, and receive the Holy Spirit as children of God.[41]

---

[40] Bruce, *Galatians*, 90.

[41] cf. I. Howard Marshall, *New Testament Theology* (Naperville, Ill.: InterVarsity, 2004), 227; Thomas R. Schreiner, *Paul, Apostle of God's Glory in Christ: A Pauline Theology* (Leicester: InterVarsity, 2001), 237.

Both Jews and Gentiles receive redemption from the curse of the law and the Holy Spirit through faith. It shows the legitimacy of God's mission. God sent his son Jesus to this earth (4:4) so he died on the cross as a substitute for the sins of "us" (both Jews and Gentiles). God resurrected the son and through him he gives all believers the Holy Spirit.[42]

## Paul's Mission: "All Nations" (πάντα τὰ ἔθνη, 3:8)

According to Paul, the gospel of God had already been given to Abraham as a promise to "all nations" (3:8). He is called by God to preach his gospel to ἔθνη (1:13-14, 16).[43] Jarvis J. Williams and Trey Moss postulate the association of ἔθνη and πάντα τὰ ἔθνη.[44] They suggest that 3:8 should be understood in the context of 3:1-14. God included the Gentiles in Abraham's blessing along with the Jews who followed Christ. Through Paul's missional hermeneutic perspective, πάντα τὰ ἔθνη spoken to Abraham includes both Jews and all Gentiles in the promise. It is evident that the promise was given to Abraham, and that through his faith his descendants became the heirs of the promise. In Galatians 3:6-9 Paul speaks of two structures:

| | |
|---|---|
| 3:6 | Abraham's faith and its reckoning as righteousness |
| 3:7 | Believers are descendants of Abraham |
| 3.8 | God justifies the Gentiles by faith. The Gospel of God: "In you (Abraham) shall all the nations be blessed." |
| 3:9 | Believers are blessed along with Abraham, a man of faith. |

In these verses Paul emphasizes three things. First, God justifies people. Second, the means is faith. Third, God blesses those who believe, along with Abraham. In verse 7, Abraham's descendants could have been referred to as those who were circumcised if they were referring to the Jews, but Paul said that they were believers. It

---

[42] Longenecker, *Abraham's God*, 62.

[43] Longenecker, *Galatians,* 157. "Ἕλλην in the NT always means a Greek of Gentile origin (cf. 2:3)."

[44] Jarvis J. Williams and Trey Moss, "Focus on 'All Nations' As Integral Component of World Mission Strategy," in *World Mission: Theology, Strategy, & Current Issues,* ed. Scott N. Callaham and Will Brooks (Bellingham, WA: Lexham, 2019), 157.

says in verse 8 that God not only justifies the Gentiles by faith, but that they are blessed along with Abraham. His claim made it possible for the Gentiles to receive Abraham's promise of "the Holy Spirit" by faith. Interestingly, however, Paul does not say that Gentiles enter the Jewish Christian community through the faith of Jesus Christ. By faith, Jews become Christians as Jews while Gentiles become Christians as Gentiles (2:7, 14-20). Their becoming children of God has nothing to do with or without circumcision, which means keeping the whole law (2:14, ἐθνικῶς "gentile way of life" and Ἰουδαϊκῶς "Jewish way of life"; Ἰουδαΐζειν "Jewish way of life to live"). It starts with the fact that all of them are beings who need to be redeemed from "the curse of the law." And through the faith of Jesus, Gentiles are justified as Jews should be, receive the Holy Spirit, and share in Abraham's blessing (3:8-9, 14, 29; cf. 2:16; 3:1-5, 6).[45] All of this is happening in the story of God's mission as planned and carried out.[46]

## Πίστις Ἰησοῦ Χριστοῦ

Paul taught that Jesus became a curse on the cross for all sinners to be redeemed from their sins (1:4, 3:13 and 2:20). They can live in it by faith and not by the works of the law (1:23, 2:16, 2:20, 3:2, 5, 7, 8, 9, 11, 12, 14, 22, 25, 26, 5:5, 6, 26, 22, 6:10).[47] Through faith, Jews and Gentiles become children of God without discrimination and receive the Holy Spirit. Scholars have been seriously discussing what 'faith' is. In particular, regarding the interpretation of πίστις Ἰησοῦ Χριστοῦ (2:16, 3:22, 26; cf. πίστις τοῦ υἱοῦ τοῦ θεοῦ, 2:20).[48]

---

[45] Williams and Moss, "Focus on 'All Nations'," 160.

[46] Regarding the discussion of "a revision of Jewish universalism," from a Christological Perspective, see Terence L. Donaldson, "'The Gospel that I Proclaim among the Gentiles' (Gal 2.2): Universalistic or Israel-Centered," in *Gospel in Paul*, eds. L. Ann Jervis and Peter Richardson, 166-93 (JSNTSup 108; Sheffield: Sheffield Academic Press, 1994), 166-70.

[47] "The faith" (τὴν πίστιν, 1:23), "the faith of Christ" (πίστεως Ἰησοῦ Χριστοῦ, 2:16, 3:22), "the faith of the Son of God" (ἐν πίστει τῇ τοῦ υἱοῦ τοῦ θεοῦ, 2:20), "by faith" (ἐξ/ἐκ πίστεως, 3:2, 5, 7, 8, 9, 11, 12, 14, 5:5), "of faith" (τῆς πίστεως, 3:25, 26, 6:10), "faith" (πίστις, 5:6, 22 [nominative singular]).

[48] Meanwhile, on the view of "πίστις as relationship", see David Downs and Benjamin J. Lappenga, *The Faithfulness of the Risen Christ: Pistis and the Exalted*

Many versions translate the phrase into English "faith in Jesus Christ" (ESV, RSV, NASB, NIV, etc). However, some translations and scholars support the "faith/faithfulness of Jesus Christ" (KJV, ISV, etc).

As a leading scholar of the latter reading, Richard B. Hays argues that 'the Faith/faithfulness of Jesus Christ' is the correct translation.[49] It is the faithful act of Jesus, which points to obedience even to death on the cross.[50] Rather than being the object of faith in Jesus, Jesus is the subject who faithfully walks toward God. Soon, the fact that "'the faith of the Son of God' is now the governing power in Paul's existence" means "the acting subject of the 'faith'."[51] The phrase "in Christ Jesus" in Galatians 3:26 and 28d is not an accusative expression that modifies faith or designates the object of faith.[52] The literary context in 3:26 is to emphasize that a new era has arrived.

Thus, πάντες γὰρ υἱοὶ θεοῦ ἐστε διὰ τῆς πίστεως ἐν Χριστῷ Ἰησοῦ is not to say that we believe in Christ as the object of our faith, but "... in Christ Jesus you are all sons of God, through faith." This is because in "the framework of a narrative Christology," it is more persuasive to read the faith, or the faithfulness of Christ Jesus.[53] To support his argument, Hays invokes interpretation of Romans 3:21-26. He notes Jesus's faith (3:26; cf. Abraham's faith [4:16]) through a theocentric perspective. The revelation of God's righteousness in 3:22 is not "through believing in Jesus Christ" but "through the faithfulness of Jesus Christ." [54] Soon, God's righteousness was revealed in the faith and righteous deeds of the dead on the cross (3:25).[55]

---

*Lord in the Pauline Letters* (Waco, TE: Baylor University Press, 2019), 84. According to them, πίστις is not simply the content of the gospel, but "the community of trust between God, Christ, and faithful humanity" in terms of "in Christ" (6:10). Above all, they note Paul's use of the phrase "entrusted with the gospel" in 2:7 (Downs and Lappenga, *The Faithfulness of the Risen Christ*, 87).

[49] Hays, *The Faith of Jesus Christ*, xxx, 141-62.

[50] R. Barry Matlock, "Detheologizing the Debate: Cautionary Remarks from a Lexical Semantic Perspective," *NovT* 42 (2000): 1-23; "'Even the Demons Believe': Paul and πιστις Χριστου," *CBQ* 64 (2002): 300-18.

[51] Hays, *The Faith of Jesus Christ*, 154.

[52] Ibid., 155-56.

[53] Ibid., 156.

[54] Ibid., 157.

[55] Ibid., 159-60.

Hays also argues that understanding Galatians as the object of faith is opaque, considering that God, who raised Jesus from the dead, is the object of faith. Instead, Christ's obedient death on the cross signifies his faithful atoning sacrifice for us.[56] Jesus Christ is the subject of the act of giving himself under a curse for our sins in 1:3-4, 2:20, and 3:13. In this act, the beneficiaries of Christ's agency are human beings.[57]

Hays' careful interpretation highlights God's work in Jesus Christ. By this, he emphasizes that God enables human beings to be rectified in the work of his new creation through Christ's faithfulness for the atonement of sinners. Believers place their trust in Christ who died for them (cf. 5:8).[58] Thus, their salvation depends on Jesus's faithfulness.[59] In this respect, faith is not a human act, but rather an interactive one in the relationship between Jesus and God.

---

[56] Downs and Lappenga, *The Faithfulness*, 84.

[57] Caneday argues for his argument that, with the exception of Galatians 2:16, the contrast between πίστις Χριστοῦ and ἔργα νόμου does not always occur in Paul's epistles (2:15-16) (Caneday, "The Faithfulness of Jesus Christ," 190). He suggests that the symmetry of Galatians 2:20 also does not imply "observing the works of the Law" and "believing in Christ" (Ibid., 190). Because πίστις Ἰησοῦ Χριστοῦ is a symmetrical structure of "works of the Law" (Gal 2:16) or "the Law" (Rom 3:22). Moreover, it is used as "the subject of 'came'" (Gal 3:23, 25) or "the object of 'revealed'" (3:23). Faith is sometimes the origin of justification (2:16, 3:24), the agency of sonship (3:26), and the means by which believers live (2:20). Faith is the means by which God's righteousness is "made known" (Rom 3:21, 22). It is the agency by which God reveals Christ as the mercy-seat (3:25). It is an agency that either gives (3:26) or allows righteousness to come from God (Phil 3:9) (Ibid., 190).

[58] Hays, *Faith of Jesus Christ*, 265, 270; Martyn, *Galatians*, 271.

[59] Martyn, *Galatians*, 272-73. J. Louis Martyn supports Hays' argument on two fronts. First, Paul emphasizes God's corrective action in Christ (Ibid., 270). Paul shows God's work centered on death as the faithful obedience of Jesus. God responds to his faithfulness by raising Jesus to life. Second, the parallel between 2:16 and 2:21 shows Paul's contrast between correction by obedience to the law and correction by God's work in Christ (Ibid., 271). From Galatians 1:1, Paul contrasts the work of God and the faithful death of Christ with the human act of keeping the law. All of these grounds claim to be influenced by the Jewish-Christian tradition, and the meaning of "rectification" is well reflected in the perspective of "redemption from slavery" (Ibid., 272). In Jewish tradition, it provides a theological and interpretive framework for understanding why the blood sacrifice of Jesus is an act of God for the forgiveness of human sins. In order to redeem "sinful human beings" from the bondage of sin, the God of the covenant fought against the "anti-God power" by entering the place of Christ's death under sin as a universal work of salvation. And he delivers men from slavery to the law in Christ (3:13, 4:5).

Then, by placing themselves in a mutual relationship with Jesus, Christians receive the work God works in Jesus, namely the promise and sonship. At this point, the faith (fullness) of Jesus is understood in connection with the new realm of life "in Christ". And "in him," that is, "in his faithfulness" Christians must live according to the order of God's new creation.[60] This is the eschatological way of life, and at the same time union, participation, and incorporation in Jesus as the fruits of the Spirit.[61] This new way of life is the self-giving love and service of Jesus's faithful deeds.[62]

However, there are several controversial objections to Hays' translation of the subjective genitive. This objection is raised by those who support the interpretation of the objective genitive case. They say πίστις Ἰησοῦ Χριστοῦ means "faith in Jesus Christ."[63] Christ is the object of faith. From the perspective of Christology, it focuses on the human act of believing in Him. First, Stanley E. Porter and Andrew W. Pitts argue that in Greek, exegesis according to context, not grammatical issues, is necessary.[64] Their "a lexical semantic approach" attempts to define the meaning of πίστις through contextual notes or syntactic or semantic interpretation.[65] They suggest that instead of analyzing the meaning of words as "a genitive construction," they should reveal the meaning of words through "contextual and co-textual features."[66] "Contextual and co-textual disambiguation criteria extend from a given discourse down to syntactical configurations."[67] The use of the Greek case is "within a semantically rigorous systemic framework"[68] ("The imposition of

---

[60] Longenecker, *Abraham's God*, 69.

[61] Ibid., 65, 71.

[62] Ibid., 65, 71.

[63] Stanley E. Porter, "The Rhetorical Scribe: Textual Variants in Romans and their Possible Rhetorical Purpose," in *Rhetorical Criticism and the Bible* (ed. S. E. Porter and D. L. Stamps; JSNTSup 195; London: Sheffield Academic Press, 2002), 403-19; *Verbal Aspect in the Greek of the New Testament, with Reference to Tense and Mood* (New York: Lang, 1989).

[64] Stanley E. Porter and Andrew W. Pitts, "πίστις with a Preposition and Genitive Modifier: Lexical, Semantic, and Syntactic Considerations in the πίστις Χριστοῦ Discussion," in *The Faith of Jesus Christ*, eds. Michael F. Bird and Preston M. Sprinkle (Milton Keynes: Paternoster, 2009), 35.

[65] Ibid., 36.

[66] Ibid., 36.

[67] Ibid., 37.

[68] Ibid., 42.

entire contexts onto the meaning of individual case forms"). [69] Through this methodology, Porter and Pitts write that "the lexical frame presents the object of the preposition as a prepositional phrase, and that "the genitive realizes an intrinsic restricting relation with specification." As such, they observed three things.[70] Firstly, when used with the article, "your faith" as a possession meaning (Matt 9:29, 1:12, 1 Thess 3:2, 7, Heb 11:39, 2 Pt 1:5), as a doctrinal meaning "the faith" (Acts 13:8, 24:24, 1 Cor 16:13, 2 Cor 13:5:5, Gal 3:23, 1 Tim 1:19, 6:10, 21, Titus 1:13) , and "through faith in Christ" and "through faith", which use the abstract meaning (Acts 3:16, Eph 3:17, Col 2:12) or "the designation for the faith" without specifying it.[71] Porter and Pitts emphasize that when πίστις is used with the article, it is not used in the sense of faithfulness in an ethical sense.[72] Secondly, when used without the article, it shows an abstract meaning whether or not an expression embodies "the designation for the faith". Thirdly, πίστις is a relator with a preposition, in which case it is written as a doctrinal usage whether or not it is used with a prepositional specifier. Another case is *anarthrous*, which has an abstract meaning. In this case, the subjective example is used only once, in Romans 4:16. [73] Consequently, Porter and Pitts argue that it is not valid to claim "faithfulness" in the lexical sense. They argue that it is possible for the use of the possessive to specify a person's beliefs or to characterize the appropriate domain of beliefs as an abstract concept.[74]

However, we did not notice in Porter and Pitts' observation of πίστις that Hays suggested τὴν πίστιν τοῦ θεοῦ (Rom 3:3) and πίστεως Ἰησοῦ (3:26).[75] To me, Hays' observation that Romans 3:3

---

[69] Ibid., 39, 40. "Case semantics encoding and decoding with grammatical categories such as "noun", which represent an output condition in the grammar."

[70] Ibid., 46.

[71] Ibid., 49.

[72] Ibid., 49. cf. William Mounce argued that the presence or absence of an article does not always determine "genitival construction" or that noun-verb combinations convey the same meaning. William D. Mounce, *Greek for the Rest of Us: Mastering Bible Study without Mastering Biblical Languages* (Grand Rapids, MI: Zondervan, 2003), 182.

[73] Porter and Pitts, "πίστις with a Preposition," 49.

[74] Ibid., 51.

[75] Hays, *Faith of Jesus Christ*, 282-83.

is an example of a subjective genitive case seems reasonable in that it contrasts "human faithfulness" with "God's faithfulness." [76] However, it is just controversial whether to regard πίστεως Ἰησοῦ in 3:26 as "the faithfulness of Jesus" in the same way. Hays argues that there is a grammatical weakness in understanding it as an objective genitive case.[77] The same applies to Galatians 3:22. Thus, Hays says that based on the use of "Abraham's faith/faithfulness" in Romans 4:16, it is reasonable to also translate Romans 3:26 and Galatians 3:22 as subjective genitive. From my point of view, in Romans 3:26, πίστεως Ἰησοῦ seems incomprehensible, excluding the expression τῆς δικαιοσύνης αὐτοῦ. If "his righteousness" means God's righteousness, it would be natural to understand πίστεως Ἰησοῦ as the faith/faithfulness of Jesus Christ. The same is true of πίστεως Ἰησοῦ Χριστοῦ which Paul uses in Galatians. If we read the context of 3:5-22 centering on God as the subject who saw Abraham's faith and counted it as righteousness or justified the Gentiles through faith,[78] then we naturally read in verse 22, "In the faithfulness of Jesus (ἐκ πίστεως Ἰησοῦ By Χριστοῦ), he gave the promise to those who believe (πιστεύουσιν)."[79]

---

[76] R. N. Longenecker, *The Epistle to the Romans: A Commentary on the Greek Text*, eds. I. H. Marshall & D. A. Hagner (Grand Rapids, MI: Eerdmans, 2016), 343.

[77] Hays, *Faith of Jesus Christ*, 150.

[78] Ibid., 150-51, 56.

[79] Hays interprets Paul quoting Habakkuk 2:3-4. He tried to understand Galatians 3:11 by focusing on the interpretation of Habakkuk's passage as Messiah's faithfulness. For a detailed discussion, see Hays, *The Faith of Jesus Christ*, 171-79). On the other hand, Francis Watson notes the preposition used by Paul (Francis Watson, "By Faith (of Christ): An Exegetical Dilemma and its Scriptural Solution," in *The Faith of Jesus Christ*, eds. Michael F. Bird and Preston M Sprinkle [Milton Keynes: Paternoster, 2009], 147). He notes that Paul's use of διὰ [τῆς] πίστεως (2:16, 3:26) and ἐκ πίστεως (3:24) reflects Paul's intention to quote Habakkuk. Habakkuk 2:4 can be interpreted in two ways: 1) "the one-who-is-righteous-by-faith will live" and 2) "the Righteous One will live by faith" (Watson, "By Faith," 148-49, 154). In the comprehensive aspect of the former, the one who is justified by faith is the Christological title of the latter, which means that the righteous live by his faith as the Messiah. But while speaking of Jesus as righteous is clearly reflected in Isaiah 53:11 (LXX), we find no direct evidence in Galatians for quoting Habakkuk as meaning faith of Christ Jesus or faith in Christ Jesus (Ibid., 158). Watson argues that the "from/by faith" formulation comes from Habakkuk but is used symmetrically with "from/by works of the Law." Rather, he said, "a faith

However, if we read ἐν τῇ πίστει τοῦ υἱοῦ τοῦ θεοῦ of 2:20 and διὰ τῆς πίστεως ἐν Χριστῷ Ἰησοῦ of 3:26 as "in the faith/faithfulness of the Son of God" and "through the faith/faithfulness of Christ Jesus", we are faced with two questions. The first question is, how did the Gentiles become the children of God through "the faithfulness of Christ"? Or the question "How is Christ's faith/faithfulness related to ours?" Richard H. Bell suggests three possibilities.[80] First, "our faithfulness is derived from Christ's faithfulness." Second, "Christ's faithfulness leads to our faith."[81] Third, faith and faithfulness cannot be separated.[82] Hays, in an expanded edition of his book *The Faith of Jesus Christ* (2002 [1983]), also adds his article "Πίστις and Pauline Christology: What Is at Stake?" He still adheres to the subjective genitive position.[83] He says in Philippians 2:6-8 that Jesus died as a human being. It means "faith/fidelity" towards God.[84] This is a way of life in which "the believing community", saved through the faithfulness of Jesus, interacts with Christ. Paul speaks of a "costly self-sacrificial burden-

---

that has its origin and content in God's reconciling act in the incarnate, crucified, and risen Jesus-an act whose scope is extended to us through the agency of the Holy Spirit in the proclaimed word and the communal and individual acknowledgment it evokes" (Ibid., 163). If Watson presupposes the possibility of two interpretations based on the quotation of Habakkuk, it can be seen that he tried to assert the righteousness of individuals who have faith in a universal way and the divine saving activity that works in Christ.

[80] Richard H. Bell favors the objective genitive interpretation, comparing πίστεως Χριστοῦ (3:9) and γνώσεως Χριστοῦ Ἰησοῦ (3:8) in Philippians. The phrase 'γνώσεως Χριστοῦ Ἰησοῦ' cannot be understood as the knowledge of Christ Jesus as Jesus's knowledge as a subjective genitive in the context. Richard H. Bell, "Faith in Christ: Some Exegetical and Theological Reflections on Philippines 3:9 and Ephesians 3:12," in *The Faith of Jesus Christ*, eds. Michael F. Bird and Preston M. Sprinkle (Milton Keynes: Paternoster, 2009), 116. cf. R. Barry Matlock, "Saving Faith: The Rhetoric and Semantic of πίστις in Paul," in *The Faith of Jesus Christ*, eds. Michael F. Bird and Preston M. Sprinkle (Milton Keynes: Paternoster, 2009), 83-86. R. Barry Matlock compares Galatians 2:16 and Philippians 3:9. First of all, Matlock notes that Paul, in Galatians 2:16, places ἐὰν μὴ διὰ πίστεως Ἰησοῦ Χριστοῦ and ἡμεῖς εἰς Χριστὸν Ἰησοῦν ἐπιστεύσαμεν symmetrical. This expression clarifies that πίστεως Ἰησοῦ Χριστοῦ is 'faith in Christ Jesus in light of that we believed in Christ Jesus.

[81] Bell, "Faith in Christ," 117.
[82] Ibid, 117.
[83] Hays, *The Faith of Jesus Christ*, 272.
[84] Ibid., 293.

bearing" life in Philippians 1:27–2:13.[85] He says having the mindset of Christ doesn't mean simply imitating him. To live in Christ a way of life defined by Christ's death and suffering is called "participation in him." Of course, this claim is quite compelling. As he says, people do not become the subject of faith so we cannot make Christ the object of faith. We can just recognize Christ to be God's faithful one and participate in his life by imitating his life, but living it fully, for he is the representative of believers. However, in his discussion, they involve the notion of "imitation" and "participation in the reconciling act" as Jesus' death and resurrection in Philippians 2 and 3.[86] However, to Bell, the serious problem is that there is no content that "faith" comes out of participation anywhere in Paul's letter.[87] However, from my point of view, the aspect of making people participate in the faith/faithfulness of Jesus Christ through the proclamation of the gospel seems difficult to rule out. Because in Galatians, the subjective genitive reading is still possible.

1) 2:15, it is through the faith/faithfulness of Jesus Christ, not the works of the law, that all sinners, Jews or Gentiles, are justified. Paul said in 2:20 that he would die and live "in the faith of the Son of God." It would mean that his way of life is not "in the flesh" but that he lives the way of Jesus.

2) 3:28, all of Jew or Greek, slave or free, male or female are one in Christ Jesus. The reason why the faith (fulness) of Jesus is the gospel to both Jews and Greeks is because Jesus's faithful death leads them to the new life in the Holy Spirit. Paul pays attention to what Jesus did, not to any human action.

3) 2:20, it can be seen that the dead can no longer do anything with the death of Jesus. Instead, they must just live in the faithfulness of Christ. Likewise in 3:22, 26, receiving promises or becoming the children of God is the result of God's work, ultimately through Jesus.

Considering the discussion so far, I come to the conclusion that πίστις Ἰησοῦ Χριστοῦ in Galatians would be appropriate to read as "faith/faithfulness of Jesus Christ." But even so, I don't think that in Galatians Paul uses all the terms of faith as "faithfulness." This is the second question we face. In other words, by '(the) faithfulness', can

---

[85] Ibid., 293, 294.
[86] Bell, "Faith in Christ," 118.
[87] Ibid., 118.

the term "the faith" be equally applied in other contexts? Ardel B. Caneday argues that the phrase "the faith" must also be translated in the same sense.[88] This argument is in line with the saying that if πίστις Ἰησοῦ Χριστοῦ is to be understood as Jesus's faithfulness, obedience, or loyalty, then "the faith" must also be interpreted as Jesus's faithfulness or loyalty. The question then arises, is it natural for the phrases "that faith came" or "that faith appeared" in chapter 3 to read "that loyalty or faithfulness or obedience came" or "appeared"? If unnatural, when Paul uses πίστις Ἰησοῦ Χριστοῦ as Jesus's faithfulness, the fundamental question arises whether he is using ἡ πίστις. Of course, Hays does not always see πίστις as faithfulness. He understands "the faith" of 1:23 in terms of the phenomenology of the Christian community's proclamation.[89] This refers to a collective movement, not an individual act of faith. When Hays understands the term faith, he is not excluding the act of faith as a response to the proclamation of the gospel. This makes it impossible to see Caneday as simply contradicting Hays' argument. However, like Caneday's position, it is highly likely that Paul will use faith as a human act. Furthermore, given that Paul uses "the faith of Christ" as an accusative genitive in his epistles, it is reasonable that Galatians also implies an accusative genitive meaning.

Regarding this discussion, we need to look at the interpretation of ἐξ ἀκοῆς πίστεως in 3:2. ἀκοῆς is "hearing" and πίστεως is "preaching" a gospel and its content containing Christ (cf. Rom 1:27, 15:19, "gospel of Christ" as "the gospel concerning Christ" or 1 Cor 1:18 and 2 Cor 5:19, "the word of the cross/reconciliation"). He saw that hearers have faith as a result of the act of hearing the word or message.[90] Paul's uses of the genitive case highlight the believing response of the hearer to what he preaches, and is christological and soteriological.[91] Therefore, Bell saw it as meaning that those who hear the content of the Word or Message believe it. It is 'the

---

[88] Ardel B. Caneday, "The Faithfulness of Jesus Christ as a Theme in Paul's Theology in Galatians," in *The Faith of Jesus Christ*, eds. Michael F. Bird and Preston M. Sprinkle (Milton Keynes: Paternoster, 2009), 187.

[89] Hays, *The Faith of Jesus Christ*, 131.

[90] Bell, "Faith in Christ," 119, 120.

[91] Ibid., 120.

proclamation/preaching message of faith as the content of the gospel'.[92]

But Hays says these phrases go beyond the genitive and each have two meanings: "ἀκοή can mean either 'the action (or sense) of hearing' or 'that which is heard' (= report, message); πίστις can mean either 'the act (or state) these two remarkable and God of believing/trusting' or 'that which is believed' (= the gospel)."[93] He says (a) "believing by hearing with faith," (b) "the faith by hearing the gospel," (c) "believing from the message that aims at (or enables) faith," (d) "the faith from the Looking at interpretations such as "gospel-message", he makes the following claim.[94] (a) and (b) are incorrect understandings based on Romans 10:16-17 and Isaiah 53:1. In Romans, ἀκοή means "report, proclamation," so it should be understood that "faith comes from the proclamation."[95] This point has the same understanding as Bell. But while Bell interprets ἀκοή as "hearing" in Galatians, Hays suggests that "the message of faith" is more plausible, as Paul suggests in (c) and (d) as in Romans.[96] He questions the parallelism of ἐξ ἀκοῆς πίστεως with ἐξ ἔργων νόμου as a human act, while (a) and (b) refer to the human act of hearing. Rather, he proposes a juxtaposition of the human act of hearing and "God's message (=ἀκοή)."[97] This, as in (c) and (d), signifies the proclamation of "the message of God" as "the gospel." In addition, πίστις is used in 1:23 and 3:23-26 as "the historical phenomenon, not personal belief." of the faith (= Christianity)."[98]

Thus, Hays understands in the independent sense of (d) to imply not only faith from the gospel-message, but also the response by which human beings come to believe because of the proclamation of the gospel.[99] In this case, ἀκοῆς πίστεως would be the message of faith ("from the message that aims at faith").[100] As Hays argues, "the faith" in 1:23 can be understood as the message or proclamation

---

[92] Betz, *Galatians*, 133.
[93] Hays, *The Faith of Jesus Christ*, 143.
[94] Ibid., 144-46.
[95] Ibid., 146.
[96] Ibid., 222.
[97] Ibid., 147.
[98] Ibid., 149.
[99] Ibid., 148-49.
[100] cf. Martyn, *Galatians*, 289.

Christians believe. In comparison with Luke 22:4, what Paul persecuted is paralleled with "the faith" and "the way." This "way" indicates Christianity (cf. Gal 1:13, "I persecuted the church of God").[101]

However, even if it is "faith" as a historical phenomenon of Christianity, it is necessary to consider the situation in which individuals believe and form a community of faith in the Gentile world. Moreover, in Paul's argument, the "I" of 2:20 is tied together with the "we" of chapter 3. There is no separation between individual beliefs and "we" beliefs. Above all, in 3:2, "works of the law" and "ἀκοῆς πίστεως" are replaced, and the subject of this is "you" (Galatian Christians). Above all, it seems difficult to deny that the cause of receiving the Holy Spirit is to refer to the act of "a hearing the gospel and believing it" (ἀκοῆς πίστεως = "hearing with faith").[102] Of course, it should be admitted that Hays insists on the purpose of proclaiming God's message and making people believe in it rather than human-centered interpretation, in that the proclaimed message causes a response of human faith.[103] As Ian G. Wallis observes, the phrase ἐν τῇ πίστει τοῦ υἱοῦ τοῦ θεοῦ in 2:20 means "God's work in Christ" while 2:17-19a reflects a "human initiative," for faith is an interactive interaction between God and humans.[104] In other words, that "faith" originates from God and causes a reaction of human faith.[105] Therefore, faith is a responsive action between the faith given by God and human beings. Faith becomes complete through mutual interaction.

In conclusion, I suggest that Paul means "in the faith/faithfulness of the Son of God" in 2:20, but also includes the meaning of man "in faith in him and his doings [contents of the message]." According to Mark A. Seifrid, "His [Paul] usage of πίστις often includes both the act of believing and the content of faith."[106] As Seifrid suggests, faith includes both the act of believing and the content of believing. This

---

101 J. A. Fitzmyer, *The Acts of the Apostles: a New Translation with Introduction and Commentary*, Vol. 31 (New Heaven, Mass.: Yale University Press, 2008), 705.

102 Bruce, *Galatians*, 149.

103 cf. Lightfoot, *Galatians*, 135; Ian G. Wallis, *The Faith of Jesus Christ in Early Christian Traditions* (London: Cambridge University Press, 1995), 107.

104 Wallis, *The Faith of Jesus Christ*, 115-16.

105 Ibid., 113.

106 Mark A. Seifrid, "The Faith of Christ," in *The Faith of Jesus Christ*, eds. Michael F. Bird and Preston M. Sprinkle (Milton Keynes: Paternoster, 2009), 131.

is the faithfulness of Jesus, and it is seen that the contents of faith and Christians' believing act can be accommodated as one set without separating them. First of all, Jesus's faith presupposes his loyalty to God. He died on the cross (3:1). He became the curse of the law and he devoted himself to what God had planned. In Galatians 3:6-14, Abraham's believing (faith) in God and his descendants by faith are paralleled by the participation of Jews and Greeks in Jesus in the event that Jesus "made a curse for us." Just as those who believe "with Abraham" are blessed, "with the death of Jesus" they receive the blessing promised to Abraham, the Holy Spirit (2:20; 3:13-14). In another expression, those who are saved through Jesus's faithfulness live in Jesus's faithfulness as "the doers of the law live in them" (3:11-13). Therefore, without denying the human act of believing, the meaning of Jesus's faithfulness can be seen as defining the faith of Jesus.

1) 5:5, "according to our faith by the Spirit," faith seems to mean something objective. However, in the end, it must also be accompanied by an obedient response from the subject, "we". Or we could read it as following the faithfulness of Jesus. Similarly, in 6:10 it is called "the assumptions of faith." Two things are possible.[107] One is the home of the faithful, and the other is the home of believers. Paul asserts the truth of the gospel through Galatians. He criticizes those who preach a different gospel and rebukes the Galatians for accepting it. He claims that the gospel he preached originated with God, and that he himself was sent to them for this purpose.

2) 5:6, "in Christ Jesus" speaks of "faith working". It means that faith is sincere or active dynamically. If so, it can be seen that faith here means the human response expressed in the faithfulness of Jesus.

For Paul, faith originates in God. It was given to the world in the faithfulness of Jesus Christ. Humans who responded to Jesus's faith/faithfulness by 'believing in' act by possessing faith. Therefore, the way for all nations to become children of God and receive the Holy Spirit is through "faith in/faithfulness of Jesus Christ." Jesus's faithfulness in his atonement, in which he obeyed even unto death, made all the nations in him the heirs of the blessings promised to Abraham. However, that faith requires

---

[107] Hubing, *Crucifixion and New Creation*, 139.

people to act of faith ("from faith for faith" cf. ἐκ πίστεως εἰς πίστιν, Rom 1:17). Just as people become Abraham's descendants by faith, so by faith in Jesus's faithfulness they participate and die and live to become his people who live in him (Gal 2:20; 3:6-14). Paul's mission is a proclamation of the atoning faithfulness of Jesus. Gentiles hear it and receive the Holy Spirit as children of God by faith. This principle applies equally to the Jews (3:28-29, 4:1-7). All of them live a national way of life, but all must live in Jesus and according to the way of life of Jesus (cf. 6:14, "besides the cross of Christ").

## The Community of God's New Creation

God sent Jesus Christ into the world to redeem those who were under the law/sin. By the faith of Jesus and believing in, they become the children of God. And they all form one community as "we-community in Christ Jesus and the Holy Spirit. They are newly created to live in the law of Jesus Christ and by the guidance of the Holy Spirit. This is the ultimate goal of God's mission.

### 'We-Community'

God's mission in the faith of Jesus is that his mission story is aimed at all nations, including Israel. [108] Paul asserts that the promise given to Abraham for all nations was fulfilled by Jesus Christ. [109] In 4:4 ("fullness of time"), God sent his Son to adopt sinners as his own. [110] "The shift in focus from what God has done in Christ (4:4-5) to Christian sonship (4:6-7) pivots on the figure of the

---

[108] Caneday notes the expression, in context, of Christ or of Abraham. If he is of Christ, whether slave or free, male or female, Jew or Greek, he/she belongs to the true lineage of Abraham (Caneday, "The Faithfulness of Jesus Christ," 193). In light of 3:29, Galatians 2:15-16 contrasts "origin from Torah and origin from Christ". Candeday's claim of "origin" is well shown in περιτομῆς, ἐθνῶν ἁμαρτωλοί, ἄνθρωπος ἐξ ἔργων νόμου, which is not an issue of "works-righteousness" in 2:12, 15, 16 (Ibid., 194). In 3:10, ὅσοι γὰρ ἐξ ἔργων νόμου εἰσίν (3:10) is ἄνθρωπος ἐξ ἔργων νόμου "a person from deeds required by the Law" (2:16) is ἑρμα forming a parallel relationship with "works-righteousness," it refers to who "origins" from Christ (Ibid., 195). Thus, the preposition ἐκ in these phrases means "origin" "affiliation." Thus, it is likely that in 3:7, 9 Paul uses ἐκ as "origin" "affiliation", also in ἐκ πίστεως. (Ibid., 196).

[109] Longenecker, *Abraham's God*, 57.

[110] Ibid., 60.

Spirit, just as God has sent the son (4:4), so God has sent the Spirit (4:6)."[111]

Paul highlights "we" (ἡμεῖς of the plural noun of ἐγώ) "in Jesus" (4:3 [3:26-29]).[112] Paul refers to both Jews and Gentiles in "us," including himself. All of them were adopted as sons of God (4:5).[113] Paul uses "us" and "you" repeatedly in his epistles, especially in the discussion of 3:15-4:7. This seems to make a distinction between "us" (Jewish Christians) and "you" (gentile Christians). Das discusses the parallel structure of Donaldson's study of "we" in Galatians 3:10-14, 23-26, and 4:4-5. Donaldson saw that "we" in 4:3 refers to Jews who were under the elements (στοιχεῖα), whereas in 4:5 it refers to both adopted Jews and Gentiles. Based on the "'influx' pattern" in 3:13-14 and 3:23-29, he suggested that the flow of "we" is similarly changed in 4:3 and 4:5.[114] However, Das insists that "we" in 4:1-7 is a group that includes Jews and Gentiles in four ways:[115] First, Paul believes that because of the beginning of Jesus's saving work (4:4-5a), "we" are adopted. Gentiles form "us" with those who are Jews. All of them are created as one community of those who have received the Holy Spirit. Second, compared to "we"

---

[111] Ibid., 60.

[112] Paul uses the 'we' plural noun as follows: 1:4 we (Jews and Gentiles) are sinners in the age of the evil generation; 1:8, 23 we (Paul and evangelists [a Greek Titus, 2:3]); 2:4 we (Jews and Gentiles) have freedom in Christ Jesus; 2:9, 15 we (Jews) were sent to Gentiles (2:9); 2:16 we (Jews only?) believed in Christ Jesus; 3:13 we (Jews and Gentiles) were redeemed from the curse of the law; 3:24, (25) we (Jews? or with Gentiles?) had the law as the guardian. and were justified by faith (cf. "you" in 3:26, 29); 4:3 we (Jews) were enslaved to "the elements of the world"; 4:6 we (Jews and Gentiles) have the Son's spirit; 4:26 we (Jews?) had a mother Jerusalem; 5:1 we (Jews and Gentiles) are set free by Christ for freedom; 5:5 we (Paul and evangelists only?) are waiting for "the hope of righteousness"; 6:14, 18 our (Jews and Gentiles) Lord is Jesus Christ.

[113] Das, Paul and the Stories of Israel, 37.

[114] In 3:10, 13, 23-24, 25, "we" refers to Jews "under the curse of the law" or "under the law or elementary learning." In 3:14, 26 "we" refers to Jews and Gentiles. Thus, "those who are under the law" refer to the Jews, and "adopted" means both Jews and Gentiles (4:5). In particular, "you" (plural) in Christ is placed between "us" and "us" adopted, referring to both Jews and Gentiles who have received the gospel of Abraham, as children of God. Longenecker thinks that in 4:3 and 4:5, the first-person plural "us" may include both Jewish and Gentile Christians. However, he argues that since 4:4-5 quotes the confessions of early Jewish Christians, "we" in v. 3 certainly refers primarily to Jewish Christians (Longenecker, Galatians, 164, 172).

[115] Das, Paul and the Stories of Israel, 38-42.

in 4:3 also referring to "you" under "elements" in 4:9, the first-person plural "we" and the second-person plural "you" are the same people under the elements of the universe. Third, while in 4:1-2 Paul speaks of the natural Israelites who were to be under "custodianship until the appointed time" (3:23), in 4:3-7 "we" are the Galatian Gentile Christians as adopted heirs. Fourth, in Paul's logic, "us" adopted through Christ's redemptive act means both Jews and Gentiles (cf. Rom. 9:4).[116]

In terms of the completion of the oneness of Jew and Gentile, Das' analysis may seem more in line with Paul's logical development. Paul went on to emphasize that both Jews and Gentiles are adopted children of God through Christ (4:3-7). In 3:28-29, "we" who are divided in terms of national distinction became one by being one in Jesus. Although he repeatedly uses "you" in distinguishing the recipients of the letter, Paul does not distinguish Jewish Christians from Gentile Christians in "us" who became children of God through the redemptive event of Jesus Christ and received the Holy Spirit.[117] From this point of view, it could be argued, as Das claims, that "we" in 4:3, 5 includes both Jews and Greeks.

However, one hypothesis is that Paul's phrase καὶ ἡμεῖς can certainly be read as making a distinction from "you". If, as in the context of 3:23, the στοιχεῖα of the world implies the law, it seems reasonable to see "we" as "Paul and his fellow believers of Jewish birth." [118] Certainly, the emphasis in 4:9 that "you" (Gentile Christians) were "enslaved to those that by nature are not gods" and were enslaved under στοιχεῖα means, after all, that Paul is saying that both Jews and Gentiles did the same thing as στοιχεῖα in the

---

[116] cf. J. B. Lightfoot, *St. Paul's Epistle to the Galatians. A revised text with introduction, notes, and dissertations* (4th ed., Macmillan and Co., 1874), 166–167. Lightfoot suggests, on the basis of 4:11, that Paul uses "us" in the overall narrative flow, regarding Jews and Gentiles as one.

[117] Martyn's interpretation is similar to Das' in two respects. First, I saw that "heirs" in 3:29 and "heir" in 4:1 were connected. Second, Paul said in 4:3-5a, "So also we… " suggests that you are using a formula. This formula contains "we" and "you" (plural), to show all of humanity "under the power of the elements of the cosmos." That formula is also used in the context of God sending his Son at the appointed time to deliver mankind from slavery (vv. 4-5). As Martyn observes, Galatian Gentile Christians being sons of God (3:26) and heirs as descendants of Abraham (3:29) are not heirs in 4:1 or "receiving" in 4:5 adoption as sons" (Martyn, *Galatians*, 384).

[118] Bruce, *Galatians*, 193.

world. It can be inferred that it meant to say that it was in a state. Also, in 3:23-4:7, we-you-us-you/we structure is formed.

| | |
|---|---|
| 3:23-25 | Until faith came, "we" were "under the law" or "under the guardians." |
| 3:26-29 | "You" are those who are to be inherited as "sons of God" through faith. |
| 4:1-5a | "We" were "under guardians and stewards," or "under the rudiments," or "under the law." |
| 4:5b | "We" are those for whom the sonship has been granted. |
| 4:6-7 | "You" are sons. "We" are the sons who receive the Holy Spirit and call God Father, and are the ones who will receive the inheritance. |

If "we" and "you" make a distinction between Jewish and Gentile Christians in 3:23-25 and 26-29, it seems natural that in chapter 4 there is also a division into two. Therefore, one presupposition is, 'Could it not be read that Jew "we" were under the law in 4:1-5, but because of the Son of God, we Jew Christians received sonship?' And just as you (Gentiles) received the Holy Spirit by becoming sons in verse 6, we (Jews) also received the Holy Spirit. In other words, through this argument, Paul asserts that just as Jew "we" were confirmed to be God's children by receiving the Holy Spirit, the Galatian believers also claim to be God's children and inheritors by receiving the Holy Spirit. By this Paul's intention is to remind the Galatian Christians that it is not by the law, but by the receiving of the Spirit, that "us" and "you" are united in the children of God. At this point, it seems reasonable that Longenecker suggests that the first-person plural "we" in 4:3 refers to Jewish Christians (cf. 2:15-16; 3:13-14, 23-25).[119]

However, even in such a reading, Paul's irregular use of the subject causes confusion to the reader. In 3:28, "you" refers to both Jews and Greeks. Ethnic divisions disappear in Christ. Similarly, in 4:6, it is contradictory in time that God sends his Son's Spirit into

---

[119] Longenecker, Galatians, 164.

"our" hearts "because you are his sons." Those who received the Holy Spirit are obviously Jewish Christians and are preaching the gospel to the Gentiles. Yet, the fact that God gave the spirit of His Son into our hearts to call God Abba Father shows that the line between "you" and "us" is ambiguous. Paul already asserted that Jews and Gentiles are one in Christ. Even though there is a racial distinction between "us" and "you" as Jews and Greeks, I think that his focus is on Jews who have become children of God in Christ and who have received the Holy Spirit. It seems that he maintains his attitude in 3:28 that Jews and Greeks became one.[120]

Paul said that "in Jesus" all of them became children of God equally. And they received the Spirit of Jesus and came to live as the heirs of God.[121] For this, God sent his Son and the Holy Spirit. Longenecker says that the formula of sending is not ontological, but functional. This formula describes God's redemptive action toward mankind.[122] After all, Paul's phrase "in Christ" is a paradigm for the realization of God's mission. He saw that both Jews and Greeks equally shared in salvation by faith "in Christ."[123]

## The Community of the New Creation: Living according to the Spirit

God sent the Holy Spirit to those who were redeemed through Jesus (4:6). They are those born of the Spirit (4:29). By the Holy Spirit, they call God Abba Father (4:6). Paul makes a distinction between those who are born according to the flesh. Those who have received the Spirit stand in the freedom given by Christ and are never again subject to a yoke of slavery (5:1). They obey the law perfectly (5:3, 5). It does not make them righteous because of it, but those who have already been justified by faith live according to faith through the Holy Spirit (5:4-5). Paul's mission had the purpose of

---

[120] F. F. Bruce, *The Letters of Paul: An Expanded Paraphrase (Ga 3:23–29)* (Grand Rapids, MI: Eerdmans, 1965), 31.

[121] Longenecker, *Galatians,* 164.

[122] Ibid., 170.

[123] Terence L. Donaldson, "The 'Curse of the Law' and the Inclusion of the Gentiles:
Galatians 3.
13-14," *NTS* 32 (1986): 94–112. The equality of 'We-community' is not limited to Jews and Greeks only. It also applies to the distinction between slave and free, male and female (3:28). In Jesus, 'We-community' is one based on equality.

leading the Galatians into the realm of Jesus's intimate and obedient relationship with God. [124] Paul said that the Gentiles were sent "a hearing the gospel and believing it," so that they might receive the Holy Spirit. While the Jerusalem community insists on circumcision, feasts, and the law, Paul proclaims faith and the Holy Spirit. Longenecker argues that Paul's proclamation as a "new creation" has meaning in Jesus Christ, whether circumcised or uncircumcised (5:6, 6:15).

The mission that God sent Paul is ultimately to continue the new creation. Paul is willing to suffer for the "church of God" and "the faith" he persecuted (1:13, 23; 5:11, 6:12; cf. Acts 9:21). [125] He boasts only of "the cross of Jesus Christ," which shows the faithfulness of Jesus Christ (Gal 6:14a). Since he has already died on the cross and lives in Jesus Christ, the Son of God, he boasts only of his cross (2:20; 6:14b). Paul urges the community of faith newly created through the cross of Jesus Christ to live according to the Holy Spirit. In 5:16, Paul contrasts the lust of the flesh with the way of the Spirit. He declares in 1:4 that "we-community" as the community of God's new creation has been redeemed from the evil age. All the members of that community were freed from sin through the cross of Jesus and became children of God. And according to the Holy Spirit given to them, they can live freely.

First, they are free to live according to the faith of Jesus and their believing
it (5:5-7). Believers do not seek righteousness by law, but choose to live "according to faith by the Spirit" (5:1-5). It means a life of choice according to the freedom they have been given. Because the goal of their life is to follow the faith of Jesus, not the desire of the flesh. Paul called this way of life "walking in the Spirit" (5:16). Another expression is that if Christians "live by the Spirit, they also walk by the Spirit." Those who are in the faith of Christ have the ability to freely choose between the works of the flesh and the fruits of the Spirit. And the result is the completion of "the hope of righteousness." If Martyn's understanding is right, "we eagerly await what we confidently hope for, rectification at God's hands." [126] This is an eschatological hope. Paul speaks of future events by using

---

[124] Longenecker, *The Triumph of Abraham's God*, 65.
[125] Hubing, *Crucifixion and New Creation*, 119-35, 138.
[126] Martyn, *Galatians*, 472.

the expressions "to inherit the kingdom of God" or "to reap eternal life" (5:21, 6:8). The fact that Paul himself has nothing to boast about except the cross of Jesus is probably because he obtained "righteousness" through faith and lives with hope in that faith (6:14). For that, he chose persecution not for "the pride of the flesh" but for "the pride of the cross of Christ" (6:13-14).

Second, they have "the law of Christ." The formula "the Law of A" has various uses in Romans (Rom 3:27, "Law of observance" or "the law of faith"; 7:22/8:7, "the law of God"; 7 :23/25, "the Law of Sin"; 8:2 "the Law of the Spirit of life in Christ Jesus").[127] Martyn saw that 7:22 and 8:7 indicates God as the source of the law. Furthermore, 3:27, 7:23, 25, 8:2 also from a syntactic point of view, "'the Law in the possession of A' or 'the Law as it has been taken in hand by A' or 'the Law as it is determined by A'." 8:2 speaks of "the life-giving Spirit of Christ" as opposed to their use, while 7:23, 25 means the law in the possession of sin.[128] And its usage is similar to Galatians 6:2, where Paul says "Christ has brought the scriptural Law to completion, restoring it to its original singularity, and thus causing it to be the whole of the Law for the church."[129] Martyn's argument helps us to understand that the church, as a new creation, was given the way Christ fulfilled the laws. The church community must live by way of Jesus's life. Paul objected to redemption from sin through the works of the law, but he did not deny the essential teaching of the law (5:14). It was not against God's promises (3:21). Paul teaches that those who have received righteousness as a gift through Jesus Christ must live according to the essential requirements of the law that Christ fulfilled. This is love. He gave his own life for "believers, us." Therefore, just as Christ bore his cross according to his faithfulness to God, so his people must bear each other's burdens as well as theirs, according to Jesus's faithfulness to God (6:2, 4-5). Bruce calls this one's responsibility before God and they have to take their own responsibility.[130] This realm is their way of life in the public realm. The law of Christ sacrificed itself to form the community of the new creation. Likewise, Christians must

---

[127] Ibid., 556.
[128] Ibid., 557.
[129] Ibid., 558.
[130] Bruce, *Galatians*, 263.

not only fulfill their responsibilities within the community, but also build the community by bearing each other's burdens.

The law of Christ is the teaching of the whole law to perfect love (5:13-14). It is to do good to everyone (6:9-10). By this, those who "hold up the hope of righteousness according to faith by the Spirit" in 5:5 achieve faith/faithfulness that works through love in Jesus Christ (5:6). Love is the fruit of the Spirit of Christ (5:22).[131] It is the essence of God-given life in Christ.[132] He sees "faith at work" as vitally produced by love. That love has already been revealed by Jesus's faithfulness (2:20). The love that God has accomplished through the faithfulness of his Son by sending him into the world is a new creation that must bear fruit more abundantly by those who are in Christ. Paul calls on Galatian Christians to choose to "serve one another through love" (5:13).

In summary, Paul explains that Jesus and the Holy Spirit were sent through God's mission, and the beginning of the work of redemption. All people trust in Christ's faith/faithfulness, and through faith are redeemed from the curse of the law and sin. And we receive the Holy Spirit and live according to it. For this work, Paul was also sent as a missionary. He lives a life of preaching the gospel that boasts only the cross of Christ, aiming not only to Galatia but also to all nations to live the life of Christ's new creation. To become a believer by accepting the faith/faithfulness of Christ is allowed to receive the Holy Spirit that God gives His children. That is why to live in the Holy Spirit is the goal of his mission.

## Conclusion

This study was to read Galatians from a missional perspective. Paul explains his gospel by focusing on the story of God's mission. First, God "redeemed those under the law" (1:4, "atoned for our sins") by sending his Son. Second, it is the story of the fulfillment of the promise of God giving the Holy Spirit to all nations (Jews and Gentiles) according to Abraham's promise (3:6-9, 11, 13-14, 23-26, 4:5). Third, it is through the faith/faithfulness of Jesus Christ that all nations can receive the Holy Spirit. For Paul, Jews and all the Gentiles became children of God through 'the faith of

---

[131] Martyn, *Galatians*, 473.
[132] Bruce, *Galatians*, 233.

Jesus/believing it.' They not only live as 'we-community' in Jesus Christ, but also walk as a new creation by the Holy Spirit. These three contents are the central story of Paul's gospel. And God is sending his apostles to Jews and nations to accomplish his mission. Paul's missionary story is placed in the middle of God's sending story.

# Bibliography

Arndt, William F. and F. Wilbur Glngrich. *A Greek-English Lexicon of the New Testament and Other Early Christian Literature*. Chicago: The University of Chicago Press, 1971.

Barrick, William D. "The New Perspective and 'Works of the Law'." *The Master's Seminary Journal* 16 (Fall 2005): 277-92.

Bell, Richard H. "Faith in Christ: Some Exegetical and Theological Reflections on Philippians 3:9 and Ephesians 3:12." In *The Faith of Jesus Christ,* edited by Michael F. Bird and Preston M. Sprinkle, 111-28. Milton Keynes: Paternoster, 2009.

Betz, Hans D. *Galatians: A Commentary on Paul's Letter to the Churches in Galatia*. Philadelphia: Fortress, 1979.

Bruce, F. F. *The Letters of Paul: An Expanded Paraphrase (Ga 3:23–29)*. Grand Rapids, MI: Eerdmans, 1965.

_____.*The Epistle to the Galatians*. Grand Rapids, MI: Eerdmans, 1982.

_____. *The Book of Acts*. Grand Rapids, MI: Eerdmans, 1960.

Caneday, Ardel B. "The Faithfulness of Jesus Christ as a Theme in Paul's Theology in Galatians." In *The Faith of Jesus Christ*, edited by Michael F. Bird and Preston M. Sprinkle, 185—205. Milton Keynes: Paternoster, 2009.

Capes, David B., Rodney Reeves, and E. Randolph Richards. *Rediscovering Paul*. Naperville, Ill.: InterVarsity, 2007.

Crandfield, C. E. B. "'The Works of the Law' in the Epistle to the Romans." *Journal for the Study of the New Testament* 43 (1991): 100.

Das, A. Andrew. "Another Look at ἐὰν μὴ in Galatians 2:16." *Journal of Biblical Literature* 119 (2000): 529-39.

_____. *Paul and the Jews*. Edited by Stanley E. Porter. Peabody, Mass.: Hendrickson, 2003.

_____. *Paul and the Stories of Israel: Grand Thematic Narratives in Galatians*. Minneapolis: Fortress, 2016.

Donaldson, Terence L. "The 'Curse of the Law' and the Inclusion of the Gentiles: Galatians 3.13-14." *NTS* 32 (1986): 94–112.

_____. "'The Gospel that I Proclaim among the Gentiles' (Gal 2.2): Universalistic or Israel-Centered." In *Gospel in Paul*, edited by L. Ann Jervis and Peter Richardson, 166-93. JSNTSup 108; Sheffield: Sheffield Academic Press, 1994.

Downs, David and Benjamin J. Lappenga, *The Faithfulness of the Risen Christ: Pistis and the Exalted Lord in the Pauline Letters*. Waco, TE: Baylor University Press, 2019.

Dunn, James D. G. "Works of the Law and the Curse of the Law." *New Testament Studies* 31 (1985): 523-92.

_____. *Christology in the Making: A New Testament Inquiry into the Doctrine of the Incarnation*. Grand Rapids, MI: Eerdmans, 1989.

_____. *The Epistle to the Galatians*. Peabody, Mass.: Hendrickson, 1993.

_____. "Echoes of Intra-Jewish Polemic in Paul's Letter to the Galatians." *Journal of Biblical Literature* 112 (1993): 459-77.

_____. "Once More, PIXTIX CRIXTOU." In *Pauline Theology: Looking Back, Pressing On*. Vol. IV of *Pauline Theology: Looking Back, Pressing On*. Edited by E. E. Johnson and D. M. Hay. 61-81. Atlanta: Scholars Press, 1997.

Fitzmyer, Joseph A. *Romans: A New Translation with Introduction and Commentary*. Anchor Bible 33. New York: Doubleday, 1993.

_____. *The Acts of the Apostles: a New Translation with Introduction and Commentary*, Vol. 31. New Heaven, Mass.: Yale University Press, 2008.

Furnish, Victor Paul. *2 Corinthians*. AB 32; New York: Doubleday, 1984.

Goulder, Michal. *St. Paul versus St. Peter*. Louisville, Ky.: Westminster John Knox, 1994.

Gundry, Robert H. "The Nonimputation of Christ's Righteousness." In *Justification: What's at Stake in the Current Debates*, edited by Mark Husbands and Daniel J. Treire. 21. Downers Grove, Ill.: InterVarsity, 2004.

Hay, David M. "*Pistis* as 'Ground for Faith' in Hellenized Judaism and Paul." *Journal of Biblical Literature* 108 (1989): 461-76.

Hietanen, Mika. *Paul's Argumentation in Galatians: A Pragma-Dialectical Analysis*. London: T&T Clark, 2007.

Hays, Richard. B. *The Faith of Jesus Christ: The Narrative Substructure of Galatians 3:1–4:11.* Grand Rapids, MI: Eerdmans. 2002.

Hong, In-Gyu. *The Law in Galatians.* Journal for the Study of the New Testament, Supplement Series 81. Edited by Stanley E. Porter. Sheffield: Sheffield Academic Press, 1993.

Hubing, Jeff. *Crucifixion and New Creation: the Strategic Purpose of Galatians 6.11-17.* London: T & T Clark, 2015.

Kim, Seyoon. *The Origin of Paul's Gospel.* Tübingen: J. C. B. Mohr, 1984.

Lightfoot, J. B. *St. Paul's Epistle to the Galatians. A revised text with introduction, notes, and dissertations.* 4th ed., Macmillan and Co., 1874.

Longenecker, B. W. *Galatians.* WBC 41. Dallas: Word, 1990.

_____. "Defining the Faithful Character of the Covenant Community: Galatians 2:15-21 and Beyond." No Pages. England, 1995.

_____. *Galatians.* Anchor Bible 33A. New York, London, Toronto, Sydney, Auckland: Doubleday, 1997.

_____. , *The Triumph of Abraham's God.* Edinburgh: T & T Clark, 1998.

_____. "Narrative Interest in the Study of Paul: Retrospective and Prospective," in *Narrative Dynamics in Paul: A Critical Assessment.* Edited by Bruce W. Longenecker. Louisville: Westminster John Knox, 2002.

_____. *The Epistle to the Romans: A Commentary on the Greek Text.* Edited by I. H. Marshall & D. A. Hagner. Grand Rapids, MI: Eerdmans, 2016.

Marshall, I. Howard. *New Testament Theology.* Naperville, Ill.: InterVarsity, 2004.

Martyn, J. L. *Galatians: a New Translation with Introduction and Commentary.* Vol. 33A; London: Yale University Press, 2008.

Matlock, R. Barry. "Detheologizing the Debate: Cautionary Remarks from a Lexical Semantic Perspective," *NovT* 42 (2000): 1-23.

_____. "'Even the Demons Believe': Paul and πιστις Χριστου." *CBQ* 64 (2002): 300-18.

_____. "Saving Faith: The Rhetoric and Semantic of πίστις in Paul." In *The Faith of Jesus Christ*, edited by Michael F. Bird and Preston M. Sprinkle, 73-89. Milton Keynes: Paternoster, 2009.

Moo, Douglas J. *The Epistle to the Romans.* New International Commentary on the New Testament. Edited by Gordon D. Fee. Grand Rapids: Eerdmans, 1996.

_____. *A Theology of Paul and His Letters: The Gift of the New Realm in Christ.* Grand Rapids, MI: Zondervan, 2021.

Mounce, William D. *Greek for the Rest of Us: Mastering Bible Study without Mastering Biblical Languages.* Grand Rapids, MI: Zondervan, 2003.

Owen, Paul L. "The 'Works of the Law' in Romans and Galatians: A New Defense of the Subjective Genitive." *Journal of Biblical Literature* 126 (2007): 562-63.

Porter, Stanley E. "The Rhetorical Scribe: Textual Variants in Romans and their Possible Rhetorical Purpose." In *Rhetorical Criticism and the Bible,* edited by S. E. Porter and D. L. Stamps; JSNTSup 195; London: Sheffield Academic Press, 2002.

_____. *Verbal Aspect in the Greek of the New Testament, with Reference to Tense and Mood.* New York: Lang, 1989.

Porter, Stanley E. and Andrew W. Pitts. "πίστις with a Preposition and Genitive Modifier: Lexical, Semantic, and Syntactic Considerations in the πίστις Χριστοῦ Discussion." In *The Faith of Jesus Christ,* eds. Michael F. Bird and Preston M. Sprinkle, 35-56. Milton Keynes: Paternoster, 2009.

Sanders, E. P. *Paul, the Law, and the Jewish People.* Philadelphia: Fortress, 1983.

Seifrid, Mark A. "The Faith of Christ." In *The Faith of Jesus Christ,* edited by Michael F. Bird and Preston M. Sprinkle, 129-46. Milton Keynes: Paternoster, 2009.

Schreiner, Thomas R. *Romans.* Grand Rapids: Baker, 2004.

_____. *Paul, Apostle of God's Glory in Christ: A Pauline Theology.* Leicester: InterVarsity, 2001.

Schliesser, Benjamin. *Abraham's Faith in Romans 4.* Wissenschaftliche Untersuchungen zum Neuen Testament 2. Tübingen: J. C. B. Mohr, 2007.

Silva, Moses. "Faith versus Works of Law in Galatians." In *Justification and Variegated Nomism: the Paradoxes of Paul.* Vol. 2 of *Justification and Variegated Nomism: the Paradoxes of Paul,* edited by D. A. Carson, Peter T. O'Brien, and Mark Seifrid, 246-47. Grand Rapids: Baker, 2004.

Wallace, Daniel. *Greek Grammar Beyond the Basics.* Grand Rapids: Zondervan, 1996.

Wallis, Ian G. *The Faith of Jesus Christ in Early Christian Traditions.* London: Cambridge University Press, 1995.

Watson, Francis. "By Faith (of Christ): An Exegetical Dilemma and its Scriptural Solution." In *The Faith of Jesus Christ,* edited by Michael F. Bird and Preston M Sprinkle, 147-84. Milton Keynes: Paternoster, 2009.

Williams, Jarvis J. and Trey Moss. "Focus on 'All Nations' As Integral Component of World Mission Strategy." In *World Mission: Theology, Strategy, & Current Issues*, ed. Scott N. Callaham and Will Brooks. Bellingham, WA: Lexham, 2019.

Witherington, Ben. *Grace in Galatia.* New York: T & T Clark, 2004.

Witherington, Ben and Darlene Hyatt. *Paul's Letter to the Romans.* Grand Rapids: Eerdmans, 2004.

Wright, N. T. *The New Testament and the People of God.* London: Fortress, 1992.

_____. "4QMMT and Paul: Justification, 'Works,' and Eschatology." In *History and Exegesis,* edited by Sang-Won Son, 104-32. New York, London: T & T Clark, 2006.

# CHAPTER 3

## WHY CONTEMPORARY APOLOGETIC INDULGENCES WITH THE IDEALITY OF SCIENCE NEEDS TO BE REFORMED

by Finney Premkumar

## Introduction

It is an absolute privilege for me to contribute to a publication in honor of Dr. Joseph Tong and Dr. Mel Loucks. If the old adage that "we stand on the shoulders of those who have come before us" is true, then its concrete embodiment is in and through the life of these two remarkable and God-fearing men. Our debt to them transcends anything that can be expressed in words. Nevertheless, I offer the following as a tribute especially in the context of their apologetic contribution to the academy and the Church of Christ.

This undertaking will explore the ways in which the Evidential[1] Approach, Reformed Epistemology and apologetic strategies (like historical and cumulative case arguments) in general take the ideality of science to be normative and offer a potential corrective to the current context. The scope of this particular work does not permit beyond a few comments to provide some context for the rise and privileged status of science within academia and culture at large. The ideality of science was concretely formulated by a period that scholars[2] often identify as the "Enlightenment", along with its consequential tailoring of the modern mindset (Toulmin 1992). This scientific ideality was and is, implicitly and explicitly, accepted by apologists as the norm for dialogue or discussion about issues

---

[1] Another close ally to the evidential approach is the cumulative case argument. The most able proponent of this perspective is Richard Swinburne. He presents quite a compelling case in Swinburne (1979). The apologetic approach that goes against this generally accepted strand is the presuppositional method advocated by Cornelius Van Til.

[2] There are a number of scholarly works that address the influence and impact of the Enlightenment in developing intellectual, social and colonial attitudes, among others. Toulmin (1992) delves into many of the unarticulated elements often overlooked by other authors.

concerning faith and science. There has been a slightly more critical stance undertaken towards science in recent times, but the basic paradigm has not shifted much in how we carry out the task of apologetics as something that is done within the purview of normative science. This apologetic approach needs to be reformed. Accordingly, first and foremost, I will briefly outline the basic position and argument forwarded by those who subscribe to these apologetic schemes in an effort to unearth their implicit and explicit assumptions about the nature of science. I will argue that these apologetic undertakings try to utilize the theories that science seems to represent, without asking the more fundamental question as to whether science has any kind of representational power and why (representational in terms of moving beyond structural-functional to access-oriented designations). In other words, they implicitly assume the ideality of science and its realistic (metaphysical) reach. Secondly, I will provide a strong case for anti-realism in science due to the fact that satisfaction of a given theory by the rules of method might warrant acceptance of the theory without thereby being truth conferring since its reliability or confirmation does not exemplify nor explain why it conduces to truth in a non-epistemic sense. I will further clarity why methodology in science (or any other discipline) aligns more with rational justification or what can be justifiably believed (sometime referred to as warranted assertability) rather than with a word-world fit (in terms of correspondence) or truth. I will conclude by briefly outlining a more "reformed" apologetic attitude in view of the non-ideality and non-representational status of the scientific enterprise focusing particularly on the kinds of possibilities open to the apologist in dialogue with the scientific discipline.

## The Approach of some Prominent Contemporary Apologists

Much of the historical and contemporary apologetic[3] measures have tried, with much success, to utilize a vast capital of resources

---

[3] When thinking about Apologetics we immediately become cognizant of St. Paul utilizing the term *apologia* in his trial speech to Festus and Agrippa or 1st

for the effective defense of the Bible in general and the Gospel in particular. The asset that seems to have gained somewhat of an exclusive reign in the complex and evolving set of means employed in current apologetic methodology seems to be science[4]. There are a number of apologists who not only see science as a valuable resource but also comprehend it as such due to its perceived realistic[5] grip (Craig 1979, 1984), (Geisler 1976), (McDowell 1972) (Moreland 1987, 1989), (Plantinga 2010, 2011), (Polkinghorne 1997, 1998).

Let us look at the commitments that pre-configure into the paradigms of some prominent contemporary apologists. John Polkinghorne observes that "it seems impossible to believe that science could have been successful as it is unless it really represents

---

Peter 3:15 where we encounter the need to provide a reason for the hope within. I agree with the basic biblical mandate and this paper in no way argues for the ineffectiveness of apologetics in general but rather focuses on specific approaches that might be ineffective.

[4] It's very difficult to configure the lines of demarcation between science and non-science disciplines. The best I think we can do is identify regularities that gain "normativity" not due to identifiable intrinsic values but rather due to practicing communities which distinguish one practice from another. The demarcation problem is not unique to science and it really brings to the fore the fundamental problem of trying to deal with fundamentals. How do we really access the seemingly objective/fundamental lines that separate regions or domains of inquiry which can only be identified as such at the expense of such inquiry?

[5] This realism functions on at least 3 levels. Metaphysically, realism is committed to the mind-independent existence of the world investigated by the sciences. More specifically, it is committed to the claim that what is described or conceptualized outruns its descriptive and conceptual content. Epistemologically, realism is committed to the idea that theoretical claims (interpreted literally as describing a mind-independent reality) constitute knowledge of the world. This contrasts with skeptical positions which, even if they grant the metaphysical and semantic dimensions of realism, doubt that scientific investigation is epistemologically powerful enough to yield such knowledge, or, as in the case of some antirealist positions, insist that it is only powerful enough to yield tentative knowledge regarding observables (Woit 2006). Semantically, realism is committed to a literal interpretation of scientific claims about the world. In common parlance, realists take theoretical statements at "face value". According to realism, claims about scientific entities, processes, properties, and relations, whether they be observable or unobservable, should be construed literally as having truth values. This semantic commitment contrasts primarily with those of so-called instrumentalist epistemologies of science, which interpret descriptions of unobservables simply as instruments for the prediction of observable phenomena, or for systematizing observation reports.

aspects of the way things really are[6]" (1998, p.7). He concludes in his book <u>Belief in God in an Age of Science</u>, based on the Terry Lectures at Yale University, that we need to take "the stance, so natural to the scientist, that concepts that have broad explanatory power, making swathes of experience intelligible, should be expected to have ontological reference" (1997, p.45). For instance, he refers to J.J. Thomson's picture of electrons as being little hard lumps of matter, tiny charged "currants" in the atomic "pudding" while he himself regards them as excitations in the quantum field of the electron. The difference, he says is in regards to the evolution of descriptive strategies and not in terms of its representational reach and suggests that there should be a "charity of reference" (1997, p.105).[7]

William Lane Craig[8], as most of us are aware, is an ardent defender of the Kalam Cosmological Argument (1984) and utilizes recent scientific theories, namely the Big Bang theory to support the second premise in his formulation of the argument[9] in his books, <u>Reasonable Faith</u> and <u>The Cosmological Argument</u>[10]. The Steady

---

[6] He ends the chapter in his book (Polkinghorne, 1998) with these words: "God has written two books for our instruction. The book of Scripture and the book of Nature and I think we need to try to decipher both books if we are to understand what's really happening." This again betrays a deep-seated commitment to scientific realism. It may be generated by an inductive or case-by-case approach rather than a naïve all-out realism that regards all pronouncements of science along these representational lines. Regardless, it considers science and its theories as actual representations or approximations that will eventually represent the quantities or entities they approximate (mature theories).

[7] Polkinghorne comments, "although social factors can accelerate or inhibit the growth ofscientific knowledge, they do not determine the character of that knowledge" (1997).

[8] It should be mentioned that although Craig is a scientific realist regarding most issues, he does reserve certain anti-realistic tendencies. For instance, he does not subscribe to platonic forms or the existence of abstract entities including numbers.

[9] See Craig (1979) and (1984) for a more detailed presentation of his arguments. I am not sure of how to conceive of his position that science confirms what are purely philosophical deductions since he does seem to suggest that theories, both philosophical and scientific, are in fact theory-laden. However, he is cautious not to identify his position with Thomas Kuhn's proposal in The Structure of Scientific Revolutions (1970).

[10] There are a host of other books that follow a similar strategy. These include Geisler (1976),Sproul, Gerstner, Lindsey (1984) and McDowell (1972), just to name a few.

State model of a beginning-less universe and the Oscillating model of a universe expanding and contracting from eternity are rejected due to their lack of experimental verifiability and contrariness to observational evidence. He then advances the Big Bang theory as that which "receives powerful scientific confirmation" since the scientific evidence concerning the expansion of the universe and the thermodynamic properties of closed systems indicates that the universe is finite in duration, beginning to exist about fifteen billion years ago. This, he sees, as a truly remarkable substantiation of purely philosophical arguments (1979, p.76). J. P. Moreland, in his book Scaling the Secular City[11] and especially in Christianity and the Nature of Science, seems to affirms a very sympathetic disposition toward scientific realism. He says for instance, after discussing the components of rational realism and the correspondence theory, that whatever difficulties may have been encountered it does not "warrant a wholesale abandonment of scientific realism, but they might show that a naïve acceptance of scientific realism is unjustified" and he proposes an "eclectic philosophy of science wherein a realist or antirealist stance is taken on a case-by case approach." However, he does not really provide any criteria for when to choose one disposition over the other (1989, p.71).

This tendency also seems to pervade the literature of those who subscribe to Reformed Epistemology. Alvin Plantinga, in a dialogue with Daniel Dennett at the APA meeting in 2009, argues that contemporary evolutionary theory as a scientific formulation is compatible with theism while its naturalistic assumptions which call for an unguided process are not (2010). He thereby, re-describes the dialogue to be a conflict between theism and naturalism while maintaining the theological solidarity and continuity with science. His well-known "evolutionary argument against naturalism" seeks to show that there is actually an incompatibility between unguided evolution and naturalism such that those who hold to the former cannot endorse the latter as a truth claim. He makes a similar point in his book, Where the Conflict Really Lies. After arguing that the world described by science is

---

[11] Moreland (1987) is a little more evidentially motivated than his later books. He is quite a bit critical of scientific realism in his more recent writings but still remains committed to a correspondence theory of truth in reference to science (that scientific terms have referential significance).

compatible in more respects than not with theism, he concludes that there is "indeed a science/religion conflict.....but it is not between science and theistic religion. It is between science and naturalism. That's where the conflict really lies" (2011, p.350). The basic motivational and undergirding element of these various approaches is that science, for the most part, does yield representational[12] value and provides real privileged access or ontological thrust through its current theories or those in the process of gaining maturity (often tied to progressive approximations that are truth-tracking).

## Problems Facing Scientific Realism

The contemporary apologetic scene shows a clear commitment to scientific realism. A position that is either pre-supposed or postulated based on pragmatic output (that science works or yields results) rather than on any identifiable intrinsic feature within the discipline.

### The Problem of Method and Truth

The problem is that these contemporary apologetic schemes seem to overlook the lack of any intrinsic connection between method which is inferential without necessarily being representational and the non-epistemic nature of truth. While satisfaction of a given theory by the rules of method might warrant acceptance of the theory, it is not thereby truth conferring since its reliability or confirmation does not exemplify nor explain why it conduces to truth in a non-epistemic sense[13]. The question has to do with what it is we are cognitively accessing when involved in utilizing scientific methodologies to represent "reality". For

---

[12] Representation and correspondence are being utilized interchangeably for the purposes of this particular paper. The reference is to a 'Word-World' fit.

[13] A scientific non-realist or one who does not find the correspondence perspective appealing need not therefore become inclined toward relativism or skeptical of objectivity. The specific contention in that the bridge between accepted epistemological systems, including scientific methodologies and the ontological thrust they seek or presume is not apparent.

instance, in Quantum Mechanics [14] , in order to resolve the measurement problem there are various approaches and methodologies that are proposed. Some have proposed that decoherence, which involves interactions between the quantum process and its radiative environment, helps resolve the problem of rapidly minimizing all but one state and by cancelling interference effects (decoherence does not have predictive ability in terms of possible outcomes). Another group believes that interaction with large systems brings about the collapse of the wavefunction. Still another,

looks at the matter involved in the interaction to determine if whether the collapse occurs, or where quantum gravity plays a crucial role. All in all, the nature of access i.e., what exactly in being represented by the various approaches/methodologies is still very much in question since we cannot clearly configure the reality of the object, the nature of the experience and how explanatory models (like the ones in quantum theory) help us create that link to access or approximate the 'real'.

## The Ambiguity of Experience

We can gain greater clarity by considering a parallel case of access-ambiguity through a simple discussion of experience in general. Suppose that an experience $E$ is not an experience or awareness of a phenomenal or intentional object $X$. Then it would seem that the relevant cognitive access has to be to $E$ itself, that is to person $S$'s having $E$. On the other hand, suppose that the relevant phenomenological experience E involves being aware of something $X$, the phenomenal or intentional object of $E$. In such a case what is it that $S$ is aware of in having experience $E$. Would the relevant cognitive access attributable to $S$ be access to $X$ or to $E$ (namely $S$'s experience of $X$)? A relevant alternative would be to ask if $X$ can be collapsed to $E$, that is, if $S$ experiencing $X$ in $E$ can be contained within $E$. This is not to say that $X$ cannot outrun $E$ (thereby making it objective). However, any such pronouncement of $X$ in $E$ for $S$ would have to be postulated. The ontological substantiation of $X, E,$ or $X$ in $E$ for $S$ cannot be verified or validated. The rules and

---

[14] See Clayton, Polkinghorne, Russell, Wegter-McNelly (1988) for a thorough discussion of the various issues in Quantum Mechanics. The latter part of the book focuses on the theological significance of these areas of inquiry.

inferences that govern scientific practice seem to display a similar ontological ambiguity when confronted with this issue of the incommensurability of methodology and truth.

## No- Miracles Argument and Tarski's T-Scheme

Rational scientific inquiry is governed by the rules of scientific method and adherence to the rules of this peculiar methodology warrants the rational acceptance of experimental results and scientific theory (as in the case of the measurement issue discussed above). As such, scientists who accept results or theories licensed by the rules of method do so on a rational basis. Thus, rational justification in science is closely connected with the scientific method. However, while it is evident that there is a close relation between method and rational justification, substantive questions remain about the relation between method and truth. The general theoretical view of method is a monistic one, according to which there is a single, historically invariant method, the use of which is the characteristic feature that distinguishes science from non-science. According to this scheme, scientific method not only encompasses justification and validation, but more importantly, a uniquely truth conferring status as well. This was essentially the argument proposed by Alan Musgrave[15] as the "Ultimate argument for scientific realism." Hilary Putnam originally called it the "No-miracles argument"[16] saying that " Realism is the only philosophy that does not make the success of science a miracle' (1975, p.73). This seems to be the implicit, and in some cases the explicit commitment of those within apologetic circles who appeal to science and scientific theories and their purported realism. The argument basically follows Tarski's *T-scheme*[17]:

(T) 'P' is true iff P.

---

[15] See Musgrave (1999) for a detailed study of the ultimate argument for scientific realism. However, much of it is a re-describing of the no-miracles argument made by Hilary Putnam is his1975 paper.

[16] For elaborations of the no-miracles argument, see Brown (1982), Boyd (1989), Lipton (1994), Barnes (2002), Lyons (2003), Busch (2008), and Frost-Arnold (2010).

[17] See Sankey (2000) for a more detailed study of Tarski's T-Scheme

While the *T-scheme* is not a definition of truth, it provides a minimal condition of adequacy that must be satisfied by any account of truth. However truth is conceived, the truth-predicate must behave in accordance with the *T-scheme* i.e. *P* cannot be true if person *S* believes that *P* and it is ~*P* or believes that ~*P* while *P*. Rather than a definition, the *T-scheme* is a schema on the basis of which meta-linguistic statements of truth-conditions may be formulated for sentences of an object-language. For example, replacing *'P'* in *(T)* by 'Electrons have negative charge' yields a statement of the truth-conditions of 'Electrons have negative charge' for the *T-sentence*:

(E) 'Electrons have negative charge' is true iff electrons have

negative charge.

Statements such as this assert the material equivalence of sentences that predicate truth and the sentences of which truth is predicated. The *T-scheme* thereby specifies a correlation between the truth of statements and the states of affairs that statements report. For it stipulates that, for any sentence *'P'*, *'P'* is true just in case a given state of affairs obtains, viz., the state of affairs that *P*. Thus, this strategy tries to bridge the gap between methodology and truth by showing that consistent methodological (empirical) success can only be explained in terms of truth. As such, all other explanations as outlined below seem inadequate to show why science has been so successful:

(i) T's predictions about observable phenomena are true

(ii) T is empirically adequate (Van Fraassen 1980)

(iii) The observable phenomena are as if T were true (Leplin 1993).

Even in cases where *T* is false or unsuccessful, the success of a theory *T* that is very wrong is explained by the approximate truth of a replacement theory *T'*. [18] It is because the unobservables

---

[18] For instance, let's assume that our best scientific theories tell us something true about the way the world "really" is, in an ontological sense. And further, for simplicity, let's assume a deterministic interpretation of those theories. In this

posited by $T'$ exist and have approximately the properties attributed to them that $T$ is successful. Indeed, we expect the very same theory that shows $T$ to be wrong to also explain $T''s$ observational success.

The basic affirmation is that $T's$ actually being true is the best explanation of why all the observable phenomena are as if it were true [19]. According to this understanding which conflates methodology and truth, truth consists in correspondence between a linguistically formulated statement of fact and an extra-linguistic state of affairs, where the state of affairs that makes a statement true is a mind-independent state of affairs.

The problem is that this conceptual relation is not as apparent as usually supposed. In fact, the non-epistemic nature of realist truth derives specifically from the mind-independent status of the

---

view, the universe as we know it began ~13.7 billion years ago. We'll set aside any questions about what, if anything, preceded the first instant and just draw a line there and call that our "initial state". Given the specifics of that initial state, plus the particular causal laws of physics that we have, the universe can only evolve along one path. The state of the universe at this moment is entirely determined by two, and only two, things: its initial state and its casual laws. But this means that the development of our scientific theories *about* the universe was also entirely determined by the initial state of the universe and it's causal laws. Our discovery of the true nature of the universe has to have been "baked into" the structure of the universe in its first instant. By comparison, how many sets of possible initial states plus causal laws are there that would give rise to conscious entities who develop *false* scientific theories about their universe? It seems to me that this set of "deceptive" universes is likely much larger than the set of "honest" universes. What would make universes with honest initial conditions + causal laws more probable than deceptive ones? For every honest universe it would seem possible to have an infinite number of deceptive universes that are the equivalent of "The Matrix" - they give rise to conscious entities who have convincing but incorrect beliefs about their universe.

[19] One might wonder, for instance, why a *particular* theory is successful (as opposed to why theories in general are successful), and the explanation sought may turn on specific features of the theory itself, including its descriptions of unobservables. Whether such explanations need be true, though, is a matter of debate. While most theories of explanation require that the *explanans* be true, pragmatic theories of explanation do not (Van Fraassen 1980). More generally, any epistemology of science that does not accept one or more of the three dimensions of realism—commitment to a mind-independent world, literal semantics, and epistemic access to unobservables—will thereby present a putative reason for resisting the miracle argument

truth-makers.[20] The point turns on the ontological independence of thought and reality, rather than on any epistemic aspect of the relation between thought and reality. Thus, instead of a multitude of particular methodologies independently or collectively tied to invariant basic laws, we have a variety of approaches with a sense of implicit interdependence looming in the background without any necessary orientation to truth[21]. The truthfulness of claims about the world is solely determined by the existence of states of affairs which obtain independently of human thought or experience. Hence, the belief that a given state of affairs obtains does not itself — i.e., *qua* belief — have any effect on the truth or falsity of that belief. The state of affairs may obtain, or fail to obtain, whether or not anyone believes that it does. This remains the case regardless of how well justified the belief may be unless truth is reduced to nothing beyond justification. Thus, given the mind-independence of the truth-makers, it is entirely possible for rationally justified beliefs about the world to be false. Indeed, given such mind-independence, the *entirety* of such beliefs might be false. Attitudes, beliefs and justifications in science, as is any area of study, are emergent properties which gain a certain amount of justification to be regarded as objective or converging on the objective due to regularities and their progressive institutionalization. This in no way structures any valuation or intrinsic correlation with the real or the ontological regardless of pragmatic success and does not in any way minimize the great strides made in science, especially in its technological application and implication.[22] However, the evident success in methodology is not translatable not computable to entailing truth in any sense.

---

[20] See Lycan (1985). He discusses the notion of signifiers which was introduced by Jacques Derrida.

[21] See Feyerabend (1999, p.36). He writes that "if science is indeed a collection of different approaches, some successful, others wildly speculative, then there is no reason why I should disregard what happens outside of it." Additionally see Rorty (2007, p.46). Pointing out the impossibility of purely objective methodologies he says, "there is really no such thing as either philosophical or scientific method."

[22] See Sankey (1997) and (2004) for a more extensive treatment.

**The Institutional and Socio-political Element**

Furthermore, the preceding view of science does not take into consideration the institutional and highly complex socio-political character of scientific pursuits. Even the current wave of excitement and aggressive promotion of string theory at the expense of other theoretical pursuits within physics can be seen as a political rather than an academic battle within the universities and contemporary culture at large. String theory attempts to comprehensively describe the macro (gravity) and micro (elementary particles) worlds by reducing them to vibrations of a single entity - a string - that obeys simple and beautiful laws. It claims to be the one theory that unifies all the particles and all the known forces in nature i.e., electromagnetism, gravity, the strong nuclear force and the weak nuclear force. However, we do not yet know what its fundamental principles are or whether there is even a complete and coherent theory that can go by the name "string theory."[23] There are strong doubts about whether string theory might be true but this skepticism is met with a sort of undermining by the community of physicists who subscribe to it. As such, the aggressive promotion of string theory has led to its becoming the primary avenue for exploring the big questions in physics (Smolin, 2007). It has gained such prominence that it's almost equivalent to a suicidal disposition for any emerging young physicist to not pursue it. Additionally, this conviction about string theory overlooks scientific pre-commitments and thereby stifles any other progressive or creative attempts to come to terms with the great problems in physics. To put this matter a different way, if a given

---

[23] See Greene (2004, p.102) where he states "Even today, more than three decades after its initial articulation, most string practitioners believe that we still don't have a comprehensive answer to the rudimentary question...What is string theory?" See also Woit (2006) and Smolin (2007, p.21), who states that "Even if we restrict ourselves to theories that agree with some basic observed facts about our universe, such as the vast size and the existence of dark energy, we are left with as many as $10^{500}$ distinct string theories - that's 1 with 500 zeros after it, more than all the atoms in the known universe." See Smolin (2007) for the five unsolved problems of physics. They are (1) the combination of general relativity with quantum theory into single theory. (2) Resolve the foundations of quantum mechanics. (3) Determine if the various forces and particles can be unified. (4) Explain how the free constants of nature came to be and (5) Explain dark matter and dark energy.

scientific community *(SC)* at a given point of time *t* accepted the standards *V*, then the preference of *SC* for theory *T* over *T'* on evidence *E* would be rational just in case the epistemic utility or conditional probability of *T* relative to *V* was higher than that of *T'*. However, in a new situation where the standards are different from *V*, it may be *T'* that is chosen over *T* making the alternate preference rational. In the case of string theory, as with any other theory in physics that is justified, the theory *T* if expanded into *T* = "string theory is true" equates to nothing more than a given SC's confirmation based on *V* that the epistemic utility of *T* (*T* = "string theory is true") is higher than *T'* on evidence *E*[24]. The point is that there is no clear agreement even on a particular theory that purportedly explains the cosmos in a beautiful or elegant way and we see the battle raging for the dominance of one scientific idea or particular narrative tradition over another in less than scientific ways.

## Apologetic Conversations with Science

Where does this leave the apologist and the apologetic task of conversing with science? A few comments will be issued before concluding. These are not meant to be comprehensive nor the final word on the topic at hand. However, the sincere hope is that it will

---

[24] For example, let's take a quick look at Mathematics, the language of science. In the case of mathematical formulations, the sort of structuralism I have outlined implies that there are no natural numbers as *particular objects*, that is, as existing things whose 'essence' or 'nature' can be individuated independently of the role they play in a structured system of a given kind. More generally, we say that there are only mathematical 'objects' as kinds of objects, that is, that there are 'objects' that can be individuated only up to isomorphism as positions in a structured system of a given kind. Thus, taking 'structured system' to mean 'model', we say that a mathematical theory, while framed by its axioms, can be *characterized* by its models, and the *kinds of objects* that the theory talks about can be *presented* by their being positions in models that have the same kind of structure. As such, the sentence '2 + 3 = 5' is not a claim about abstract objects (the numbers 2, 3, and 5); rather, it's a claim about piles of physical objects that exist in mathematical space. A person *S* within this theoretical structure may use elliptical statements and count proposition *P* {2 + 3 = 5} as pointing to *"P"* (Tarski scheme *P* iff *P*) as long as the latter *P* is a reaffirmation of the former *P*. The structural objectivity of *P* in no way implies or validates the truth of *P* in any ontological sense for *S* at *T* or in a sequence of $T_n$.

lead to an on-going and productive discussion on the intersection between faith and science.

Firstly, I affirm without any reservation, the authority and priority of Scripture. All disciplines and avenues of thought and investigation are circumscribed by axioms that cannot be proven within the system. These axioms are not something that we "argue to" but "argue from." This foundational level is the unarticulated constituent of every conceivable paradigm of thinking. Accordingly, the Christian takes the Bible to be the foundational and navigational axiom in his or her thinking just like the scientist, mathematician or anyone else involved in mental activity. The Christian, therefore, is not operating below par in terms of intellectual standards by invoking axioms because 'thinking' in any discipline or dimension of life is foundationally axiomatic.

Secondly, if science is in fact structurally constituted as I have argued, and the socio-linguistic and epistemic motivations are constitutive of this structure, then it seems that a more reformed approach will see the indulgence with science and its formulations in less rigorous and comprehensive terms. That is, if science does not provide the perceived ontological thrust assigned to its formulations historically, it can still be utilized in apologetic positions but in an *instrumental* but not *intrinsic* manner. The unquestioned acceptance of "scientific facts" due to a perceived word-world fit does not seem to hold when we view the enterprise from a structural standpoint. The structural regularity that ensues (what Thomas Khun called 'normal science') though validated observationally and experimentally thereby catapulting theories into a "mature" status still seems to fall short of representational or metaphysical value. Accordingly, objectivity, validation, experimentation etc. in science are given a purely structural status, retaining success without translating it into truth (as was done in the "no miracles" argument).

Thirdly, if science and its methodological reach does not compute to realism then it should not be regarded as an ideal within academic circles and certainly not within the apologetic community. The need to somehow show the rationality of theological truth as well grounded because they complement science (which as I have argued is falsely seen to represent reality to a greater extent or more ideally that the other disciplines) needs to be rejected. The unfortunate consequence, in some cases of trying to make theology more like a science, has resulted in very reductionistic or naturalistic conclusions by exorcising the supernatural from theological discourses or by re-describing any of its vocabularies not in alignment with a 'scientific' perspective as mythological or somehow reserved for purely narrative purposes. However, if the representational link is not intact and the supposed realistic or truth-tracking nature of science is very much in question then it opens up quite a bit of space for the apologist in terms of possible discourses and dialogues. In fact, it will provide the context for a more inter-disciplinary outlook on the part of the apologist when science is no longer seen as the ideal but as one among the various disciplines within the academy exemplifying what Alasdair Macintyre (1981) calls "tradition-constitutedness" and therefore manifesting similarly limited ways.

Finally, the apologist is accordingly free to reject any scientific theories that do not align with his to her theological convictions since the conclusions and confirmations in each respective structure, although there may be structural inter-penetrations at various points, will necessarily yield inconsistencies due to how science is in fact practiced in our contemporary context. This rejection can be maintained even in the face of observational validation of scientific theories since these inferential claims are not meta-structural and therefore do not yield anything like a final vocabulary. All in all, the apologist may freely and calmly be a scientist or *refer* to science for the defense of the faith as long as faith is not *exclusively or primarily* defended by science.

## Bibliography

Barnes, E. C. (2002). 'The Miraculous Choice Argument for Realism', *Philosophical Studies*, 111: 97–120.

Boyd, R. N. (1983). 'On the Current Status of the Issue of Scientific Realism', *Erkenntnis*, 19: 45–90.

Brown, J. R. (1982). 'The Miracle of Science', *Philosophical Quarterly*. 32: 232–244.

Busch, J. (2008). 'No New Miracles, Same Old Tricks', *Theoria*, 74: 102–114.

Cartwright, N. (1983). *How the Laws of Physics Lie*, Oxford University Press: Oxford.

Clayton, Polkinghorne, Russell, Wegter-McNelly (1988). *Quantum Mechanics: Scientific Perspectives on Divine Action*. Vatican Observatory Publication: Vatican State.

Craig, W. L. (1979). *The Kalam Cosmological Argument*. Wipf & Stock Publishers: New York

Craig, W.L. (1984). *Reasonable Faith: Christian Truth and Apologetics*. Cross Way Books: Wheaton.

Devitt, M. (2005). 'Scientific Realism', in F. Jackson& M. Smith (eds.), *The*
*Oxford Handbook of Contemporary Philosophy*. Oxford University Press: Oxford.

Feyerabend, P. (1999). *Conquest of Abundance*. University of Chicago Press: Chicago.

Fine, A. (1986). 'Unnatural Attitudes: Realist and Antirealist Attachments to Science', Mind, 95: 149–177.

Frost-Arnold, G. (2010). 'The No-Miracles Argument for Realism: Inference to an Unacceptable Explanation', *Philosophy of Science*, 77: 35–58.

Geisler, N. (1976). *Christian Apologetics*. Baker Book House: Grand Rapids.

Giere, R. N. (1988). *Explaining Science: A Cognitive Approach*. University of Chicago Press: Chicago.

Kuhn, T. S. (1970). *The Structure of Scientific Revolutions*. University of Chicago Press: Chicago.

Laudan, L. (1981). 'A Confutation of Convergent Realism', *Philosophy of Science*, 48: 19–48.

Leplin, J. (1993). 'Surrealism', *Mind*, **97**: 519-524.

Lipton, P. (1990). 'Prediction and Prejudice', *International Studies in the Philosophy of Science*, 4: 51–65.

MacIntyre, A. (1981). *After Virtue: A Study in Moral Theory*. University of Notre Dame Press: Notre Dame.

McDowell, J. (1972). *Evidence that Demands a Verdict*. Thomas Nelson Publishers: Nashville.

Moreland, J.P. (1987). *Scaling the Secular City: A Defense of Christianity*. Baker Book House: Grand Rapids.

Moreland, J.P. (1989). *Christianity and the Nature of Science*. Baker Book House: Grand Rapids.

Musgrave, A (1999). *Essays or Realism and Rationalism*. Oxford University Press: Oxford.

Papineau, D. (2010). 'Realism, Ramsey Sentences and the Pessimistic Meta-Induction', *Studies in History and Philosophy of Science*, 41: 375–385.

Plantinga, A. (2010). *Science and Religion: Are they Compatible?* Oxford University Press: Oxford.

Plantinga, A. (2011). *Where the Conflict Really Lies: Science, Religion and Naturalism*. Oxford University Press: Oxford.

Polkinghorne, J. (1997). *Belief in God in an Age of Science*. Yale University Press: New Haven.

Polkinghorne, J. (1998). *Quarks, Chaos and Christianity*. Crossroad Books: New York.

Rorty, R. (2007). *Philosophy as Cultural Politics*. University of Cambridge Press: London.

Sankey, H. (1997). *Rationality and Incommensurability.* Princeton University Press: Princeton.

Sankey, H. (2000). 'Methodological Pluralism, Normative Naturalism and the Realist Aim of Science', in Robert Nola and Howard Sankey (eds.), *After Popper, Kuhn and Feyerabend: Issues in Recent Theories of Scientific Method.* Kluwer Academic Publishers: Dordrecht.

Smolin, L. (2007). *The Trouble with Physics.* Houghton Mifflin Co: New York.

Sproul, R.C., Gerstner J., Lindsley, H. (1984). *Classical Apologetics.* The Zondervan Corporation: Grand Rapids.

Swinburne, R. (1979). *The Existence of God.* Oxford University Press: Oxford.

Van Fraassen, B. (1980). *The Scientific Image.* Oxford University Press: Oxford.

Toulmin, S. (1992). *Cosmopolis.* The University of Chicago Press: Chicago.

Woit, P. (2006). *Not Even Wrong.* Harvard University Press: Cambridge.

# PART II

# MISSION

# CHAPTER 4

## ETHNIC/RACIAL RECONCILIATION: ROLE OF CHRISTIAN MISSION IN A GLOBALIZING WORLD

by Lami Rikwe Ibrahim Bakari, PhD

### Introduction: Setting the Stage

Discussions about racial and ethnic reconciliation are common, but there is little evidence of racial or ethnic[1] reconciliation to show.[2] Human brutality is on the rise,[3] cultures and nations are confronting each other right at their doorsteps.[4] In the global south, cultures are thriving despite Europeans' attempts, for example, to

---

[1] I will use race and ethnicity interchangeably. Andreas Wimmer (2008) writes "First, treating race as fundamentally different from ethnicity overlooks the fact that the same group of individuals might be treated as a race at one point in history and as another type of ethnic category at another: in the 16th and 17th centuries, African slaves in the United States were primarily defined as pagans and their English masters as Christians. Only after about 1680 was this ethnoreligious distinction gradually replaced by the ethnosomatic differentiation between "white" and "Negro" (Jordan 1968). Second, phenol typical differences are often evoked as one among *other* markers of ethnic distinction, as the racialization of ethnicity in Rwanda and Burundi and many other contexts with a history of ethnic violence shows. Third, distinguishing between race as fixed, imposed, and exclusionary, on the one hand, and ethnicity as fluid, self-ascribed, and voluntary, on the other hand, would not do justice to constellations (such as among Serbs in Kosovo, Albanians in Serbia) where ethnic groups experience degrees of forced segregation, exclusion, and domination usually associated with race" (Andreas Wimmer, "The Making and Unmaking of Ethnic Boundaries: A Multilevel Process Theory," *American Journal of Sociology* 113/4 (2008): 974).

[2] For detail discussion on this subject see, for example, Emmanuel Katongole, *A Future for Africa: Critical Essays in Christian Social Imaging* (Chicago: University of Scranton, 2005); Michael Emerson & Christian Smith, *Divided by Faith: Evangelical Religion and the Problem of Race in America* (New York: Oxford University Press, 2000); Colin E. Gunton, *The Theology of Reconciliation* (New York: T&T Clark, 2003).

[3] See Mark Omi Hay, *Ukunbuyisana: Reconciliation in South Africa* (South Africa: Cluster, 1998).

[4] Duane Elmer, *Cross-Cultural Conflict: Building relationship for effective ministry* (Downers Grove, Ill.: InterVarsity, 1993); and Simon Harrison, "Cultural Boundaries" (Ulster University: EBSCO, 2003).

make "black Europeans" out of Africans.[5] In the global north, even within the same nation, people are becoming aware of their cultural and ethnic differences. This thriving culture and re-awareness of ethnic and cultural differences has few implications—I will mention only three. First it makes the belief that emerging globalization and urbanization would eradicate commitment to individual cultures too simplistic at best.[6] Second, it shows how human understanding of these differences often slowed down the process of reconciliation. Third, failure to address human differences has a high probability of impairing every effort toward reconciliation.[7]

For Christians, however, ethnic and cultural differences provide the opportunity for us to prove that the gospel message is for all people as they accept each other and work on their differences.[8] As a result, ethnic and racial reconciliation should have a greater impact on the theory and practice of Christian mission today than ever before. Wilbert R. Shenk, in his article "Christian Mission and the Coming Clash of Civilizations," observes that reconciliation has not played a significant role in Christian mission and that in a world torn by rivalries of many kinds, only the gospel of Jesus can bring healing. He said this will happen when reconciliation becomes central to missionary motivation and theological rationale for

---

[5] For a critical discussion on the European experiment see, Kwame Bediako, *Theology, and Identity: The Impact of Culture upon Christian Thought in the Second Century and in Modern Africa* (Oxford: Regnum Books International, 1999).

[6] See Richard Shweder, *Recipes for Cultural Psychology: Why Do Men Barbecue?* (Cambridge, Massachusetts: Harvard, 2003). Globalization has made it possible for people to encounter and engage each other at their doorstep. But encountering each other this way has resulted in more conflict than ever before. Scholars such as Dennis Walker, Shmuel Shamai, Zinaida Ilatove, Richard Alba, and others observe that this is due to identity crises that occur at the boundary of relationships and the conflict of cultural change.

[7] See, Stewart Copper and Fredrick T.L Leong, "Introduction to the Special Issue on Culture, Race and Ethnicity in Organizational Consulting Psychology," *American Psychological Association and the Society of Consulting Psychology* 60/2 (2008); Shmuel Shamai and Zinaida Ilatove, "Assimilation and ethnic boundaries: Israeli students' attitudes toward Soviet Union student immigrants," *Adolescents*, 36/144 (2001).

[8] Paul Hiebert, "The Missionary as Mediator of Global Theologizing," *Globalizing Theology: Belief and Practice in an Era of World Christianity* (Grand Rapids: Baker, 2006), 296.

missionary witness. [9] To explore this opportunity, this study explores a theological understanding of reconciliation as a mission and the nature of reconciliation, and the content and context of reconciliation as mission.

## Theological Implications of Reconciliation

Differences are inherently part of God's design for his world, and ethnic boundaries, as we have seen, do not signify exclusion. They are elastic. They can meet the demand for change by contacting others who are different. Despite the accommodating nature of ethnic boundaries, reconciliation has not been achieved. We can point to some pockets of racial, political, and religious reconciliation processes going on in the world. But in the wider sense of the word, we are far from reconciliation worldwide. Especially today, the need for reconciliation has escalated beyond what we can imagine.

The difficulty in achieving racial reconciliation and the wider spectrum of social, political, economic, and class segregation, etc., indicates a basic problem in our understanding and in the handling of the hostility that is prevalent, not just in America but in the world today. [10] Some scholars blame this on an inability to take reconciliation seriously, insufficient knowledge of biblical reconciliation, the limiting of racial reconciliation to political institutions and public education, and the fear of liberalism. [11] While others argue that the demands of true reconciliation can be enormous, they consider the Christian's fear of the cost of bridging the gap between "us" and "them" as one key hindrance to racial

---

[9] Wilbert R. Shenk, "Christian Mission and the Coming Clash of Civilizations," *Missiology* 3 (2000): 303. Also see, David W. Shenk, "The Gospel of Reconciliation within the Wrath of Nations," *International Bulletin of Missionary Research* (2008): 3-9.

[10] Robert L. Gallagher and Paul Hertig (ed.), *Landmark Essays in Mission and World Christianity* (New York: Orbis Books, 2009), 29.

[11] This issue is treated in a few studies, for example, J. Robert Priest and Alvaro Nieves, *This Side of Heaven: Race, Ethnicity, and Christian Faith* (New York: University Press, 2007); Craig Ott, *Encountering Theology of mission: biblical foundations, historical developments, and contemporary issues* (Grand Rapids, Mich.: Baker, 2010); and Alvin Sanders, *Reconciliation 101: A Handbook for Ministry Leaders* (Minneapolis: EFCA Publication, 2009).

reconciliation. [12] As Shenk observes, reconciliation will not be achieved until reconciliation becomes the motivation for missionary thought and practice.

In what follows, we will explore the theological perspective of reconciliation as it relates to the mission of the church, taking into account the meaning and significance of reconciliation and the nature, content, and context of reconciliation.

## The Meaning and Significance of Reconciliation

The discussions of the meaning and significance of reconciliation go hand-in-hand with the history and meaning of race and racism. Some scholars observe that race and racism are recent developments in the West. [13] For such scholars, reconciliation is viewed as a social and political issue, probably only between blacks and whites in America. Conversely, others argue that, although racism and any kind of alienation and hostility directed at other human beings by others have a social and political face, the root cause of disharmony and hostility in the world is spiritual. [14] It may be true that the call for reconciliation in the West today might have at its core the black-and-white social discrimination and racism of the eighteenth century. However, reconciliation has always been a scriptural mandate for Christians for every human division (Rom. 5:6-11; 2 Cor. 5:17-20).

Alvin Sanders, writing from the above position, uses the family metaphor to demonstrate that sin interrupted the blissful relationship experienced by Adam and Eve and indeed all of creation in the Garden of Eden. The intended unity of the family was disrupted, causing disharmony. God, all through the ages, has worked to restore the human family, starting with the call of

---

[12] See David P. Gushee, "More Free, At Least Racial reconciliation is making some unexpected demands on me" in *Christianity Today* (2007); Ferdinand Nwaigbo, "Christ Jesus: Our Peace and Reconciliation" African Ecclesia! Review (n.d.): 356-384.

[13] See, for example, Ivan Hannaford, *Race: The History of an Idea in the West* (Maryland: The John Hopkins University Press, 1996); George Fredrickson, *Racism: A Short History* Princeton, NJ: Princeton University Press, 2002).

[14] Murray J. Harris, *The Second Epistle to the Corinthians: A Commentary on the Greek Text* (Mich.: Grand Rapids, 2005), 436; Sanders, Reconciliation 101, 33; and Jarvis Williams, *One New Man: The Cross and Racial Reconciliation in Pauline Theology,* Nashville, TN: B&H Publishing, 2010), 9.

Abraham and, consequently, the promise of a blessing for the whole human race (Gen. 12:1-2). This culminated in the birth and death of Jesus. Through the death of Jesus, reconciliation was achieved between God and man, and reconciliation between humans became possible. In this sense, "reconciliation is God's initiative in restoring a broken world to Himself. God's intentions by reconciling 'to himself all things' through Christ include the relationship between people and God, between people, and with God's created earth. Christians participate with God by being transformed into ambassadors of reconciliation."[15]

Understanding human hostility, damnation, and alienation concerning sin enlarges the scope of hostility and the demand for reconciliation. Sanders holds that reconciliation is an expression of God's work within. He believes that reconciliation is the primary mission of God in a fallen world and compels the Christian to genuinely seek and practice reconciliation. He sees Genesis 3:15 as the announcement of the conflict that will continue to dominate the world until Christ returns. Although agreeing with the above, Emmanuel Katongole observes that theological discussions of racial reconciliation have always remained at the theoretical level, perpetuating racism. He, therefore, argues for a historical, sociological, and pragmatic approach to reconciliation. On the contrary, Jarvis Williams' numerous biblical examples force the point beyond doubt that social alienation and historical hostility today are part of a long history that has as its base the fall of Adam and Eve in the Garden of Eden.

Katongole maintains that the theological approach to racial reconciliation puts reconciliation on a universal scale that does not address the particular struggles of Africa. Synthesizing Williams and Katongole, Nwaigbo and Sanders insist that Christian reconciliation must have a theological and philosophical base but must be accompanied by practical social action. Racism and racial categorization are based on the fall of God's creation. Therefore, theology must inform the way men and women carry out the work of reconciliation in the world. Priest and Nieves agreeing with this point of view, observes that history shows that the church has acted in weakness with regards to the issue of race, but he insists that a

---

[15] Sanders, Reconciliation 101, 67.

proper understanding of racial reconciliation from a proper biblical or theological perspective will stimulate true racial reconciliation.[16]

Placing reconciliation on a theological pedestal challenges each person to experience reconciliation with God and to rediscover his or her humanity in the process. Out of that will flow the call to a ministry of reconciliation.[17] A Hausa adage says, "*In mutum yace zan baka riga, ka dubi ta wuyarsa.*"[18] (We cannot give what we do not have.) Reconciliation, then, becomes pertinent to the mission of God in the world. It is important to briefly explain what these two concepts, mission and reconciliation, entail.

1. *Mission:* Mission is the creative use of the whole biblical tradition in teaching and content. The Christian mission is motivated by compassion and passion in our dealings with human beings.[19] "The mission of the church, then, has all the dimensions and scope of Jesus' ministry and may never be reduced to church planting and the saving of souls. It consists in proclaiming and teaching, but also in healing and liberating, in compassion for the poor and the downtrodden." [20] So the mission is ultimate for God, but human beings are invited to participate with Him. [21] God is the Creator, Redeemer, and Sanctifier for the sake of the world, a ministry in which the church is privileged to participate. "Mission has its origin in the heart of God. God is a fountain of love. There is a mission because God loves people."[22] Mission as reconciliation is then the instrument by which the love of God is expressed to people, anywhere and everywhere, by all means.

---

[16] See J. Robert Priest and Alvaro Nieves, 2007, *This Side of Heaven: Race, Ethnicity, and Christian Faith* (New York: University Press, 2007).

[17] Robert Schreiter, *Reconciliation: Mission and ministry in a changing social order* (Maryknoll, NY: Orbis, 1992), 68.

[18] If someone says they are giving you a dress, look at the one they are wearing. The implication is that people do not usually give what they do not have. If they promise you a fine new dress and the one they are wearing is dirty, tattered, and torn, it will be difficult to believe them.

[19] Gallagher, *Rethinking the Color Line*, 6-12.

[20] Ibid., 15.

[21] Andrew Walls and Cathy Ross (eds.), *Mission in the 21st Century: Exploring Five Marks of Global Mission* (Maryknoll: Orbis, 2008), 104.

[22] David Jacobus Bosch, *Transforming Mission: Paradigm Shifts in Theology of Mission*, New York: Maryknoll, 1991), 393.

2. *Reconciliation:* When the word *reconciliation* is mentioned, the first thing that comes to many minds is social justice. We picture two warring parties—individuals or communities—that need to be settled, hence the idea of justice and peace. Embedded in these words is a call for fairness in judging the situation and the expectant result, which is peace. Christian reconciliation includes this, but it is definitely much more. Christian reconciliation is rooted in Christological, ecclesiastical, and cosmic theological realities. Grounded as such, reconciliation is, finally, a mode of being rather than a strategy.[23]

## The Nature of Reconciliation

In the New Testament, the person who declares faith in God through Christ becomes a member of God's family. Every believer has direct access to the family table through faith, just like Abraham (so Sanders). Conversely, Ephesians 2:1-3 and 11-22 show the horrible situation of humanity, alienated not only from fellow human beings but also from God. However, Yusufu Turaki observes that through the work of God, humans are reconciled not only to God but also to fellow human beings. Reconciliation placed in the realm of the redeeming mission of God in the world provides the freedom that the church needs in responding to the different needs that readily confront God's creatures in the world.[24] Reconciliation, as the task of mission, has two dimensions: the vertical and the horizontal.[25]

### The Vertical Dimension

Reconciliation has a theocentric dimension. When God is missing in talks and plans for reconciliation, good plans and strategies fail to achieve peace and harmony.[26] Only as people are reconciled to God their maker, experiencing the forgiveness offered in Christ alone, do they find the power to forgive and to reconcile

---

[23] Robert Schreiter, *Reconciliation: Mission and ministry in a changing social order* (Maryknoll, NY: Orbis, 1992), viii.

[24] Ott, *Encountering Theology of mission: biblical foundations*, 141.

[25] Ibid., 96.

[26] See See Robert Schreiter, *The Ministry of Reconciliation: Spirituality and Strategies*, (New York: Orbis, 1998).

human relations at the deepest level, forgiving one another as Christ forgave them (Eph. 4: 32).[27] Echoing this, Rick Richardson emphasizes the important place of live testimony in evangelism and conversion. [28] A personal and daily connection with God is necessarily a part of reconciliation.

## Horizontal Dimension

The horizontal dimension of reconciliation was never seriously considered as part of the Church's mission, but the evils done to humans by other humans all over the world have made this a very important topic in the list of mission problems.[29] Human beings need to be reconciled with other human beings. There are many broken relationships among individuals and communities in the world that must be repaired. In every situation, we need to tell each other the truth, give forgiveness, and receive forgiveness and consolation from one another.[30] Reconciliation demands that the agents of this reconciliation be reconciled to one another as a sign to those they seek to reconcile and also as hope for them that reconciliation can be achieved as individuals and communities.

Believers are called into a community, not only for the nurturing fellowship that we need to grow into who we ought to be as a sign of the Kingdom, but also because it provides a place to practice our vocation as people charged with the task of reconciling the world to God. [31] The Christian community points the way to eternal reconciliation, which leads to present reconciliation. The essence of the community is to equip Christians to take up their cross and follow Christ (Mark 8:34). How far should they take up the cross, and what is their message?

Next, the vertical and horizontal dimensions have few implications for Christians. But for the purpose of this study, I will discuss only two in what follows.

---

[27] Ott, *Encountering Theology of mission: biblical foundations*, 96.

[28] Rick Richardson, *Evangelism Outside the box: new ways to help people experience the Good News* (Downers Grove: Intervarsity, 2000), 119.

[29] Ott, *Encountering Theology of mission: biblical foundations*, 96ff.

[30] See Andrew J. Kirk, "What is mission?" A Lecture Presented at the Swedish Mission Council's Bi-Annual Meeting Swedish Mission Council, 2002), 16.

[31] Ott, *Encountering Theology of mission: biblical foundations*, 95.

## Restoration of Human Beings to God

"Everyone has sinned and is far away from God's saving presence. But by the free gift of God's grace, all are put right with him through Christ Jesus, who sets them free" (Rom. 3:23-4 GNT). Reconciliation must start where brokenness started. The need for restoration cannot be overemphasized. It is costly, but worth it. Restoration demands that all those who want to see their relationship restored must take practical steps to bring reconciliation and healing.[32] Andrew Kirk outlines five steps to that effect:

1. Recognizing and accepting the situation.
2. Admitting wrong.
3. Confessing wrong.
4. Repenting from the wrong,
5. Giving forgiveness, accepting the same unconditionally, and being willing to pay the price, no matter *what it is,* is very important to reconciliation.

Restoration is costly, not only because of the shame that we risk or our inability to achieve it, but also because it costs God His son. Jesus had to die so that the wrath of God might be appeased (Isa. 53:6). It took God Himself to provide us with the quickening of our spirit. Ephesians 2:1-10 gives a beautiful picture of this. This finished work of Christ on the cross of Calvary is the gospel message, which leads to the reconciliation of the human being with God. Through this event, human beings plug into the source of ultimate power—God, Himself—through the agency of the Holy Spirit to deal justly with God, one another, and the environment.[33]

### A Daily Personal Walk with God

Thomas V. Frederick, in "Discipleship and Spirituality from a Christian Perspective," infers that daily contemplation of how Jesus lived leads to a life empowered by Him who is with us always, even to the end of the age. We then begin an intentional imitation of Christ. We learn to "walk in his steps" (1 Pet. 2:21). It is on this

---

[32] Kirk, "What is mission?" 16.
[33] See Francis Anekwe Oborji, *Concepts of Mission: The Evolution of Contemporary Missiology* (Maryknoll: Orbis, 2006);

journey with God that we can find out where He is at work today so that we can join Him. It is here that we find the power to face the inadequacies that readily confront us.[34] Through this, we confess our sins and our weaknesses. Only then can we discuss the situation of the world we want to reach with the gospel.

## The Content and Context of Reconciliation as Mission

The content of reconciliation as the mission is the whole redemptive story of God found in the Old and New Testaments, from creation to eternity.[35] However, this story needs to be told in ways that bring dignity to people and liberate them and their culture to participate with the bearers of this message as partners in the reconciling process.[36] The whole story of God's love and His act of redemption in history, as recorded in the Bible and experienced by people everywhere, needs to be creatively told. The context of reconciliation then is the whole of God's creation (Gen. 3:17-18; Rom. 8:20-23). The whole creation groans under the weight of the fall.[37] This idea is widespread in the Scriptures. The context of reconciliation then becomes cosmic, wherever the curse is found. It is for everyone, everywhere, in every language. Racial reconciliation is a preview of Revelation 7:9-10, the great multitude standing before the throne and in front of the Lamb. Reconciliation presents an important opportunity for the Christian to partner with God in restoring His creation.

## The Opportunity in Reconciliation

Darrell Whiteman, agreeing with Sanders, says, "Human cultural diversity is necessary to give us a fuller picture of God's creation and how we need all of these perspectives from different languages and cultures to be able to understand God in all of God's fullness."[38] God is the initiator of ethnic diversity. It can be seen as different

---

[34] Thomas Frederick, "Discipleship and Spirituality from a Christian Perspective," *Pastoral Psychology* 56/6 (2008): 553-560.

[35] Christopher J. H. Wright, *The Mission of God's People: A Biblical Theology of the Church's Mission* (Grand Rapids: Erdmann, 2010), 39-46.

[36] Shusaku Endo, *Silence* (New York: Taplinger, 1969), 88.

[37] Ott, *Encountering Theology of mission: biblical foundations*, 85.

[38] Whiteman, "The role of ethnicity and culture in shaping Western mission agency identity," 67.

patterns on a mat or in a quilt. The beauty of the quilt is lost if there is only one piece of cloth, one pattern, or one color. It becomes inexpensive and common. Also, among the Irigwe people of Nigeria, plainness or colorlessness signifies lifelessness or death. A plain mat or plain wooden spoon is used only during mourning. In everyday life, a mat must have a mixture of designs and colors. "God's creational design is far from cookie-cutter uniformity. In the melodious mélange of Genesis 1, the Creator seems to delight in making opposites—but opposites that complement, not clash, opposites that harmonize, not antagonize."[39] God said that all He created, with all their differences, was good.

Christians can consciously choose to understand ethnic differences from God's perspective. When this happens, it is at this point that ethnic differences can become an opportunity to extend reconciliation and the means of reconciliation to others.[40]

## Means of Reconciliation

The redemptive work of Christ on the cross made reconciliation between God and human beings possible. The effect of this work of reconciliation between God and human beings forced those who had experienced reconciliation to become agents of reconciliation, and this is the total mission of God to the dying world. Gallagher notes, "The mission of the church, then, has all the dimensions and scope of Jesus' ministry and may never be reduced to church planting and the saving of souls. It consists in proclaiming and teaching, but also in healing and liberating, in compassion for the poor and the downtrodden. The mission of the church, as the mission of Jesus, involves being sent into the world to love, to serve, to preach, to teach, to heal, to save, to free."[41] The world requires love, salvation, healing, and freedom, and mission is how God, through the ministry of the church, extends mercy and the grace of reconciliation to all people.

As suggested above, brokenness in the world has as its source humanity's fall in the Garden of Eden. Isaiah 53:6 shows that it affected all of creation. This continues to enrage God. It took God

---

[39] Ken L. Davis, "Building A Biblical Theology of Ethnicity for Global Mission" in *The Journal of Ministry and Theology* (2003): 91-126, esp. 93.

[40] Davis, "Building A Biblical Theology of Ethnicity for Global Mission" 92.

[41] Gallagher, *Rethinking the Color Line: Readings in Race and Ethnicity*, 15.

Himself to provide us with a quickening of our spirit. Ephesians 2:1-10 gives a beautiful picture of this. Now we have a way out through the finished work of Jesus on the cross of Calvary. This finished work of Christ on the cross is the gospel message, which is the power of God for salvation from past, present, and future sin. This is the core of the Christian mission. This is the message that leads to the conversion (change of heart) of a person.

Conversion plugs human beings into the source of ultimate power. God, Himself, through the agency of the Holy Spirit, allows us to deal justly with God, one another, and the environment. Man's restoration to God, or *vertical* reconciliation, is the beginning of a transformation. Man's spirit, which was quickened at the entrance of God's word at conversion and then empowered by the Holy Spirit, puts on a new nature that is more in tune with God and doing right. Someone may say, "If this is true, why all these wars and hostilities among Christians, countries that are 'Christian', institutions, communities,[42] or even individuals?" I think I will be simplistic about this and point out that one major reason for the hostilities is that *horizontal* reconciliation has been neglected. Missions focusing on both the spiritual and physical situations of people then become the means for racial reconciliation. Healthy relationships and communities give a preview of the glory of God that is yet to be revealed; that is the hope of all God's creation.[43] The church must concern itself with both dimensions of reconciliation. They are inseparable.

The vertical reconciliation I will call it the birthing of a *new self* (1 Cor 5:17). It is spiritual, mysterious, and intellectual. The horizontal dimension of reconciliation provides the opportunity for the *new self* to express itself. Here, the words in James 2:14-18 become very relevant in that the vertical may be considered faith while the horizontal can be considered work. Vertical (faith) reconciliation without horizontal (work), or vice versa, is a missed opportunity. Real transformation starts with individuals who are reconciled to God and one another. In their newness of life and their relationships, they begin to thirst for more newness in their lives,

---

[42] Frederick, "Discipleship and Spirituality from a Christian Perspective," 559.

[43] Ernest M. Ezeogu, "From evangelization to reconciliation, justice and peace: Towards a paradigm shift in African mission priorities," *SEDOS Bulletin* 41/9 (2009): 353.

others' lives, and their environment, therefore increasing their involvement in the ultimate mission of God.

Mission provides how the church can reach the world with its liberating message. It offers an opportunity for people to accept the freedom and salvation that are in Christ. It also allows us to become agents of reconciliation. The mission can be summed up as the church mending or serving a broken world in the name of Jesus. The human structures that were erected under the influence of sinful minds also need to be dismantled. Men and women under such structures, either as oppressors or the oppressed, need to be set free. Leslie Newbigin observed that Christians can never stand in-between in a case of injustice; they are either on the side of the oppressed or the side of the oppressor. God chooses to mediate the message of reconciliation through his church.[44]

## Agent of Reconciliation on Earth

The agent of reconciliation on earth, as we have already seen above, is the church, the community of God's people and the apprentices of God for the work of reconciliation. The Christian faith has functioned as a force that brings together people who, hitherto, had been locked in irresolvable antagonism.[45] Though we are aware of situations that we wish we had done differently, we cannot deny the fact that the gospel, in dramatic ways, has through the centuries brought enemies face-to-face with each other in fellowship. Mark Omi writes of the important role the church played in the reconciliation process and attainment in South Africa. It was when the church rose up that reconciliation was achieved. It was possible because:

1. They articulated the problem. It was no longer white versus black. It was "Christians oppressing Christians using the Scripture."[46]

---

[44] Lesslie Newbigin, *The Gospel in Pluralist society* (Grand Rapids: Eerdmans, 1989).

[45] Romanucci-Ross and De Vos, Ethnic Identity: Problems and Prospects for the Twenty-First Century, 414.

[46] Hay, *Ukunbuyisana: Reconciliation in South Africa*, 37.

2. There arose prophetic voices among church leaders denouncing both the white and government oppression of the blacks.[47]
3. By the 1960s, the church had become active in conflict resolution.[48]
4. By 1975, the Catholic Bishop had drafted a letter requesting the repentance of whites.[49]
5. The church's resistance to government imposition on the people.[50]
6. The Kairos Document challenged Christians to take a greater stand for justice.
7. Church media for education were established.[51]
8. Rustenburg's conference was a call for the church to be united. It was titled "Toward a United Christian Witness in a Changing South Africa.[52]

From the time the church became conscious of the need to speak out for justice to the time the nation achieved its reconciliation process, it took about fifty years. It was an appropriate length of time for the process. When the time came for national reconciliation, it was the political leaders who were calling for reconciliation, not the church.[53] I believe it was because the church had already prepared them.

If truth-telling is a big part of reconciliation, as seen in South Africa, those with the spirit of truth are better prepared for it. Gallagher observes that the work of salvation and redemption of people is solely God's work, but it is He who chooses to use feeble human beings to this end. "To recognize that it is God, rather than any one of us who brings reconciliation, it is to acknowledge the breadth and the depth of pain and trauma that evil and violence wreak on us. Nor are we able to assess the persisting damage they continue to bring to human lives and communities." [54] Schreiter

---

[47] Ibid., 39.
[48] Ibid., 41.
[49] Ibid., 42.
[50] Ibid., 43.
[51] Ibid., 46.
[52] Ibid., 47-48.
[53] Ibid., 50.
[54] Gallagher, *Rethinking the Color Line: Readings in Race and Ethnicity*, 68.

insists that if we recognize that reconciliation is the work of God, this will strip us of our pride and the superiority complex that often characterizes those who seek, through Christ, to be agents of reconciliation. God then becomes the center of our attention. The church, His new community, will participate with Him in reconciling the world to Him because it is his ultimate desire to save his creation.

The church, as the community of those who have experienced reconciliation and are enjoying the fruit of it daily, becomes an agent of reconciliation here on earth. Through the work of Jesus on the cross and the indwelling power of the Holy Spirit, the church is enabled to demonstrate to the world the power of God to save and to completely save those who trust in Him. Clarence D. Weaver observes rightly that,

If peace (and justice) are the fruits of the Spirit, then they arise with an enduring and dynamic force, not simply from informed, articulate persons or astute ecclesial-politicians or statesmen, but primarily from those spiritual communities that the Spirit creates, nurtures, and sustains. One approach to moral and ethical questions is to attempt to build spiritual communities from which group solutions arise or in and through which conflicts are either resolved or reduced to the level where they no longer feed gross distortions of reality, keep social systems rigid, or are punitive when the central focus of peacemaking is peacemaking.[55]

It is through spiritual communities that God can properly serve peace and justice in the world. The church becomes the physical representative, or agent, of reconciliation, directing people to God's grace and power that can change them and continuing to build a community of reconcilers.

As a reconciler, the church has a double role that should help her be the best agent of reconciliation. The church's position as both a receiver and a giver of reconciliation is very strategic, making it serve with fear and trembling. The superiority complex that characterized early Western missions to other parts of the world signified that the church forgot its two-sided role. Weaver advises, "As agents of reconciliation, we were submitting ourselves to a

---

[55] Clarence D. Weaver, "Mutual mission: spiritual formation and the questions of reconciliation, peace, and justice" *Austin Seminary Bulletin* (Faculty ed.) 99/3 (1983a): 37.

process which would change us as much as it would change them."[56] Chris Rice and David P. Gushee hold that anyone who truly understands the effect of being reconciled will find that the natural self loses its power to hold and control others. They insist that the desire to do wrong will be there, but the power to do right is invested in us by God through the Holy Spirit. This is why I have difficulties understanding why ignorance should be a reason for the lack of racial reconciliation in America, especially when it concerns evangelicals.

## Conclusion

The works of literature indicated that there are differences in the world that are hurting relationships. Sin is deeper than the hurt we see. Reconciliation is God's way of bringing both spiritual and physical healing to his creation. He invites the church to be a partner with him in this. The mission is the means that he has provided for the church to carry out this mission. Situations may be different, but the message is the same.

God's love is one basic reason for our being reconciled to Him and the rest of His creation. But bigger than that is the establishment of God's power over the Kingdom of Darkness. Jesus came that He might save people but also that He might destroy the works of Satan that are readily displayed by the power of sin in humanity.[57] The Rigwe people believe that they are the only people that are well-cultured (they think they are the center of the universe, as Gladis Depree put it). The name Rigwe directly translates as "well-cultured and of good manner." This refers only to human beings. The Rigwe people, with such a misconception of themselves, are prone to look down on other people. Yusufu Turaki, commenting on Ephesians 2:11-22 in the *African Bible Commentary*, illustrates the situation between the Jews and the Gentiles in the story of an African man from a rural village who went to church for the first time. He discovered that someone from another tribe—one that his people despised—was also in the same church. He became angry and demanded to know what the person was doing there. He

---

[56] Clarence D. Weaver, "Mutual mission: spiritual formation and the questions of reconciliation, peace and justice," *Austin Seminary Bulletin* (Faculty ed.) 99/3 (1983b): 43

[57] Sanders, Reconciliation 101, 67.

called him names and embarrassed him in front of everyone. He was judging the other tribesman by old standards, e.g., where he came from, his tribe, and probably his abilities. Paul beautifully reminded the Ephesian church in his letter that those things that used to divide them (religion, culture, and race) no longer affect them because Jesus Christ has now united them in a new community, the Church.[58]

In 1 John 4:20, the Bible reiterates to believers that it is not possible to claim love for God and hate others—their brothers. The love of God is demonstrated only in our relationships with one another. The essence of a new community, a community free of hostility, signifies togetherness. The Christian is reconciled to God and others. Under this reconciliation, he or she becomes a reconciler of others. This is the essence of the mission of God that was enacted by Christ and continued by the church. This understanding sets our feet on the path to truly celebrating our "differentness" on the one hand and our unity on the other. To set our feet on the path of appreciating our differences is good, but it is not good enough until we walk on that path—that is what reconciliation is. It is walking on paths that bring healing and restoration to the whole creation. In the following paragraph, I will conclude with some practical steps to reconciliation.

If Christians are going to truly show the way from the negative view of racial differences to the positive and create the opportunity to give the world a preview of the glory to come, we must engage in deliberate acts that allow us to be the salt and light of the world as we were meant to be. Scholars such as Kirk, Hiebert, Sanders, and others view truth-telling, self-identification, acceptance, and grace in interpersonal relationships as key ingredients in social relationships that can lead to true reconciliation. I wish to recommend that Christians:

1.  Need to consciously reflect on their thoughts, words, and actions when they meet other people. The influence of race on our thinking or our interactions with other people is often buried deeper in our minds than we can imagine.

---

[58] See Yusufu Turaki, "Ephesians" in *African Bible Commentary*, edited by Tokunbo Adeyemo (Nairobi, Kenya: *Zondervan,* 2006).

2.  Spend time with people who are different from them. Individual Christians should take it upon themselves to make friends with believers and non-believers from other ethnicities and cultures. These include issues of interracial marriage, especially if they are both believers (Priest, Sander).

3.  Take time to identify their heritage. For instance, considering what it means to be a black Nigerian Christian or a white European Christian can allow each of us to accept who we are and then enable them to accept others. This kind of reflection can help them see that, though they are different from each other, they are not strangers to each other based on human nature and the image of God in us.

4.  Tell each other the truth, but in love. This demands that they listen to each other. Many years ago, one of my professors, addressing the issue of forgiveness, said that sometimes people are hurt by actions that we never thought were going to be offensive. She advised, "If somebody says I am offended by your action, even if you did not intend it, you owe that person an apology. Not that you were wrong or you intended it, but because they were hurt and they told you." I have found that very helpful in my relationships.

5.  Need to associate with others. It is natural to want to associate with those who are like us, but if Christians are going to fulfill their role as the bearers of reconciliation for this generation, they must also seek to relate positively with those within and outside the church who are different from them, sometimes completely the opposite of them (Matt. 5:46-48). It is in these kinds of relationships that the light of the glory of God shines brighter. This is why the church exists.

6.  Give and accept forgiveness. Kirk considers this the most difficult step in reconciliation when it involves actual people facing each other. Racial reconciliation, as observed by Sanders, starts with one person at a time. Giving and accepting forgiveness are crucial not only in human relationships but also in our worship of God, according to Jesus in the Gospels.

# Bibliography

Alba, Richard, 2006, "On the Sociological Significance of the American Jewish Experience: Boundary Blurring, Assimilation, and Pluralism, Albany, Sociology of Religion, 67:4 347-358

Appiah, K. A. "The Uncompleted Argument: DuBois and the Illusion of Race" at http://reconciliation101.wordpress.com, accessed January 2012.

Barth, Fredrik, 1998, *Ethnic Groups and Boundaries.* Prospect Heights, IL: Waveland Press.

Bediako, Kwame, 1999, *Theology, and Identity: The Impact of Culture upon Christian Thought in the Second Century and in Modern Africa,* Oxford: Regnum Books International.

Bosch, David Jacobus. 1991 *Transforming mission: paradigm shifts in theology of mission,* New York: Maryknoll.

Buell, Denise K. 2005, *Why This New Race: Ethnic Reasoning in Early Christianity.* New York: Columbia University Press.

Copper, Stewart and Fredrick T.L Leong, 2008, Introduction to the Special Issue on Culture, Race and Ethnicity in organizational consulting Psychology, *American Psychological Association and the Society of Consulting Psychology,* Vol. 60, No. 2, 1065-9293/08/$12.00 DOI: 10.1037/0736-9735.60.2.133

Davis, Ken L., Fall 2003, "Building A Biblical Theology of Ethnicity for Global Mission" in The Journal of Ministry and theology, Pp 91-126.

Du Bois, "The Conservation of Races" at http://reconciliation101.wordpress.com, Accessed January 2012.

Elmer, Duane, 1993, *Cross-Cultural Conflict: Building relationship for effective ministry* Downers Grove, Ill.: InterVarsity

Emerson, Michael & Smith, Christian, 2000, *Divided by Faith: Evangelical Religion and the Problem of Race in America,* New York: Oxford University Press.

Endo, Shusaku, 1969, *Silence,* New York: Taplinger.

Ezeogu, Ernest M. 2009, "From evangelization to reconciliation, justice and peace: Towards a paradigm shift in African mission priorities", SEDOS *Bulletin* 41, no. 9.

Frederick, Thomas. 2008. Discipleship and Spirituality from a Christian Perspective. *Pastoral Psychology* 56, no. 6 (July): 553-560. Doi: 10.1007/s11089-008-0148-8

Fredrickson, George, 2002, *Racism: A Short History.* Princeton, NJ: Princeton University Press.

Gallagher, Charles, 2009, ed. *Rethinking the Color Line: Readings in Race and Ethnicity,* 4th edition, New York: McGraw-Hill.

Gallagher, Robert L., and Paul Hertig, 2009, ed., *Landmark Essays in Mission and World Christianity,* New York: Orbis Books.

Gilbreath, Edward, *Reconciliation Blues: A Black, Evangelical's View of White Christianity,* Downers Grove: InterVarsity.

Gunton, Colin E., 2003, *The theology of Reconciliation,* New York: T&T Clark.

Gupta, Akhil and James Ferguson, 2007, "Beyond "Culture": Space, Identity, and the Politics of Difference", *Ethnographic fieldwork: an anthropological reader,* Malden, MA: Blackwell.

Gushee, David P., 2007 "More Free, At Least Racial reconciliation is making some unexpected demands on me" in *Christianity today.*

Hannaford, Ivan, 1996, *Race: the History of an Idea in the West,* Maryland: The John Hopkins University Press.

Harris, Murray J. 2005. *The Second Epistle to the Corinthians: a commentary on the Greek text,* Mich.: Grand Rapids.

Harrison, Simon, 2003 "Cultural Boundaries" Ulster University: EBSCO.

Hiebert, Paul, 2006, "The Missionary as Mediator of Global Theologizing", *Globalizing Theology: Belief and Practice in an Era of World Christianity, Grand Rapids:* Baker.

_____ 1983, *Cultural Anthropology,* Grand Rapids: Baker.

Katongole, Emmanuel, 2005, *A future For Africa: Critical Essays in Christian Social Imaging,* Chicago: University of Scranton.

Kirk, Andrew J. 2002. What is mission? – Lecture at the Swedish Mission Council's bi-annual meeting Swedish mission council

Lott, Tommy L., "Du Bois on the Invention of Race" at http://reconciliation101.wordpress.com, Accessed January 2012.

Loury, Glenn C, 2002, *The Anatomy of Racial Inequality,* Massachusetts: Harvard University Press.

Newbigin, Lesslie, 1989, *The Gospel in Pluralist society,* Grand Rapids: Eerdmans.

Nwaigbo, Ferdinand, "Christ Jesus: Our Peace and Reconciliation" African Ecclesia!   Review; pages 356-384.

Oborji, Francis Anekwe, 2006 *Concepts of Mission: The Evolution of Contemporary   Missiology.* Maryknoll: Orbis.

Omi, Mark, Hay, 1998, *Ukunbuyisana: Reconciliation in South Africa,* South Africa: Cluster.

Ott, Craig. 2010.   *Encountering Theology of mission: biblical foundations, historical developments, and contemporary issues,* Grand Rapids, Mich.: Baker

Padilla, C. René, 2010, *Mission between the Times: Essays,* Grand Rapids: Eerdmans.

_____. Wholistic mission: evangelical and ecumenical. *International   Review of Mission* 81/323 (1992): 381-382.

Priest, J. Robert and Alvaro Nieves, *This Side of Heaven: Race, Ethnicity, and   Christian Faith,* New York: University Press, 2007.

Putnam, Robert and David E. Campbell, *American Grace: How Religion Divides and Unites Us.* New York: Simon and Schuter, 2010.

Shamai, Shmuel and Zinaida Ilatove, 2001, Assimilation and ethnic boundaries: Israeli students' attitudes toward Soviet Union student immigrants, *Adolescents,* vol 36/144.

Rice, Chris, March. "Born Again...In my ministry of racial reconciliation, I had to move from a culture of effort to a culture of grace", *Christianity Today* (2010): 34-37.

Richardson, Rick. 2000. *Evangelism Outside the box: new ways to help people experience the Good News /.* Downers Grove: Intervarsity.

Roberts, J W. 1972. "The meaning of ekklesia in the New Testament." *Restoration Quarterly* 15 (1) (January 1): 27-36.

Romanucci-Ross, Lola and George De Vos, (ed.), 2006, *Ethnic Identity: Problems and Prospects for the Twenty-First Century,* Fourth Edition. Walnut Creek, CA: Alta Mira Press.

Sanders, Alvin, 2009, Reconciliation 101: A Handbook for Ministry Leaders, Minneapolis:   EFCA publication.

Sanders, Jimy M.2002, "Ethnic Boundaries and Identity" in Plural Societies in Annual Review Sociology.

Schreiter, Robert, 2001, Mission *in the third millennium /.* Maryknoll, N.Y.

_____, 1998, *The Ministry of Reconciliation: Spirituality and Strategies,* New York: Orbis

_____, 1992, *Reconciliation: Mission and ministry in a changing social order.* Maryknoll, NY: Orbis.

Shenk, David W, January 2008, "The Gospel of Reconciliation within the Wrath of          Nations", *International          Bulletin          of Missionary Research:* pp. 3-9.

Shenk, Wilbert R, 2000, "Christian Mission and the Coming Clash of Civilizations," *Missiology* No3

Shweder, Richard, 2003, *Recipes for Cultural Psychology: Why do men barbecue?*          Cambridge, Massachusetts: Harvard

Turaki, Yusufu, 2006, "Ephesians" in *African Bible Commentary.* Nairobi, Kenya: *Zondervan.*

Walls, Andrew and Cathy Ross, 2008, eds. *Mission in the 21st Century: Exploring Five Marks of Global Mission.* Maryknoll: Orbis.

Ward, Roy Bowen. 1958. "Ekklesia: a word study." *Restoration Quarterly* 2 (4) (January 1): 164-179.

Ware, Carles, 2002, "Crossing the divide: God's way to unity is through reconciliation, *Light* Nov/Dec, Lifeway.

Weaver, Clarence D. 1983a. Mutual mission: spiritual formation and the questions of reconciliation, peace, and justice. *Austin Seminary Bulletin (Faculty ed.)* 99, no. 3 (October 1): 37-52.

———. 1983b. Mutual mission: spiritual formation and the questions of reconciliation, peace and justice. *Austin Seminary Bulletin (Faculty ed.)* 99, no. 3.

Wimmer, Andreas 2008, The Making and Unmaking of Ethnic Boundaries: A Multilevel Process Theory, *American Journal of Sociology,* Vol. 113, No. 4, pp. 970-1022.

Whiteman, Darrell L, 2006, "The role of ethnicity and culture in shaping Western mission agency identity," *Missiology* 34 (1).

Williams, Jarvis, 2010, *One New Man: The Cross and Racial Reconciliation in Pauline Theology,* Nashville, TN: B&H Publishing.

Wright, Christopher J. H., 2010, *The Mission of God's People: A Biblical Theology of the Church's Mission.* Grand Rapids: Erdmann.

# CHAPTER 5

# THE REFORMED CHURCH OF EAST AFRICA: A BRIEF HISTORY OF ITS ORIGIN, GROWTH, AND EXPANSION IN KENYA

by Patrick Nasongo, PhD

## Introduction to Reformed Theology

In 2017, Churches with their roots in the 16th-century Reformation celebrated the 500-year legacy of the Reformation. This radical event transformed the life of the Church. It also changed Christians' perspectives on the authority of the Bible, faith, Christ, Sacraments, etc. The Medieval Church was suppressed by the Roman Catholic Church for over 1000 years. For example, the average believer was restricted from owning the Bible. Furthermore, traditions superseded Scripture. This practice culminated in the Reformation Movement. Reformers (Martin Luther, John Calvin, John Knox, Huldrych Zwingli, etc.) risked their lives, but their message spread fast, far, and wide within Europe. The epicenter was in Wittenberg, Germany by Luther; carried over to Geneva, Switzerland by Calvin; extended to Scotland, by Knox; and crossed over to England by William Tyndale, Robert Barnes, and Martin Bucer, but not in Nairobi or Johannesburg. Thus, the movement was a European affair, although with a global impact. The continent of Africa is of particular importance to this writer. But before embarking on the issue, the thesis of this article will follow.

## Thesis Statement

It is a fact that African theologians did not participate directly in the Reformation Movement of the 16th century. Additionally, it is known that African fathers of the fourth and fifth centuries significantly influenced the theology of the 16th-century Reformers. The nonparticipation of African theologians in the Reformation Movement does not imply all is lost. Three hundred years later, Reformed theology is slowly finding inroads into Africa. This paper examines the state of the Reformed Church of East Africa in Kenya specifically, its inception, history, expansion, and challenges. More importantly, this author affirms that Reformed theology will continue to expand through the faithful preaching and teaching of God's Word. So, the theme of the Word of God is a centerpiece of this article. Before embarking on this issue, the definition of Reformed theology follows.

## Definition of Reformed Theology

The word 'Reformed' comes from Webster's dictionary meaning 'change, transform, radical, etc.' Most Evangelical churches conceive of Reformed theology in terms of key figures such as Luther, Calvin, Zwingli, etc. But what actually does being 'Reformed' mean? Is it a mere commitment to the ideals of the Reformers? This author agrees with Thomas Hinson who observes that Reformation is more than principles. Hinson notes that "being Reformed involves a serious commitment to sound biblical doctrine and deep personal faith."[1] Reformed doctrines are derived directly from the Bible. The tenets of Reformed theology are hereby examined.

## Tenets of Reformed Theology

Reformed theology started with basic elements that bind it together. Leith lists four of them as (a) a theology of the holy catholic church; (b) a theocentric theology; (c) a theology of the Bible; (d) predestination; etc. These tenets are briefly discussed. First, Reformed theology is "a theology of the holy catholic church." This implies that Reformed theology is a comprehensive faith that is built upon the work of the ancient church, but not isolated. This theology adheres to the teaching of major creeds and doctrines of the universal church. John Leith notes, "The Protestant Reformation accepted with little modification the great formulations of the ancient church, namely the Apostles' Creed, the Nicene Creed, and the Chalcedonian Definition of the person of Jesus Christ. ... All who affirm it are united in the basic Christian affirmation that God is

---

[1] Thomas Hinson, The Reformed Church in Africa: How We Got this? accessed February 22, 2023, The Reformed Church in Africa: Have We Got This? - TGC Africa (thegospelcoalition.org)

defined by Jesus Christ."[2] However, this statement does not imply that the Protestant Reformation subscribed to anything the medieval catholic [universal] church taught. There were major disagreements on issues such as sacraments and salvation. The Roman Church erroneously taught and edified the church as the offeror of salvation. Leith concludes, "The Protestant Reformation concentrated upon God's way of salvation and insisted that salvation is wholly by the grace of God and not by any merit of man."[3] The Reformed Church continues to uphold this important tenet.

Second, Leith observes that Reformed theology is "A Theocentric theology." Simply, Reformed theology is centered on God the Father. He writes, "The central theme of theology ... is not man and his plight or his possibilities, not even Jesus Christ, but God, who is the creator and who was uniquely present in Jesus Christ." [4] For clarity, God here implies the Triune God (Father, Son, and Holy Spirit). Leith concludes, "Christian theology has to do with one God who is personally and always related to his creation in three ways."[5] This is a fundamental affirmation. God the redeemer is also the creator and the object of our faith. Leith correctly concludes: "The theocentric character of Reformed faith is set over against every ethic of self-realization, against inordinate concern with the salvation of one's own soul, against excessive preoccupation with questions of personal identity. The great fact is God, and the true vocation of every human being is trust in him and loyalty to his cause."[6]

Third, Reformed theology is rooted in the Bible. This tenet is popularly understood as *sola scriptura*. The five adages of Reformed theology are sola *gratia*, sola *fidei*, sola *scriptura*, sola *dei gloria*, and sola *Christos*. Since Sola Scriptura aligns with this tenet: the theology of the Bible, thus, will be revisited.

Fourth, Reformed theology is a theology of predestination. This tenet focuses on the believer's faith and the church. On this note, Leith writes, "The origin of the faith of the believer and of the church

---

[2] John H. Leith, *Introduction to the Reformed Tradition* (John Knox Press: Atlanta: GA, 1981), 97.

[3] Leith, *Introduction to Reformed Tradition*, 97.

[4] Leith, *Introduction to Reformed Tradition*, 98.

[5] Leith, *Introduction to Reformed Tradition*, 98.

[6] Leith, *Introduction to Reformed Tradition*, 99.

must be found first in the action of God, not in any human effort. ...Reformed theologians ... insisted that the root of this life was not first in the decision of individuals or of the community but in the election of God."[7] Thus, predestination implies that the source of human life is rooted in the eternal decree and will of God. Leith notes, "God thought of each person before he was and called him into being, giving him his name, his individuality, his identity as a child of God, and his dignity that no man should dare abuse."[8] Simply, our salvation today is not based on chance but on election by God. This is biblical teaching.[9] After this analysis, the third element turns to focus.

## A Fervent Commitment to the Bible.

Reformed theology has always been intensely Biblical. As noted earlier, the Medieval Roman Catholic Church emphasized traditions over Scripture. But the Reformers decisively made the Bible the only rule for faith and practice. To emphasize this theme, the three Reformers are selected to highlight their views on the biblical text.

The first and foremost is Luther. Regarding the authority of the Scripture, Luther writes, "This queen [the Scripture] must rule and everyone must obey and be subject to her. The pope, Luther, Augustine, Paul, an angel from heaven—these should not be masters, judges, or arbiters but only witnesses, disciples, and confessors of Scripture."[10]

Luther also viewed the Scriptures as a Christ-centered interpretation. He observes:

> Therefore dismiss your own opinions and feelings, and think of the Scripture as the loftiest and noblest of holy things, as the richest of mines which can never be sufficiently explored, in order that you may find that divine wisdom which God here lays before you in such a simple guise as to quench all pride. Here you will find the swaddling clothes and the manger in which Christ lies, and to which the angel points the shepherds (Luke 2;12).

---

[7] Leith, *Introduction to Reformed Tradition*, 104.

[8] Leith, *Introduction to Reformed Tradition*, 104.

[9] Predestination Scriptures: Acts 13:48; Rom. 8:28-30; Rom. 9:11-13 [Jacob over Essau]; Rom. 11:7; Eph. 1:4-6; 2 Thess. 2:13

[10] *LW* 26:58 ("lectures on Galatians," hereafter, "Lectures").

Simple and lowly are the swaddling clothes, but dear is the treasure, Christ, who lies in them.[11]

Although Luther expressed an unfavorable opinion about certain books such as Esther, Ezra, Nehemiah, James, Jude, and Revelation, generally, he adhered to the inspiration of Scripture to the very letters. But Luther's important slogan was *sola scriptura*. It was established to repudiate Roman Catholic dogma and the power of the Pope.

Concerning Zwingli, he deliberately preached from the books of the Bible. He read the Scriptures from their natural sense. Zwingli was a gifted preacher but seldom wrote his sermons. He preached word for word from almost every book of the Bible. Jean Rilliet observes Zwingli's devotion to the Bible:

After St. Matthew, in 1520 he commented on the Acts of the Apostles; in 1521, he commented on the First Epistle to Timothy, and on Galatians; then, ... two epistles of St. Peter. In 1522 he tackled Hebrews, then came back to the Gospels; in 1523 St. Luke, in 1524 St. John, while in the first term of 1525 he went back to various Pauline texts. ... Genesis (which he finished on March 2, 1527) Joshua, Judges, Ruth, Samuel, 1 and 2 Kings (1527), Isaiah (1528). Jeremiah and other prophets, Ezra, Nehemiah, Esther, Chronicles, fill up the last years.[12]

Last, John Calvin. Calvin's views on Scripture are stated in the *Institutes*. Calvin writes:

When that which professes to be the word of God is acknowledged to be so, no person, unless devoid of common sense and the feelings of a man, will have the desperate hardihood to refuse credit to the speaker. But since no daily oracles are given from heaven, and the Scriptures alone exist as the means by which God has been pleased to consign his truth to perpetual remembrance, the full authority which they obtain with the faithful proceeds from no other consideration than that

---

[11] Martin Luther, *Luther's Works*, Volume 35:236 ("Old Testament"), Editor, E. Theodore Bachmann

[12] Zwingli, *Third Man of the Reformation* (Philadelphia: The Westminster Press, 1959), 58.

they are persuaded that they proceeded from heaven, as of God had been heard giving utterance to them.[13]

Calvin also ascribes the authorship and durability of Scripture to God. He asserts, "God is the author of the Scriptures. The Scriptures themselves manifest the plainest signs that God is the speaker (*manifesta signa loguentis dei*). We are never established in the faith of this doctrine until we are indubitably persuaded that God is its author."[14] Calvin further notes, "We feel the firmest conviction that we hold an invincible truth. 'Between the apostles and their successors' ... the apostles were the certain and authentic amanuenses of the Holy Spirit and therefore their writings are to be received as the oracles of God, but others have no other office than to teach what is revealed and deposited in the holy Scriptures."[15]

Calvin also encouraged preaching that develops theology from the Bible. He writes:

> If they call a foreign word one that cannot be shown to stand written syllable by syllable in Scripture, they are indeed imposing upon us an unjust law which condemns all interpretation not patched together out of the fabric of Scripture ... we ought to seek from Scripture a sure rule for both thinking and speaking, to which both the thoughts of our minds and the words of our mouths should be conformed. But what prevents us from explaining in clear words those matters in Scripture which perplex and hinder our understanding, yet which conscientiously and faithfully serve the truth of Scripture itself, and are made use of sparingly and modestly and on due occasion?[16]

In the writing of the Scripture, Calvin asserts, "The law and the Prophets are not a doctrine delivered according to the will and pleasure of men but dictated by the Holy Spirit." Calvin also attributes the task of dictating the Scripture to the Holy Spirit. As a result, the written words "are those of God, and not of men." Therefore, Calvin upheld the Scriptures as verbally authoritative

---

[13] John Calvin, *Institute*, I, vii, I.
[14] Calvin, *Institutes*, I, vii, 4 *passim*.
[15] Calvin, *Institutes*, IV, viii, 9.
[16] Calvin, *Institutes*, 28.

and originating directly from God. His view on Scripture was later altered slightly but maintained over the years by Calvinism.

Before his death, Calvin commented on every book in the New Testament except 2 and 3 John and Revelation. He published commentaries on the book of Genesis and the harmony of the rest of the Pentateuch, Joshua, Psalms, Isaiah, Ezekiel 1-20, Daniel, Jeremiah, Lamentations, and all the Minor Prophets.

As illustrated by Luther, Zwingli, and Calvin above, Reformed theology has stayed true to the teaching of the Bible. Leith concludes, "Reformed theologians have been in intent and in fact theologians of the Bible. Reformed theology has always been more Biblical than philosophical, just as it has been more practical than speculative."[17] This Reformed principle has been practiced by many churches with Reformed roots. But why is it significant to Reformed theology? The answer is provided below.

### Significance of the Word of God.

This writer was once awestruck by a statement made by Dr. Mel Loucks, a long-time professor at International Theological Seminary. He asserted, "The Church in Africa is one kilometer [or mile] wide and one inch deep."[18] No one knows what the originator of this statement meant. But at face value, it implies the shallowness of the Christian faith in Africa. Since Dr. Loucks travels to East Africa to Preach and Teach God's Word, he may have a clue.

Whether this statement is true or not, the church in Africa is expanding numerically at a fast rate. In fact, Phillip Jenkins alludes to this trend. He writes, "Whatever Europeans or North Americans may believe, Christianity is doing very well indeed in the global South—not just surviving but expanding."[19] The West is slowly realizing the future of Christianity lies more to the South of the equator than to the North. The church in the West is trending toward liberalism while churches in Africa remain conservative for the most part.[20] If this prediction is true, then Africa is in a unique position to seize the opportunity and preach the gospel. But the

---

[17] Leith, *An Introduction to the Reformed Theology*, 103.

[18] Dr. Mel Loucks, Professor, International Theological Seminary.

[19] Philip Jenkins, *The Next Christendom: The Coming of Global Christianity*, 3rd Edition (New York: Oxford University Press, 2011), 2.

[20] Jenkins, *The Next Christendom*, 8.

church in Africa, including Kenya, must strive to grow in quality (sound hermeneutics) and quantity (numbers). When the balance is maintained, true growth is realized. There is a need to train men and women in the Word of God. This was the Reformer's mantra: *Sola Scriptura*. A proposal for achieving this tenet is illustrated in the Reformed Church of East Africa. We now examine the roots of Reformer's theology, then the history of the Reformed Church of East Africa.

## African's Seedbed for Reformed Theology

As noted earlier, African fathers [North Africa] were the architects of Western Theology. It was mentioned that Luther, Zwingli, and Calvin were impacted by the theology of Tertullian of Tunisia, Origen of Alexandria, and Athanasius of Alexandria. Calvin was influenced by the theology of Augustine and Cyprian (both from Algeria) in his *Institutes*. These fourth and fifth-century theologians laid the foundation for the sixteenth-century Protestant Reformation. For instance, Calvin's reliance on Augustine's theology is evident. There are striking similarities between Calvin's and Augustine's theology, but with minor variations. Calvin embodied the Augustinian view on Grace, Predestination, Reprobation, God's Will, etc.

Additionally, while refuting the notion that God prefers one person over another in the election, Calvin alludes to Augustine. He writes, "Augustine testifies that men are not chosen because they believe, but on the contrary, are chosen that they might believe."[21] Similarly, Augustine wrote to Sextus saying, "As to the great deep— why one believes and another does not, why God delivers one person and not another, let him who can, search into that profound abyss..." Additionally, on Reprobates, Augustine says, "Who created the reprobate but God? And why? Because He willed it. Why did He will it? Who art thou, O man, that repliest against God?" [22] Furthermore, Calvin's reliance on Augustine is indicated in the *Institutes of the Christian Religion*. He mentions Augustine about 370 times and quotes him over 150 of those times. Thus, Calvin

---

[21] John Calvin, *Calvin Calvinism: Eternal Predestination of God* (Eugene, OR: Wipf and Stock, 2019), 40

[22] Calvin, *Calvin Calvinism: Eternal Predestination of God* (Eugene, OR: Wipf and Stock, 2019), 40

seized the opportunity and utilized the resources of St. Augustine from North Africa in his teaching during the Reformation Movement, a thousand years earlier.

Luther, Calvin, Zwingli, etc., applied these doctrines to rebut the false teachings of the Medieval Roman Catholic Church. This church's doctrines undermined salvation by grace and the authority of Scripture. Augustine laid the foundation for Calvin. Reformed theology to flourish. Therefore, when we read the Reformer's work, we are reading the thoughts of the fourth and fifth-century African theologians. Trevor Sutton rightly observes:

Before Luther in Wittenberg, there was Augustine in Algeria. Before Calvin in Geneva, there was Cyril in Egypt. Before Zwingli in Zürich, there was Tertullian in Tunisia. These African theologians had a profound influence on Reformation theologians. Indeed, many of the influential texts of the 16th century—including The Book of Concord and Calvin's Institutes—are loaded with references to African theologians. The Reformation in Europe has roots in earlier theologians in Africa.[23]

In sum, African church leaders should never ignore their earliest African Christian ancestors. They should instead stay true to Reformed Theology ideals propagated by them.

## The Birth of the Reformed Church of East Africa

### The First Protestant Mission Organizations in Kenya

As noted earlier, the Dutch Reformed Church arrived in Kenya way too late when other mission organizations had already been established. The Church Mission Society (CMS), Lutherans from Germany had sent John Ludwig Krapf (1844) and Johann Rebmann Jr (1846). These missionaries established a center near the coast of Mombasa, reaching tribes such as the Wanyika, especially the Giriama, Akamba, Chagga, and Moshi. But the missionaries were faced with setbacks such as a rejection of the salvation message and an attack by the tribes they were reaching. These missionaries later returned home with less success. Mark Shaw observes, "In 1874 Rebmann, his sight nearly gone, returned

---

[23] A. Trevor Sutton, *The Reformations Roots in Africa*, accessed February 16, 2023, https://www.thegospelcoalition.org/article/reformation-african-roots/

to Germany to die, closing the first chapter of the CMS story in Kenya."[24]

CMS extended its mission to Freretown and *Kitoto* Christianity. The mission was named after Sir Bartle Frere after arriving in Zanzibar in 1872 from Britain. Frere replaced David Livingston, who died later in 1873. Livingston was famous for his push to abolish slavery. He described slavery as "an open sore of the world."[25] After realizing this vice of human slavery, Sir. Frere ended it and established refuge centers for recaptured slaves. The Arabs slave owners resisted the move and attacked Freretown Mission. Although the Freretown mission had some success, it was plugged by paternalism and favoritism of white missionaries over local church leaders.

The Church of Scottish Mission, led by James Steward was established in 1891. He was inspired by Livingston.[26] The Africa Inland Mission was established in 1895 by Peter Cameron Scott, a Scottish-American Missionary.[27] It included Baptists, Methodists, Presbyterians, and Anglicans. The Roman Catholics started their activities in East Africa later than the Protestants. The French Congregation of the Holy Ghost was established around 1863 in Zanzibar by bishop Maupoint. The mission later expanded to Kibwezi in the 1890s, then later to Kikuyu near Nairobi in 1898.[28] The United Methodists Free Church established a station in 1862 by Thomas Wakefield at Ribe in Mombasa among the Mijikenda.

## The History of the Reformed Church of East Africa (RCEA)

The RCEA is part of several family churches known as Reformed/Presbyterian churches in Kenya. Examples are Trinity Reformed Baptist, Reformed Baptist Church, Independent Reformed Church, Presbyterian Church of East Africa, Christian

---

[24] Mark R. Shaw, *The Kingdom of God in Africa: A Short History* (Grand Rapids, MI: Baker Books, 1996), 188-189.

[25] Shaw, *The Kingdom of God in Africa*, 189.

[26] Mark, *The Kingdom of God in Africa*, 191.

[27] Van Zyl, "The impact of Reformed Missions on the Origin, Growth, and Identity of the Reformed Church of East Africa" (PhD dissertation. Stellenbosch University, 2001), 26.

[28] Zablan Nthamburi, *The Beginning and Development of Christianity in Kenya: A Survey*, accessed March 1, 2023, https://dacb.org/histories/kenya-beginning-development/

Reformed Church of Eastern Africa, Reformed Church in Kenya, etc. All these churches claim some roots in the original Protestant Reformation of the 16th century. This chapter examines the inception, naming, history, and expansion of the RCEA in Kenya.

*Geographical Location of Kenya*

Kenya is an African country in East Africa. It lies along the equator. It currently has roughly 50 million people, of which 85% are Christians, 14% Muslims, and 1% animism. Kenya was once a British colony from 1895 to 1963. The country attained independence in June 1963. Kenya has 42 major tribes, but the two required official languages are English (former British colony) and Swahili (a mixture of Arabic and a blend of African languages). Kenya is home to major wildlife with renowned parks such as Amboseli, Masai Mara, etc. Tourism is the third backbone of Kenya's economy. Global tourists flock to Kenya to encounter the "big fives" such as Lion, Leopard, Rhino, Elephant, and Buffalo.

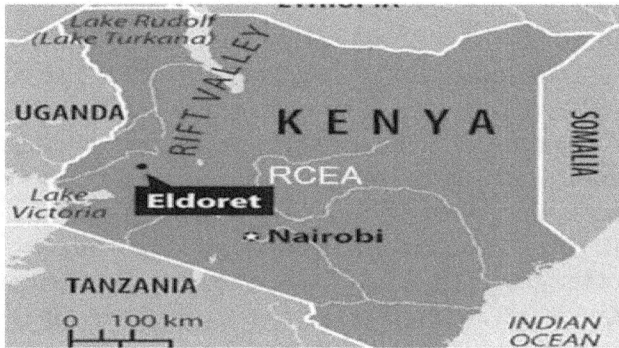

Thus, the RCEA was established in Eldoret, Kenya in the early 1900s by migrant farmers known as the Boers. These farmers had ties with the Dutch Reformed Church (DRC) in South Africa. The Dutch Reformed Church has its roots in the Netherlands. John Leith observes that DRC first came to South Africa in 1652.[29] Thus, the

---

[29] John H. Leith, *Introduction to the Reformed Tradition* (John Knox Press: Atlanta: GA, 1981), 50.

Dutch immigrants, commonly called Huguenots [30] brought the tradition of Reformed theology to South Africa in the mid-17th century. Years later, the Boers extended the same Reformed traditions to Kenya.

Ekitala observes, "The RCEA has been in Kenya for close to a century since the first missionaries founded it in Lynden consistory of the Dutch Reformed Church in South Africa (DRC), this took place on 29th August 1908 outside Nakuru on the farm of Mr. Arnoldi."[31] The migrants were tired of traveling back and forth to South Africa. As a result, they established the *Vergenoeg* congregation. The name Vergenoeg is significant. Gideon van der Watt notes "... when translated means 'far enough from British rule'."[32] In sum, it took roughly 400 years for the Reformed Church to establish in Kenya. This is indeed a long time considering when the Reformation took place in Germany (1517).

The name 'Reformed Church of East Africa' was first used in July 1963 by the Evangelist Joshua Bibiko. It was chosen as "indicative of the desire of the young church to embrace their reformed heritage on the one hand, but on the other hand, to become a self-sustainable church." [33] Therefore, the RCEA was established in Kenya as an independent church then. However, the name *East Africa* implies the church is in Kenya, Uganda, and Tanzania. Yet this church is in a small region in Kenya. Why was this name chosen if it didn't capture its vision or geographical location? On this note, Van Zyl observes,

The Reformed Church of *East Africa* did not represent the real picture of the geographical range of the Church. East Africa included Kenya, Zanzibar, Tanganyika (Tanzania), and Uganda. In reality, the

---

[30] The Huguenots were devoted Protestants from France and Southern Netherlands. They were devoted to the teachings of the theologian, John Calvin. Most of them were escaping Catholic persecution after abandoning her false teaching. They were identified as "house fellows" or house worshippers, thus "Huis Genooten." Who Were the Huguenots? Retrieved January 31, 2023, www.nationhuguenotsociety.org.

[31] Luka Ariko Ekitala, "Constitution or Church Order? A Church Judicial Analysis of the church documents in the Reformed Church of East Africa" (PhD diss., Stellenbosch University, 2018), 107

[32] Gideon van der Watt & Mariette Odendaal, *A Family of Reformed Churches in Africa: Remembering Stories of God's Grace*, 2nd Edition, Wellington: CLF Publishers, 2022), 116.

[33] Ekitala, "Constitution or Church Order..." 132.

ministry of the RCEA was limited to a very small area in the western part of Kenya with a few thousand members. As indicated before, two of the three ministers trained by Eybers were from Tanzania. The vision lived in the hearts of the Tanzanians to take the Reformed tradition back to their own country. [34] Efforts to establish the Reformed Church of East Africa church in Uganda and Tanzania are ongoing.

## Efforts to Evangelizing Indigenous People

When the missionaries arrived, they first reached out to their white farmers. Ekitala notes, "While most of the other churches started off as direct mission enterprises to the indigenous people, the Dutch Reformed Church in Kenya set off as a church for the white farmers." [35] The early DRC was basically a white church, although it made an effort to evangelize the black farm workers. The white farmer attempted to evangelize the indigenous farm worker at first. However, when that effort failed, the DRC appointed the first missionary named Rev. Benjamin Beaumann Eybers (1944) to carry on the gospel.[36]

But why did the white farmer's effort to evangelize the locals fail? Bisem observes, "Of course, these were purely white services as the Boers discriminated (against) the Africans on their farms on a racial basis, such that they could not dare worship together. The question of reaching out to these people with the gospel was unthinkable."[37] Thus, discrimination hampered evangelistic efforts. However, we applaud some white farmers who viewed locals as deserving of salvation.

Furthermore, Bisem observes that three South African 'white only' churches, based on Reformed tradition, split due to their different views on the status of Africans. He writes, "

---

[34] Van Zyl, "The impact of Reformed Missions on the Origin, Growth, and Identity of the Reformed Church of East Africa" (PhD diss., Stellenbosch University, 2001), 175.

[35] Ekitala, "Constitution or Church Order..." 131.

[36] Ekitala' "Constitution or Church Order... of RCEA..." 107.

[37] Bisem, CP, "A historical account of Kimarer (Kerio- Valley) Parish of the Reformed Church of East Africa - 1971 to 1981" (Diploma in Theology, Makerere University, 1983), 7.

In the process of establishing the Church, there arose a split amongst themselves as the status of the Africans were raised. The problem arose when some members of the Dutch Reformed Church felt that a Mission to the African labourers should be started. The hardline racialists even went to the extent of declaring that an African seems not to have a soul, but instinct, and so he does not need salvation. But the other group, who can be described as evangelicals insisted that the African like any other fallen man needed salvation. Rev. Tini Loubser, who was their pastor, did not only advocate the extension of the gospel to the Africans, but led the way in reaching out to the African laborers on the settler farms.[38]

According to Bisem, the local Reformed Churches perceived the division in the three South African Reformed Churches as rooted in racism. He writes, "His (Rev Loubser's) actions was not well received by all his Dutch members. So, a confrontation of views ensued which led to the division in places of worship."[39]

Despite the aforementioned setbacks, RDC established four Reformed congregations. The first congregation was established in Meru Tanzania on 30th September 1905. The second congregation, Vergenoeg, was established on 29th August 1908 in British East Africa Territory (Kenya). The third congregation was established in Nairobi, while the fourth was the Loubser congregation in Nakuru. Conclusively, Van Zyl observes, "These congregations in East Africa became part of the Presbytery of Lydenberg of the Transvaal Synod of the Dutch Reformed Church." [40] These congregations were established in the farms where settlers dwelled.

## Autonomy of RCEA

When Kenya started to fight for independence from British rule in the early 1960s, most South African migrants began to flee Kenya due to their safety. In this haste, work was handed over to the

---

[38] Bisem, CP, "A historical account of Kimarer (Kerio- Valley) *Parish of the Reformed Church of East Africa* - 1971 to 1981" 8.

[39] Bisem, "A Historical Account ...." 8.

[40] Van Zyl, "The impact of Reformed Missions on the Origin, Growth, and Identity of the Reformed Church of East Africa" (PhD diss., Stellenbosch University, 2001), 49.

Gereforormeerde Zendingsbond (GZB) of the Netherlands in July 1961.[41]

However, in July 1963, the first synod of the newly established RCEA convened with three congregations. With the unanimous agreement with GZM mission in the Netherlands, the RCEA was formally made independent. All properties and resources were transferred to the church as well. The church also adhered to Reformed theology and polity. Watt & Odendaal observes, "The church adhered to the Creed of Athanasius, the Nicene Creed, the Canons of Dort, the Heidelberg Catechism, and also the Westminster Confession of Faith."[42]

Ekitala, the General Secretary of RCEA based in Eldoret Synod observes that the RCEA is largely autonomous today with 1 Synod and 17 Presbyteries, 120 Parishes, and 150, 000 communicant members as of March 2023.[43] These Presbyteries form the RCEA Synod. The first constitution of the RCEA was based on the structure of the Constitution of the Presbyterian Church of East Africa (PCEA). The Presbyterian church governance, therefore, influenced majorly the church judicial development of the RCEA.[44]

RCEA also established the Reformed Institute for Theological Training (RITT)[45] in 1969 to train Evangelists. The institute is located at Plateau near Eldoret. The ministers seeking advanced studies enroll at St. Paul United Theological College in Limuru.

## Expansion of Reformed Theology

### 16th-Century Strategies

First, the message was spread by university students. He writes, "One of the most important factors was the influence of virtually thousands of students who studied at the University of Wittenberg and were indoctrinated into Lutheran theology and ecclesiology. ...

---

[41] Watt & Odendaal, *A Family of Reformed Churches in Africa: Remembering Stories of God's Grace*, 2nd Edition, Wellington: CLF Publishers, 2022), 117

[42] Watt & Odendaal, *A Family of Reformed Churches in Africa: Remembering Stories of God's Grace*, 118.

[43] Luka Ariko Ekitala is the General Secretary of the Reformed Church of East Africa located in Eldoret Parish.

[44] Ekitala, "Constitution or Church Order..." 130.

[45] Reformed Institute for Theological Training, accessed 3/25/2023, https://keweb.co/reformed-institute-for-theological-training/

the university became pivotal for the dissemination of Reformation ideas."[46] Second, through the invention of the printing press. Sproul writes, "The printing press made it possible for Luther to spread his ideas through the many books that he published, not to mention his tracts, confessions, catechisms, pamphlets, and cartoons ..."[47] The other methods Sproul lists are music, religious drama, and fine arts. However, we emphasize the first two strategies due to their relevance.

## 21st -Century Strategies

Several methods were effective in spreading the 16th-century Reformation. Two are discussed below. First, the university students. These students were taught by Luther and faithfully carried his message across Germany and beyond. Likewise, Calvin's students in Geneva spread Calvinism in Switzerland. The same applies to Zwingli, John Knox, etc. The sixteenth-century strategies are applicable today. University and Seminary students are expected to carry out the Great Commission mandate of "disciplining ... baptizing, ..., and teaching" the Word of God to neighbors and across the globe (Matt. 28:19-20). No school is better equipped and prepared to carry this solemn mandate than International Theological Seminary. Since its inception in 1982, ITS has trained over 1000 students from 30 different countries.[48] After completion of studies, ITS students return to their respective countries to plant churches, establish Bible colleges, and engage in teaching the Bible to institutions of higher education and engagement in community development.

Second, the Reformation message spread through the publication of theological books. The invention of the printing press propelled Luther's publication beyond Germany. The same method applies today. Christian Publishers such as Zondervan, Baker Academics, Moody, Thomas Nelson, Harper Collins, etc. are open to publishing Reformed/other theological books. No one knows the impact these articles will have on the next generation.

---

[46] R. C. Sproul, *How The Reformation Spread*, accessed February 15, 2023, https://www.ligonier.org/learn/articles/how-reformation-spread

[47] Sproul, *How The Reformation Spread*, accessed February 15, 2023, https://www.ligonier.org/learn/articles/how-reformation-spread,

[48] Current data per Susan Liu, ITS librarian, 03/23/2023.

## The Challenges Facing Reformed Church of East Africa in Kenya

Despite steady growth in the past, RCEA is currently experiencing some challenges. Firstly, leadership wrangles, inequality, and corruption are rampant. The election of officials such as a Bishop, Presbyter, and General Secretary is not peacefully settled. Secondly, RCEA has problems maintaining a steady relationship with people from other religions, such as Catholics, Charismatics, and Muslims. This relationship is further eroded by political instability in the region. Several religions tend to align with either the ruling government or the opposition. Watt notes that "political instability in the region also influences church life." [49]

Thirdly, RCEA suffers from financial stability. The financial budget is never met and thus the church tends to depend on foreign missions to meet her needs. Watt observes, "Although the church has plenty of resources, they are not always utilized properly."[50]

Finally, aspiring pastors/leaders are trained at institutions outside of the Reformed tradition. Watt notes, "… some students are trained at open faculties and therefore the church's identity is not well defined."[51] After graduation, these students decide whichever direction they so desire to go serve.

## Conclusions

We briefly examined how the Reformers of the 16th century were exposed to and significantly influenced by the works and writings of the fourth and fifth-centuries African fathers. We also discussed how African theologians failed to participate in the Reformation, thus, delaying its message from reaching Africa for nearly 400 years. Although there were reasons to justify Africa's absence such as cultural, military, and Islamic influence in the North, they were inexcusable.

We also traced the establishment of the Reformed Church in Kenya. Now that Reformed theology is within reach, what should we do with the legacy of those who sacrificed? Hinson asks, "…, what are we doing with that legacy? Are we, as the current

---

[49] Watt, *A Family of Reformed Churches in Africa*, 119.
[50] Watt, *A Family of Reformed Churches in Africa*, 119.
[51] Ibid., 119.

custodians of the gospel message in Africa, staying true to the early Church fathers? Are we faithfully shepherding the Reformed church in Africa today? Are we staying true to Reformation principles and sharing the good news?"[52] The remedy is to faithfully Preach and Teach the Word of God as the Reformers aspired.

Conclusively, the Reformed Church in Kenya should seize the opportunity and preach the Word. Hinson sums: "The Reformed Church in Africa is in a strong position with almost endless potential, given the moral and spiritual collapse of many churches in the West. Therefore, we must seize the opportunity. We must let our love of the truth cause us to share it with others."[53] Amen.

## Bibliography

Bisem, CP, "A historical account of Kimarer (Kerio- Valley) Parish of the Reformed Church of East Africa - 1971 to 1981." Diploma in Theology, Makerere University, 1983.

Calvin, John. *Institutes of Christian Religion*.

Calvin, John. *Calvin Calvinism: Eternal Predestination of God*. Eugene, OR: Wipf and Stock, 2019.

Ekitala, Luke Ariko. "Constitution or Church Order? A church judicial analysis of the church documents in the Reformed Church of East Africa." PhD Diss., Stellenbosch University. March 2018.

Leith, John H. *Introduction to the Reformed Tradition*. John Knox Press: Atlanta: GA, 1981.

Luther, Martin. Luther's Works, Volume 35:236 ("Old Testament"), Editor, E. Theodore Bachmann

Hinson, Thomas. *Fathers of the Reformation: Africans in the Early Church*. Accessed February 22, 2023. Fathers of The Reformation: Africans in The Early Church - TGC Africa (thegospelcoalition.org)

———. The Reformed Church in Africa: Have We Got This? Accessed February 22,

---

[52] Thomas Hinson, *Fathers of the Reformation: Africans in the Early Church*, accessed 2/22/2023, Fathers of The Reformation: Africans in The Early Church - TGC Africa (thegospelcoalition.org)

[53] Thomas Hinson, accessed February 22, 2023, *The Reformed Church in Africa: Have We Got This?* https://africa.thegospelcoalition.org/article/have-we-got-this-reformed-christianity-in-africa/

2023,https://africa.thegospelcoalition.org/article/have-we-got-this-reformed-christianity-in-africa/

Jenkins, Philip. *The Next Christendom: The Coming of Global Christianity*. 3r Edition. New York: Oxford University Press, 2011.

Nthamburi, Zablan. *The Beginning and Development of Christianity in Kenya: A Survey*, Accessed March 1, 2023. https://dacb.org/histories/kenya-beginning-development/

Reformed Institute for Theological Training, accessed 3/25/2023, https://keweb.co/reformed-institute-for-theological-training/

Shaw, Mark R. *The Kingdom of God in Africa: A Short History*. Grand Rapids, MI: Baker Books, 1996.

Sproul, R. C. *How The Reformation Spread*. Accessed February 15, 2023. https://www.ligonier.org/learn/articles/how-reformation-spread.

Sutton, Trevor. A. *The Reformations Roots in Africa*. Accessed February 16, 2023. https://www.thegospelcoalition.org/article/reformation-african-roots/

Watt, Gideon van der & Odendaal, Mariette. *A Family of Reformed Churches in Africa: Remembering Stories of God's Grace*. 2nd Edition. Wellington: CLF Publishers, 2022.

Zyl, Van. "The Impact of Reformed Missions on the Origin, Growth, and Identity of the Reformed Church of East Africa." PhD diss., Stellenbosch University, 2001.

Zwingli, *Third Man of the Reformation*. Philadelphia: The Westminster Press, 1959.

# CHAPTER 6

## RECONCILIATION AND TRANSFORMATIONAL CHANGE:FROM THE PERSPECTIVES OF NARRATIVE FRAMEWORK AND RELATIONAL INTERACTIONISM[1]

by Enoch Wan, PhD

## Introduction

The purpose of this paper is to missiologically study "reconciliation" and
"transformational change" from the perspectives of narrative framework and relational interactionism. For the sake of clarity, below are definitions of some key-terms. As shown in the proposed relational definition of Christian "mission" below, the terms and concepts of "reconciliation" and "transformation" are embedded.

- **"Christian Mission"** – The term "mission" (singular), derived from *"Missio Dei,"* refers to the entire biblical understanding of the Church of Jesus Christ[2] to continue and carry out the *Missio Dei* of the Triune God at both the individual and institutional levels spiritually (saving soul) and socially (ushering in *shalom*) for redemption, reconciliation, and transformation. [3] Mission also is the divine activity of sending intermediaries, whether supernatural or human, to speak or do God's will so that His purposes for judgment and redemption can be furthered.[4]

---

[1] This paper was originally presented at Northwest Regional Meeting of Evangelical Missiological Soceity (EMS), March 12, 2022.

[2] Harold A. Netland and Charles Edward Van Engen, "Missiology": *Evangelical Dictionary of World Missions*, (Ada, MI: Baker Books, 2000).

[3] Wan, *Diaspora Missiology: Theory, Methodology and Practice,* IDS, 2014: 6-7.

[4] Netland and Van Engen, "Missiology": *Evangelical Dictionary of World Missions,* (Ada, MI: Baker Books, 2000).

- **"culture"** – the context/consequence of patterned interaction of personal Beings/beings[5]
- **"reconciliation"** – Based on the atonement of Jesus Christ (the Son) sinners are restored to *"shalomic* relationship"[6] with God (the Father) vertically and ending estrangement between personal beings horizontally.[7]
- **"narrative framework"** - a story-based structure for describing a person's understanding of and approach to life. Narrative framework includes both macro and micro views of history. The macro view is God's eternal meta-narrative, centered around Christ and his redemptive relationship with creation. The micro view describes a person's individual story within that metanarrative, combining one's experiences and self-identity with their worldview, including their foundational assumptions, values, and beliefs.
- *"relationship"* – the interactive connection between personal being (Beings); whereas "relationality" is the generic quality of being connected.[8]
- **"relational interactionism"** – an interdisciplinary framework that develops from practical considerations of dynamic interaction of personal Beings/beings, forming realistic relational networks in multiple contexts and with various consequences.
- "transformational change" – The dynamism and process of change, originated vertically from the Triune-God and ushered in the relational reality horizontally, through the process of interaction between personal Beings (the Triune

---

[5] Enoch Wan, "A Critique of Charles Kraft's Use/Misuse of Communication and Social Sciences in Biblical Interpretation and Missiological Formulation," *Global Missiology*, October 2004:1. @_www.globalmissiology.net

[6] Enoch Wan and Jace Cloud, *Doxological Missiology: Theory, Motivation, and Practice* (Western Academic Publishers, 2022).

[7]7 This is an evangelical (and relational) definition which is different from the ecumenical definition (i.e. "Reconciliation is the *process* of addressing conflictual and fractured relationships and this includes a range of different activities. We see reconciliation as a voluntary act that cannot be imposed." (Yaacov Bar-Siman-Tov 2004:2). See Daniel Bar-Tal and Gemma H. Bennick, "The Nature of Reconciliation as an Outcome and as a Process," IN *From Conflict Resolution to Reconciliation. By* Yaacov Bar-Siman-Tov, editor. Oxford University Press, 2004:12-24.

[8] Enoch Wan, "The Paradigm of Relational Realism" EMS, *Occasional Bulletin*, Spring 2006:1.

God) and human beings (at micro and macro levels) multi-dimensionally, i.e. spiritual, moral, social, behavioral dimensions at personal and/or institutional levels.

- "**relational reality**" - the complex of networks formed by patterned interaction of dynamic personal Beings/beings at different levels (micro & macro), in multiple contexts (of socio-cultural variations)
- "**relational realism paradigm**" – the systematic understanding that "reality" is primarily based on the 'vertical relationship' of God and the created order and secondarily 'horizontal relationship' within the created order. Reality and truth are best to be comprehended and experienced in relational networks of God and the created orders (3 systems in existence: angels, humanity and the natural order).[9]
- "**society**" – the consequence of dynamic interactions of personal Beings/beings, leading to the formation of a social entity.

## "Culture" and "Christian Mission" – From the Perspectives of Narrative Framework and Relational Interactionism

### Narrative Framework of Culture

Though Clifford Geertz made a distinction between "models of" (as descriptive) and "models for" (as normative) that is useful,[10] "narrative framework" is preferred in this study as a descriptive approach (in contradistinction to the popular options of

---

[9] Enoch Wan, "Relational Theology and Relational Missiology," *Occasional Bulletin* 21, no. 1 (Winter 2008): 1-7, <www.emsweb.org> (July 15, 2009), 7n1. See also, Enoch Wan, "The Paradigm of Relational Realism," *Occasional Bulletin* 19, no. 2 (Spring 2006): 1-4, <www.emsweb.org> (July 15, 2009).

[10] Clifford Geertz, *The Interpretation of Cultures* (New York: Basic Books, 1973).

rationalistic, [11] historical [12] or normative [13] approaches in the literature).

In evangelical missiology, "culture" is a reference to the closed system of human existence, whereas God and angel are designated as "supra-cultural"[14] as shown in the figure below. The concept of the supra-cultural and the cultural seeks to make explicit the culture boundness of human beings, on the one hand, and the freedom from culture boundness of God on the other. The "supra-cultural" serves a very useful purpose in signifying the transcendence of God apart from culture, exclusively of the human realm. That is God, being completely unbound by any culture is "supra-cultural." The above figure shows three categories: (a) the super-cultural, absolute God; (b) the supra-cultural non-absolute beings (angels, demons, Satan); and (c) the relative cultural context of human beings.

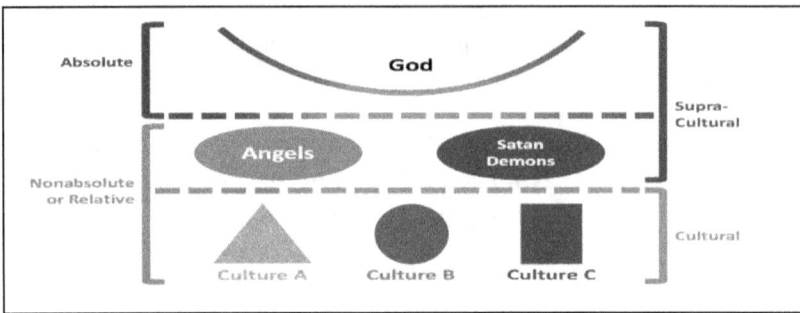

**Figure 6.1. Cultural and Supra-Cultural**[15]

However, in this paper, culture is a reference to the narrative convergence of three realms of (a) God, (b) angel and (c) human being as shown in the figure below. In terms of ontology, there are

---

[11] Carl F.H. Henry. *Basic Christian Doctrines*. Baker Books. 1981.

[12] David Bosch, *Transforming Mission: Paradigm Shifts in Theology of Mission*. (Maryknoll, NY: Orbis, 1991).

[13] Nicole, Roger R. *Standing Forth: Collected Writings of Roger Nicole*. Christian Focus Publishers. (2002).

[14] See detailed discussion on the term and concept of "supra-cultural" in Charles Kraft in *Christianity in Culture*. Orbis, 1979: chapter 12.

[15] Charles H. Kraft, *Christianity In Culture: A Study In Biblical Theologizing In Cross-Cultural Perspective*, 25th Annv edition. (Maryknoll, N.Y: Orbis Books, 2005), 95.

two levels: creator (Being - divinity) and created order (angelic beings and human beings). Instead of the popular understanding that Beings (of the Triune God) and angelic beings (of two kinds: rebellious and obedient) being "supra-cultural" (i.e. apart from "culture" of human beings), relational interactionism acknowledges that it is in God "we live, and move, and have our being" (Acts 17:28).

Ontologically, relational interactionism is a narrative framework that embraces "relational reality" as previously defined: "the complex of networks formed by patterned interaction of personal beings at different levels (micro & macro), in multiple contexts (of socio-cultural variations)." As shown in the figure below, interaction of personal Beings/beings crossing the boundary of theo-culture, angel-culture and human-culture resulting in complex relational networks, multi-level and multi-dimensional reality. "Reality is interpersoned because it is a gift from the Creator."[16]

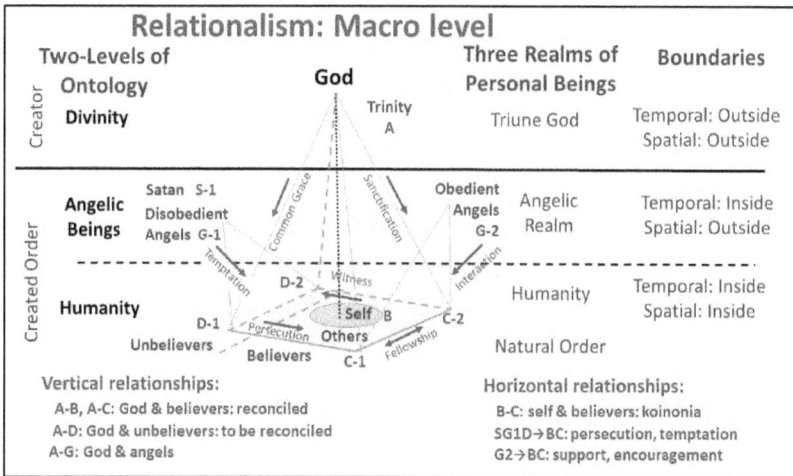

Figure 6.2. Relational Interactionism – Narrative Framework at Macro-level

Relational Interactionism describes the dynamic interaction of personal Beings/beings, which forms realistic relational networks in multiple contexts and with various consequences. Since "culture"

---

[16] Ryan Gimple and Enoch Wan, *Covenant Transformative Learning: Theory and Practice* (Portland, Oregon: Western Press, 2021), 39.

is defined in this book as "the context and consequence of patterned interaction of Beings/being," it is important to narratively describe the multiple **contexts** of patterned interaction.

- Theo-culture: the context where Father, Son and Holy Spirit interact internally and horizontally;
- Angel-culture: the context where obedient angels and rebellious angels interact internally and horizontally;
- Human-culture: the context where human beings (transformed beings of Christians and unregenerate non-Christians) interact internally and horizontally.

In the figure above, various patterns of interaction of personal Beings/beings are being identified vertically e.g. A-B, A-C, A-D, A-G) and horizontally (e.g. B-C, SG1D→BC, G2→ BC). There are various **consequences** of patterned interaction between the Triune God and the created angelic and human beings who exist within the created order:

- The resultant relationships and relational networks emerged from the "interaction of unmerited favor" from the Triune God towards (a) all people (common grace); (b) His own: redemption, provision, glorification, etc. (special grace);
- The resultant relationships and relational networks emerged from the interaction of the Triune God towards (a) rebellious angels – judgement, and (b) obedient angels – worship and glory.

## Relational Interactionist Understanding of Christian "Mission"

Relational interactionism is a framework that helps understand how socio-cultural reality is formed, preserved, and changed through dynamic, repeated, and meaningful interactions between personal Beings/beings. The relational process that occurs between interacting participants helps create and recreate relational network, create perceived meaning, [17] and perform functions. In contrast to functionalism and conflict theory, symbolic interactionism emphasizes the micro-processes through which

---

[17] Gimple and Wan, *Covenant Transformative Learning*, Appendix I.

people construct meanings while relational interactionism emphasizes the micro- and macro- processes through which relational reality of complex networks are dynamically formed, maintained and changed.

The theological foundation of relational interactionism began with the narrative understanding of interactive relationship within the Trinity as shown in the figure below.

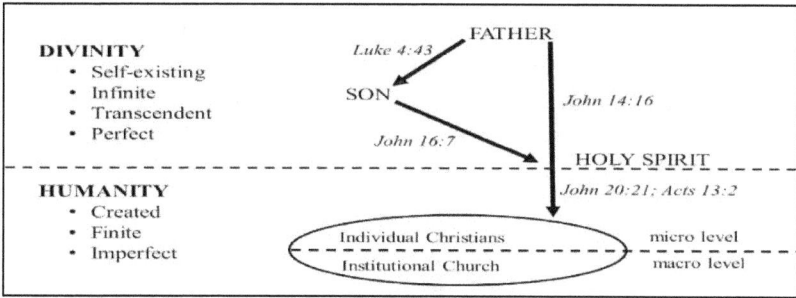

**Figure 6.3. The interactive relationship within the Trinity[18]**

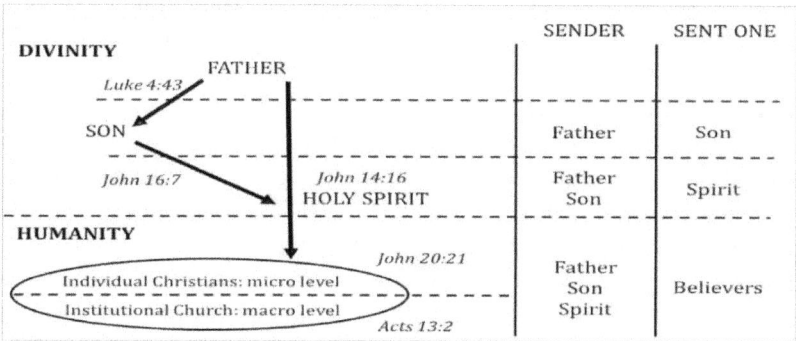

**Figure 6.4. The interactive relationship beyond the Trinity**

The two figures above show the relational interactive pattern of "sending and being sent" within the context of the Triune God (transcendent) and within the context of human existence (temporal and spatial). "Mission" therefore is missio Dei - the same

---

[18] "Mission" and "Missio Dei": Response to Charles Van Engen's "Mission Defined and Described," In Missionshift: Global Mission Issues in the Third Millennium, Edited by David J. Hesselgrave and Ed Stetzer, (2010):44.

interactive pattern eternally within the Trinity, and within humanity temporally/spatially. The following quotation is helpful for this relational and interactive understanding of "mission" theologically and theoretically:

> It is worth remembering that until the sixteenth century the term "mission" was used to describe the activity of the Trinity – the Father's sending (missio) of the Son and the Father and the Son's sending (missio) of the Holy Spirit. We have the Jesuits to thank for extending the term "mission" beyond the activity of the Trinity to include the church spreading the Christian faith. It is always helpful to keep this order in mind: that the church's mission is always an extension of God's prior mission.[19]

The term *perichoresis* is a Greek word, with the literal sense of 'rotation.' Historically, it was used by the early father of the Eastern Church to refer to the relationship between the personhood within the Triune God in the sense of "mutual dance of deep commune." Contemporary author J. J. Davis observes, "*Perichoresis* can be understood to involve a relationship of shared interiority, in which two (or more) persons share, at a deep level, their inner lives with one another. It involves an 'opening of the heart' to the other, and a giving of permission to the other to 'get inside' my life."[20]

In "relational interactionism," the term *perichoresis* is used to narratively describe the reality of transformational change of Christian in: (a) individual regeneration, growth/maturation, and (b) institutional church life in Christian faith and practice horizontally by the (vertical) dynamism of the Trinity (i.e. originated from the Triune God who is graciously involved actively in the believer's relational reality of multi-phases: **being, belonging** and **becoming**).

---

[19] Rowan, Peter. "The Church as God's Agent: A Study in Reflecting the Trinity." Mission Round Table 10:1 (January 2015) 16-20. @ https://www.academia.edu/36284562/The_Church_as_Gods_Agent_A_Study_in_ Reflecting_the_Trinity (access Feb. 1, 2022).

[20] John Jefferson Davis, "What Is 'Perichoresis'—and Why Does It Matter? Perichoresis as Properly Basic to the Christian Faith," *Evangelical review of Theology* 39, no. 2 (April 2015): 146.

| interaction | ONTOLOGY | | CREATOR | CREATED | |
|---|---|---|---|---|---|
| | BEING LEVEL | | TRINITY | ANGEL | HUMANITY |
| | Macro (dimension) | | horizontal and vertical | | |
| | Micro | Horizontal | inward | | |
| | | vertical | downward | upward | upward |

**Figure 6.5. Narrative Framework of "Relational Interactionism" – dimension & direction**

Relational interactionism comes from an interdisciplinary perspective of theology, anthropology, sociology, psychology, missiology, linguistic and communication sciences. It is a study of cultures being formed, and the social world of relational networks being created through interaction between personal Being/beings at: (a) micro- (individual), and (b) macro- (institutional) levels.

Methodologically, relational interactionists generally conduct research through various qualitative approaches, such as narrative studies (e.g. ethnography or participant observation), action research (e.g. individual research and collaborative research) and analytical studies (e.g. dynamics of relational interaction and complexity of networks). Relational interactionists continue to investigate the complex relationships between individuals and institutions, societies and cultural units, relational phenomena and contexts, peoples and places at both micro- and macro- levels.

These proposed definitions of "culture" and Christian "mission" are based on the theological understanding of the intra-interaction of the Triune God and the paradigms of narrative framework and relational interactionism.

# Missiological Understanding of Reconciliation and Transformational Change

## "Reconciliation" and "transformational change" as Missiological paradigms

The choice of narrative approach in this study on the topics of reconciliation and transformational change is not a novelist attempt. Decades ago, Robert J. Schreiter published two books, using narrative approach in his masterful study on "reconciliation" as witnessed by Rodney L. Petersen:

> Oppressors, in Schreiter's reading of situations of violence, distort reality as another story, a "narrative of the lie," which is put forward to enfold their victims in another's—the violent one's—reality. This lie can only be overcome by a stronger, **redeeming narrative**. To develop such a narrative, Schreiter argues, pushes us beyond orthodoxy and orthopraxy to an orthpathema, a right way of suffering, that enables us to regain our humanity.

The writings of Paul provide Schreiter with the lens by which to understand Christian reconciliation and the **Gospel as the stronger narrative.** Through images of death, blood, and cross (reminding us of his earlier book *In Water and in Blood: A Spirituality of Solidarity and Hope* [1988]), Schreiter helps us to see Christian reconciliation as rooted in three different theological realities: Christological, ecclesiastical, and cosmic. Grounded as such, reconciliation is, finally, a spirituality or mode of being more than a strategy. It comes upon us like healing.[21] (emphasis added)

## Understanding "reconciliation"

Etymologically, the Greek word _katallage_ = _katá_ + _allásso_ was used by the Apostle Paul in the following passages:

- Romans 5:11: believers "received reconciliation;"

---

[21] Rodney L. Petersen, "Forward" IN Robert J. Schreiter. Reconciliation: *Mission & Ministry in a Changing Social Order*. NY: Urbis. 1996.

- Romans 11:15: by grace gentiles can enjoy reconciliation, subsequent to the rejection of the Messiah by Jews – "the reconciliation of the world;"
- 2 Cor 5:18 believers are given the "ministry of reconciliation;"
- 2 Cor 5:19 believers are entrusted with "the word of reconciliation."

The broken relationship between God and man (i.e. sinners with iniquities - Is 59:2 and enmity - Col 1:21) is reconciled at God's initiative for man's blessings. [22] Those who have enjoyed reconciliation (i.e. previously alienated) with God are to share the **message** of "be reconciled with God" and to engage in the **ministry** of reconciliation (see row #1 in the figure below). After being changed and transformed by God's reconciliation, they are to become agents of God's transformational change of others in terms of "reconciliation."

The following quotation on God's *hesed* is helpful for a better understanding of relational definition of Christian "mission." It also illustrates "reconciliation" and "transformation" from a relational interactionist perspective:

> The mission of the church is to follow *missio Dei*. Since the Fall, humanity has been hiding from God (Gen 3:9-10), or, perhaps, God has been hidden from humanity, on account of the severance of the relationship between God and humanity due to sin (Is 59:1-15; Micah 3:4). One of the greatest aspects of *magnalia Dei* is God's self-disclosure to humankind. This is not an end in itself, but a means of reconciling humanity to God for human redemption (**being: God works in us**). Thus, it becomes imperative for those who have tasted of God's *hesed to* both testify to it in the congregation of the faithful (**belonging: God works among us**) and to bear witness to it in declaring God's redemptive grace among the nations (**becoming: God works through us**). There are various approaches to carrying out the

---

[22]For a theological and relational study on reconciliation and atonement, see recent publication: Early, Alex, and Enoch Wan. *The Cross and the Kaleidoscope: Substitutionary Atonement and Our Relationships*. Western Academic Publishers, 2021.

witness-bearing among the nations. (Robert Schreiter and Knud Jørgensen. 2013:97 – emphasis added).

### Understanding "transformation"

The Greek word which usually stands behind the words 'transformed' and 'transfigured' in English translations of the Bible is the verb μεταμορφόω. Specifically, it can be found in four passages: Matthew 17:2, Mark 9:2, Romans 12:2, and 2 Corinthians 3:18 (it does not occur in the LXX). In Paul's usage of μεταμορφόω, the substance or inward quality of a person is transformed by the revelation of God in Christ, and this will bear the visible, bodily fruit of godly living, even though the outward transformation of the physical body still awaits the return of the Lord (Rom. 8:23, Phil. 3:21).

Μεταμορφόω can be used to talk about *a change in external appearance*, as we have seen in our examination of the transfiguration narratives in Matthew and Mark. However, it can also describe *a change of substance or inner being*. This usage is what we are interested in and covers both of Paul's uses of the word.

However, we should add that Paul's context in both instances makes the word about an ongoing change, rather than a one-time transformation. In view of this, the meaning of μεταμορφόω in both Pauline passages is best summarized as: "An ongoing, progressive, inward change toward the being formed into the image of Christ and into a true, thoughtful worshiper." Furthermore, this is, "a change driven by perceiving the revelation of God in Christ, described as 'the mercies of God' in Romans and the glory of God in Christ in 2 Corinthians."

## Paradigms of "Reconciliation" and "Relational Transformational Change"

Though there are many publications on "reconciliation,"[23] there are few helpful references on "reconciliation" as a missiological paradigm:

---

[23] Below are some samples:

- Robert J. Schreiter. *Reconciliation: Mission & Ministry in a Changing Social Order.* NY: Orbis. 1996.
- Robert Schreiter and Knud Jørgensen. *Mission as Ministry of Reconciliation.* Regnum Edinburgh Century Series. 2013.
- Ralph Martin. *Reconciliation: A Study in Paul's Theology.* London: Marshall, Morgan & Scott, 1981.

As in this paper, the use of narrative approach on "reconciliation" is found in one of them as quoted below:

"there are powerful stories of reconciliation, such as that of Esau and Jacob, and of Joseph and his brothers. Even in the New Testament, the language of reconciliation is largely to be found only in the Pauline writings. Indeed, Paul's message has been called a "Gospel of reconciliation" inasmuch as he had experienced being reconciled to God and the followers of Jesus by a gracious act on the part of God, not due to anything he himself had done." (Robert Schreiter and Knud Jørgensen. 2013:12)

"Reconciliation" as a missiological paradigm is conceptualized as being Trinitarian, and closely tied with *missio Dei*:

What we see in these Pauline passages is how reconciliation is a central
way of explaining God's work in the world. Through the Son and the Spirit, God is making peace – between God and the world, and thus also within all of creation itself. When this insight is brought together with the concept of the ***missio Dei*** developed a few decades earlier in missiology, we see the biblical foundations for reconciliation as a **paradigm of mission**, a

---

- A Ritschl. *The Christian Doctrine of Justification and Reconciliation: The Positive Development of the Doctrine.* 2004
- Yaacov Bar-Siman-Tov, editor. *From Conflict Resolution to Reconciliation.* Oxford University Press 2004.
- Claire Moon. *Narrating political reconciliation: South Africa's truth and reconciliation commission.* Rowman & Littlefield. 2009
- Jidoth Renner. *Discourse, normative change and the quest for reconciliation in global politics.* Oxford University Press. 2018.
- Forgiveness and reconciliation
- A Kalayjian, RF Paloutzian. Eds. *Forgiveness and reconciliation.* New York : Springer. 2010.

paradigm that began taking on a particular poignancy and urgency in the last decade of the twentieth century. (Robert Schreiter and Knud Jørgensen. 2013: 14; emphasis added)

In addition, "Reconciliation" as a missiological paradigm[24] is also cosmic and ecologically relevant:

The two passages from the hymns at the beginning of the letters to the Ephesians and Colossians point out the **cosmic dimensions** of Christ's reconciling acts. The cosmic dimension not only forms the basis for a comprehensive understanding of reconciliation but is now being drawn upon especially to draw attention to the **ecological imperative** arising out of climate change on our planet. (Robert Schreiter and Knud Jørgensen. 2013: 14; emphasis added)

"Reconciliation" as a paradigm, in the words of Robert L. Petersen, is a relatively new approach:

As a new paradigm, reconciliation may take us beyond some of our old paradigms, such as liberation, evangelism (*marturia*), service (*diakonia*), proclamation (*kerygma),* fellowship (*koinonia*) and worship (*leitourgia*). At the same time, it carries forward and includes these perspectives and dimensions." (Schreiter 1996: Forward)

Throughout the years, the topic of "transformation" had been addressed by authors of evangelical orientation,[25] including the

---

[24] According to Robert Schreiter and Knud Jørgensen (2013:14-18). There are 5 principles within "reconciliation" as a missiological paradigm.

[25] Sample publications by evangelical authors are listed below:

- Bosch, David J. *Transforming Mission: Paradigm Shifts in Theology of Mission.* 20th Anniversary edition. Maryknoll, N.Y: Orbis, 2011.
- Hiebert, Paul G. *Transforming Worldviews: An Anthropological Understanding of How People Change.* Grand Rapids, Mich: Baker Academic, 2008.
- Lingenfelter, Sherwood. *Transforming Culture: A Challenge for Christian Mission.* Grand Rapids: Baker Book House, 1992.
- Shaw, Perry. *Transforming Theological Education: A Practical Handbook for Integrative Learning.* Langham Global Library, 2014.

author of this paper.[26] There are 7 aspects in the paradigm of transformational change that begins with reconciliation as a first step:

1. Reconciled (relational connectivity)
2. Redeemed (salvific efficacy)
3. Justified (forensic standing)
4. Regenerated (life condition)
5. Rescued with obligations (new identity & responsibility)
6. Sanctified (positionally) (Deut 7:6; 1Cor 1:1)
7. Adopted (children of God)

The figure below is an attempt to diagrammatically list out the 7 aspects of the paradigm of transformational change of "being → belonging → becoming," with reconciliation as the starting point:

---

- Tizon, Al. *Transformation after Lausanne: Radical Evangelical Mission in Global-Local Perspective*. Regnum Studies in Mission. Oxford: Regnum Books International, 2008.
- Jayasooria, Denison. *Social Transformation: Theology and Action*. Kuala Lumpur: Malaysia Care. 1990.

[26] Listed below are some samples:

- Wan, Enoch. "Narrative Framework for Relational Transformational Change." Paper presented at EMS National Conference, Virtual, September 2021: Pre-Publication Material. Do not circulate, 2021.
- _____. "Relational Transformational Leadership — An Asian Christian Perspective." *Asian Missions Advance* (2021). http://www.asiamissions.net/asian-missions-advances/.
- _____. . "Rethinking Urban Mission in Terms of Spiritual and Social Transformational Change." 16. Paper presented at MSG/WAMS Biennial International Conference, Ghana, October 26, 2021: Pre-publication material: do not duplicate or circulate, 2021.
- _____ & Mark Hedinger. "Transformative Ministry for the Majority World Context: Applying Relational Approaches." *EMS Occasional Bulletin* (Spring 2018). https://www.emsweb.org/images/occasional-bulletin/volume-31/OB_Spring_2018.pdf
- Gimple, Ryan, and Enoch Wan. *Covenant Transformative Learning: Theory and Practice for Mission*. Western Academic Publishers, 2021.
- Wan, Enoch, and Mark Hedinger. *Relational Missionary Training: Theology, Theory & Practice*. Skyforest, Calif.: Urban Loft Publishers, 2017.
- Wan, Enoch, and Howard Shauhau Chen. *Marketplace Transformation: Motivating and Mobilizing Chinese Churches in the Silicon Valley for Gospel Transformation*. Western Press, 2021.

| TRANSFORMATIONAL CHANGE | | |
|---|---|---|
| **Point (beginning)** → **p r o c e s s** → **positive outcome** | | |
| **BEING** <br> *God working in us - vertical* | **BELONGING** <br> *God working among us – vertical + horizontal* | **BECOMING** <br> *(God working thru us – vert.+horiz.)* |
| 1. Reconciled (relational connectivity) | Reconciled with God vertically & horizontally with one & other through Christ, a dwelling of the Spirit | ***Nicene Creed /van Engen*[27]** <br> Catholicity /reconciling | Christians: agents of reconciliation |
| 2. Redeemed (salvific efficacy) | Members of the Body of Christ are joined to Christ in salvation, with diversity of gifts to edify/care (*koinonia*) for one & other (1Cor 12-14; Eph 4:15-16) | Unity/ unifying | With the fullness of Christ as visible witness (Eph 1:22-23) |
| 3. Justified (forensic standing) | Justified by grace through faith, working through love, & forgiving one & other (Mt 5:23-24; Mk 11:25-26; Rom 4:25; Gal 5:6; Col 3:13-14) | | Known as His disciples by forgiving/loving one & other (Jn 13:35; Col 3:13) |
| 4. Regenerated (life condition) | The Church (*ecclesia*) of the living God (1Tim 3:15) is the organism to grow into the statue of Christ, being built up with unity (Eph 4:1-16) | | With unity: witness to the world (Jn 17:11, 21-23) |

---

[27] "I believe in one, holy, catholic and apostolic church…" (Nicene Creed of 381) as rephrased by Charles van Engen. *God's Missionary People: Rethinking the Purpose of the Local Church*. Grand Rapids: Baker. 1991:59-71.

| TRANSFORMATIONAL CHANGE Point (beginning) → process → positive outcome | | |
|---|---|---|
| **BEING** *God working in us - vertical* | **BELONGING** *God working among us – vertical + horizontal* | **BECOMING** *(God working thru us – vert.+horiz.)* |
| 5. Sanctified (positionally) (Deut 7:6; 1Cor 1:1) | -Sanctifying progressively (1Cor 1: 1-3; 1Pet 1:15-16)  Holiness/ sanctifying  -Temple of God: collectively & individually, (1Cor 3:16-17, 6:20) fitly built together with Christ as the corner stone (Eph 2:19-22) | - OT: "light *for the* nations" (Isaiah 42:6, 49:6) - NT: city on the hill (Mt 5:12) |
| 6. Rescued with obligations (new identity & responsibility) | - Fellow citizens of Kingdom of light (Col 1:13) - "...chosen generation, royal priesthood, holy nation.." to offer spiritual sacrifice (1Pet 2:9)  Apostolicity /proclaiming | - declare the praises of Him (1Pet 2:9) - be salt & light in witnessing (Mt 5:13-16) |
| 7. Adopted (children of God) | - Family/household of God: brotherly affection (Gal 3:26; Rom 8:17, 29; 12:10; 1Tim 5:1-2) - Fellow-heirs with Christ (Rom 8:17; Heb 2:10-18)) | - honor God (1Cor 10:31) - glorified with Christ (Ro 8:17) |

**Figure 6.6. Narrative Framework of Reconciliation and Transformational Change**

Narratively speaking, reconciliation is relational change initiated by God for sinners: from alienation to acceptance, from hostility to harmony, from displeasure to appeasement, and from enmity to friendship. The first row in the figure above is a brief

134

sketch of the transformational change brought about by reconciliation.

> "Reconciliation is not our achievement. God is at work in our world turning hopeless and evil situations into good so that his "Kingdom may come" and his "Will be done on earth as it is in heaven". (Robert Schreiter and Knud Jørgensen. 2013:Foreword)

The transformational power of the Gospel of reconciliation can help breaking down barriers of race, ethnicity, social class and cultural tradition, forming a reconciled faith community in a fallen world.[28]

Transformational change begins with "God working in us" **(being)** as a starting point. In the process of "God working among us" **(belonging)**, leading to the positive outcomes of "**becoming**." The quotation below delineates clearly the narrative description above:

> "From a theological point of view, only God can bring about reconciliation, as set forth in Romans 5 **(being: God working in us)**. It is based in the very *missio Dei* of God in the world. And the ministry of reconciliation is entrusted to us, as ambassadors for Christ's sake God begins the reconciling process with the healing of the victim **(belonging: God working among us)**...And the ministry of reconciliation is entrusted to us, as ambassadors for Christ's sake. Our work for reconciliation, then, is dependent upon God's action and always occurs through co-operating with God's grace **(becoming: God working through us)**." (Robert Schreiter and Knud Jørgensen, 2013:14-15; *words in brackets in italic added*)

"Reconciliation" as a missiological paradigm is a composite of multiple elements of "the transformation of violence, the redeeming narrative, the biblical dynamics of reconciliation, the ministry of reconciliation in our own time and shifting social contexts..." (Shreiter 1996:81)

Reconciliation and justification are linked closely together in Romans 5:10, *"For if when we were enemies, we were reconciled to God through the death of His Son, much more having been reconciled,*

---

[28] Jayasooria, Denison. *Social Transformation: Theology and Action.* Kuala Lumpur: Malaysia Care. 1990:19-20.

*we shall be saved by His life."* In the 2nd row of the figure above, individual Christians are people firstly experiencing salvific efficacy (**being: God working in us**) then become members of the Body of Christ to form ecclesia and enjoy koinonia (**belonging: God working among us**). Together they are to grow into the statute of Christ and becoming visible witness for Christ (**becoming: God working through us**).

In the figure above, the 3rd row shows that believers are being justified (by the atonement of Christ - **being: God working in us**).[29] They then are to unite together through love, forgiving one and other as Christ did so for them all (**belonging: God working among us**). By their unity and the bond of love, then the world will know that they are His disciples (**becoming: God working through us**). The same interactive pattern is found in rows 4, 5, 6, and 7.

Christian paradigms are to be re-examined from a scriptural and theological perspectives (see extensive critique elsewhere by Enoch Wan).[30] A simple comparison of popular Christian approach is shown diagrammatically in the table below.

---

[29] Alex Early and Enoch Wan. *The Cross and the Kaleidoscope: Substitutionary Atonement and Our Relationships.* Western Academic Publishers, 2021.

[30] For critique of popular paradigms (chapter 7) and proposal of "relational paradigm" (chapters 13-14), see Enoch Wan, *Diaspora Missiology: Theory, Methodology, and Practice.* (2nd ed.) IDS, 2015. (available @ Amazon.com)

| Element | Popular | Relationally Transformative |
|---|---|---|
| What to be achieved? (dimension) | Skills, knowledge, etc. (horizontal dimensions) | Christian transformative change (first vertical then horizontal) |
| Focus | Program and process | People and relationship (Christianity – true to Scripture) |
| Strategy | Traditional | Interactive and personal (Beings of Triune God & beings) |
| Succes s/ evalua tion | Measurable outcome | Not lineal/individualistic; but holistic & communal |
| What to be achieved | A proficient leader with followers; leaving a legacy. | An exemplary follower of Christ who inspires others (1st character + 2nd career) |
| Focus | Making a leader according to prevailing cultural norms; success, authority and fame | Cultivating a leader according to the Kingdom of God: God's attributes & Kingdom values. Authority is based on humility (character) and mutuality (relationship). |
| Strategy (dimension) | Leadership style: programmati c, managerial and entrepreneur | - Primarily vertical and secondarily horizontal relationships<br>- Convergence of vertical and horizontal dynamism, leading to transformational changes: levels (personal & institutional) & multiple dimensions (1st vertical + 2nd horizontal)<br>- Process: inspiration → initiative → implementation → influence (chain of transformative change) |

| Element | Popular | Relationally Transformative |
|---------|---------|------------------------------|
| Success /evaluation | popular contest & quantifiable outcomes | 1st Faithfulness to God vertically and 2nd fruitfulness by God's empowerment and provision horizontally |

**Figure 6.7. Two Christian Paradigms: Popular and Relationally Transformative**[31]

The narrative framework[32] begins with the internal interaction within the Trinity then extends to the created order. Christians being transformed are to be agents of transformational change in the practice of Christian mission.

---

[31] Enoch Wan, "Relational Transformational Leadership — An Asian Christian Perspective," *Asian Missions Advance* (2021), http://www.asiamissions.net/asian-missions-advances/.6.

[32] Enoch Wan & Paul Hiebert, "Missional Narrative and Missional Hermeneutic for the 21st Century." Published in "Featured Article" of www.GlobalMissiology.org January 2009.

| Level \ Approach | | programmatic/ managerial/entrepreneur | Relationally transformative changes at 2 levels |
|---|---|---|---|
| Individual (discipleship) | goal | Knowledge & skills | Personal relationship |
| | focus | Program & procedure | Personal brings/Beings interacting |
| | strategy | Event, formulaic | Relationship: 1st vertical + 2nd horizontal |
| | Desired outcomes | Quantitative success & measurable goal: bigger is better | Qualitative and relation-oriented growth and maturity |
| Institutional (pastoral & social) | goal | Effort-optimism: <br> • Profit, benefit, fame <br> • Win by all means & all cost | Network & nurturing relationships: vertical + horizontal <br> • Building up the body <br> • Growing in Christ <br> • God-honoring growth |
| | focus | Popularity & fashionable | Triune God = foundation of being/doing & fount of blessings |
| | strategy | Careful planning, systematic, strategic, striving for success | -Networking & nurturing -relationships (as track) for leadership (function: the train) to move & perform |

| | Desired outcomes | - Measurable outcomes of success (i.e. obsess with quantitative growth); <br> - Increase of power, prestige & property; <br> - Bigger is better (non-transformative change that is merely horizontal) <br> - Strive for success at all cost, <br> including the sacrifice of relationship. | • All submit to the Lordship of Christ; <br> • Guided and empowered by the Holy Spirit (who endows gifts) & Scripture <br> • Godly relational network: edifying horizontally & God-glorifying vertically <br> • Holistic transformative change with Kingdom-orientation |
|---|---|---|---|

**Figure 6.8. Programmatic and Relationally Transformative Changes[33]**

As shown in Figure 5, there are three phases in "transformational change" that begins with "reconciliation," i.e. "being" → "belonging" → "becoming."

The figure above shows that sinners, being reconciled to God, form the faith community universally (the Church) and locally (congregations). Together as "God's new humanity"[34] they can experience the ongoing transforming power of **God working among us** as "…one, holy, catholic and apostolic church…" (Nicene Creed of 381). The figure below shows how Charles van Engen elaborated the four distinctives of the Church in a diagrammatic format.[35]

---

[33] Enoch Wan, "Narrative Framework for Relational Transformational Change," EMS National Conference, Sept. 17-18, 2021. EMS National Conference, Sept. 17-18, 2021

[34] Stevens, David. *God's New Humanity*. Oregon: WIPF & Stock. 2012.

[35] Charles van Engen. *God's Missionary People: Rethinking the Purpose of the Local Church*. Grand Rapids: Baker. 1991:66

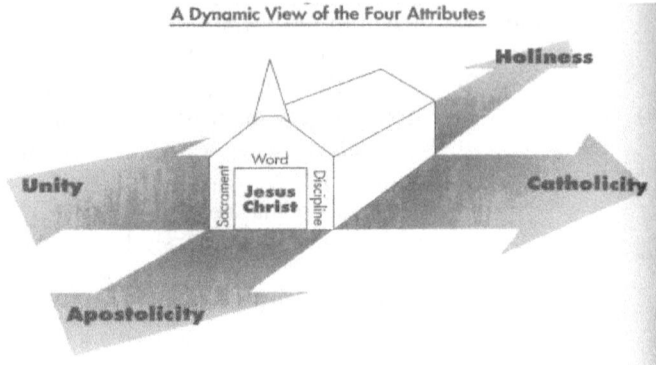

**Figure 6.9. A Dynamic View of the Four Attributes of the Universal Church**

Charles van Engen in his missiological reading of the Book of Ephesians leads to his outward looking perspective on the Church and the transformative impact of unifying, sanctifying and proclaiming:[36]

> The Church's mission in Unity (Eph 4:1-16)
> The Church's mission in holiness (Eph 1:1-14; 4:17-5:5; 5:6 – 6:20; 3:14-21)
> The Church's mission is mission to all (Eph 1:15-23; 2:1-22; 3:1-13)

In other words, the Church within the context of a fallen world is an aggregate of reconciled sinners (i.e. "**transformed individuals**") forming the Church universally and congregations locally (i.e. "reconciled faith community)." Together, they are to be **agents of God's transformative change horizontally** in the context of the fallen world, and should be collectively carrying out Christian "mission," serving "in His name, for His sake, by His power and to His glory" **vertically**.[37]

---

[36] van Engen. *God's Missionary People* 59-71.

[37] Please note the definition of "mission" at the beginning of this paper and the extensive discussion on relational definition of "mission" in Wan, Enoch. *Diaspora Missions to International Students.* Western Seminary Press. 2019: chapter 2.

## Conclusion

In this paper on "reconciliation" and "transformational change," a missiological paradigm is proposed from the perspectives of narrative framework and relational interactionism.

Relationship, especially the vertical connection with the Triune God, is foundational and dynamic to transformational change; though it is missing or neglected from the popular Christian approach. In Christian relational and transformative approach, relationships (both vertical and horizontal) are not to be exploited as a means to the end (i.e. quantifiable outcomes of "success") for the purpose of change.

## Bibliography

Bosch, David J. *Transforming Mission: Paradigm Shifts in Theology of Mission*. 20th Anniversary edition. Maryknoll, N.Y: Orbis, 2011.

Early, Alex, and Enoch Wan. *The Cross and the Kaleidoscope: Substitutionary Atonement and Our Relationships*. Western Academic Publishers, 2021.

Engen, Charles E. Van. *God's Missionary People*. Grand Rapids, Mich: Baker Publishing Group, 1991.

Geertz, Clifford. *The Interpretation of Cultures: Selected Essays*. Harper Colophon Books. New York: Basic Books, 1973. https://purl.fdlp.gov/GPO/gpo12195.

Gimple, Ryan, and Enoch Wan. *Covenant Transformative Learning: Theory and Practice*. Portland, Oregon: Western Press, 2021.

Henry, Carl F. H. *Basic Christian Doctrines*. Twin Brooks Series. Grand Rapids, Mich.: Baker Book House, 1971.

Hesselgrave, David, and Ed Stetzer, eds. *MissionShift: Global Mission Issues in the Third Millennium*. Illustrated edition. B&H Academic, 2010.

Jayasooria, Denison. *Social Transformation: Theology and Action*. Selanfor Darul Ehsan, Malaysia: Malaysian CARE, 1990.

John Jefferson Davis. "What Is 'Perichoresis'—and Why Does It Matter? Perichoresis as Properly Basic to the Christian Faith." *Evangelical Review of Theology* 39, no. 2 (April 2015): 144–56.

Kraft, Charles H. *Christianity In Culture: A Study In Biblical Theologizing In Cross-Cultural Perspective*. 25th Annv edition. Maryknoll, N.Y: Orbis Books, 2005.

Moreau, A., ed. *Evangelical Dictionary of World Missions*. Grand Rapids, Mich. : Carlisle, Cumbria, UK: Baker Academic, 2000.

Nicole, Roger R. *Standing Forth: Collected Writings of Roger Nicole*. Fearn, Ross-shire: Mentor, 2002.

Rowan, Peter A. "The Church as God's Agent: A Study in Reflecting the Trinity." Accessed April 1, 2024. https://www.academia.edu/36284562/The_Church_as_Gods_Agent_A_Study_in_Reflecting_the_Trinity.

Schreiter, Robert J. *Reconciliation: Mission and Ministry in a Changing Social Order*. Boston Theological Institute Series. Maryknoll, N.Y., Cambridge, Mass.: Orbis Books ; Boston Theological Institute, 1992.

Stevens, David E. *Gods New Humanity: A Biblical Theology of Multiethnicity for the Church*. Eugene, Or: Wipf & Stock Pub, 2012.

Wan, Enoch. "A Critique of Charles Kraft's Use/Misuse of Communication and Social Sciences in Biblical Interpretation and Missiological Formulation." *Global Missiology*, October 2004. http://ojs.globalmissiology.org/index.php/english/article/viewFile/120/346.

———. "Narrative Framework for Relational Transformational Growth." Virtual: Evangelical Missiological Society National Conference, September 2021.

———. "Relational Theology and Relational Missiology." *Occasional Bulletin* 21, no. 1 (Fall 2007): 1–7.

———. "Relational Transformation Leadership - An Asian Christian Perspective." *Asian Missions Advance*, April 2021. http://www.asiamissions.net/relational-transformational-leadership-an-asian-christian-perspective/.

———. "The Paradigm of 'Relational Realism.'" *Occasional Bulletin* 19, no. 2 (2006): 4.

Wan, Enoch, and Jace Cloud. *Doxological Missiology: Theory, Motivation, and Practice*. Western Academic Publishers, 2022.

Wan, Enoch, and Paul Hiebert. "Missional Narrative and Missional Hermeneutic for the 21st Century." *Global Missiology*, January 2009. www.GlobalMissiology.org.

Wan, Enoch Yee-nock. *Diaspora Missiology: Theory, Methodology, and Practice*. 2nd ed. Portland, Or.: Institute of Diaspora Studies : Western Seminary, 2014.

# PART III

# LEADERSHIP

# CHAPTER 7

# CHARLES SPURGEON'S SERVANT-LEADERSHIP IN PASTORAL TRAINING AND APPLICATION FOR TODAY'S SEMINARIES

by David J. McKinley, ThD

## Introduction

In 1856 a small college in London opened its doors with two students who wanted to be trained for pastoral ministry. From its humble beginnings, the Pastors' College (hereafter called "College") would continue to grow in numbers and impact. By 1890, 827 graduates had completed their two-year studies and the numbers would continue to grow in the following years. The graduates became pastors of existing churches and planted new churches in London and throughout the United Kingdom. Others ministered in continental Europe, Africa, Asia, New Zealand, Australia, South America, the Caribbean, and North America. At the beginning of the twenty-first century, the College (renamed Spurgeon's College) was reputed to be the "largest evangelical institution for theological training in Europe."

The driving force behind the College was Charles Haddon Spurgeon who is best known as a preacher and pastor of the Metropolitan Tabernacle for thirty-seven years. He was also a prolific author, an entrepreneur who began innumerable ministries, and a spokesman on international issues. It is fair to say, "Perhaps no leader had a greater impact on the evangelical world in the nineteenth century than Spurgeon."

More than a century later, another small academic institution opened its doors in Los Angeles. Under the vision and influence of Dr. John Eui-Whan Kim, International Theological Seminary (ITS) came into existence to train international students, primarily for pastoral ministry. During the following years, these men and women have come from nearly fifty countries throughout the world. They have been taught by faculty members who have grown up and ministered in their own home countries in Asia and Africa. Other faculty members have extensive short-term and long-term ministry experience in various regions of the world. The multi-cultural experience in the classroom and the cultural diversity of the metropolitan area of Los Angeles has enhanced the training for ITS students. After graduation, they have returned to their home countries further equipped to minister in churches and academic institutions, and with mission agencies. Over eleven hundred alumni have had an invaluable impact on the global church during the last forty years.

## Spurgeon's "Servant Leadership" & ITS

Spurgeon's influence on the College reminds us that leadership is an essential factor in order for an organization's long-term effectiveness. In light of this fact, this essay acknowledges the invaluable contributions of Drs. Joseph Tong and Mel Loucks who have invested many years with ITS, as presidents, board members, and faculty professors. In these various roles, they have left an indelible mark on the seminary, as well as churches and seminaries around the globe. Now, their legacy lives on through the women and men who have served and are continuing to serve Jesus Christ around the world. During almost fifteen years of teaching at ITS, I have been fortunate to witness the impact of these two men by listening to the students' respect and love for their two professors.

By examining the style of leadership exercised by Spurgeon at a school which is different but is also similar to ITS, we will discover that he was a servant-leader, committed to training men for pastoral ministry. He led in this particular way even though the concept of "servant-leadership" was not introduced as an organizational model until the 1970's by Robert Greenleaf. Spurgeon once told his students, "Let us remember we are servants in our Lord's house . . . He is highest who makes himself lowest; he is greatest who makes himself less than the least." Michael asserts, "Spurgeon believed that leaders must first be servants. When they became servants, it placed them in a position from which they could lead." However, further evidence is needed to establish the thesis that Spurgeon was a servant-leader. Based on a servant-leadership model, in addition to further research, a brief survey of Spurgeon's relationship to the College leads one to conclude he was truly a servant-leader. His particular leadership approach made it possible for him to have a significant long-lasting impact on those involved with the school. This essay supports the belief that servant-leaders do have a profound positive influence on academic institutions of higher learning, such as the ITS community.

## Understanding the Concept of Servant-Leadership

For some, the idea of "servant-leadership" may appear to be an oxymoron. In their minds, servants do not lead, and leaders do not serve. It is assumed that the notion of serving others only diminishes strong leadership. However, "servant-leadership" does not represent two distinct roles but rather, one inter-related approach. While servant-leadership may appear to weaken one's influence with others, this particular leadership approach is paradoxically very effective within organizations including academic institutions of higher education, such as ITS. For example, Don Page, who taught at a Christian university, defines a servant-leader as "one whose primary purpose for leading is to serve others for investing in their development and well-being for the benefit of the common good."[1] Jesus is the perfect embodiment of servant-leadership. He came to this world in order serve (Mk 10:45). He served by giving his time and energy in order to invest in the development of twelve men over a period of three years. He gave instructions to these disciples before sending them out to gain ministry experienced (Mk 6:7–13; Lk 9:6). Sometimes, they failed but Jesus de-briefed with them which contributed to new insights for their future ministry (Mt 17:19). He also led them by giving them a vision of the kingdom of God, teaching them about a life with God, modeling compassion to needy people, and sacrificing his life even to the point of death for the sake of building a Spirit-empowered community who would unreservedly follow him.

In the following centuries, men and women adopted Jesus' servant-leadership approach to ministry. Charles Spurgeon was one of them. He contributed to the College by leading with vision, mission, and values. He also served by equipping others for their God-given calling, and by deeply caring for the faculty and students.

---

[1] Don Page, *Servant Empowered Leadership: A Hands-on Guide to Transforming You and Your Organization* (Langley, BC: Power to Change Ministries, 2009), 90; Ken Blanchard, Servant-Leadership Revisited," in Insights on Leadership: Service, Stewardship, Spirit, and Servant Leadership, ed. Larry C. Spears (New York: John Wiley & Sons, 1998), 25-26;

Servant-leadership is best conceptualized with the "diamond model" which consists of two triangles, one upright and one inverted triangle (see the figure below).

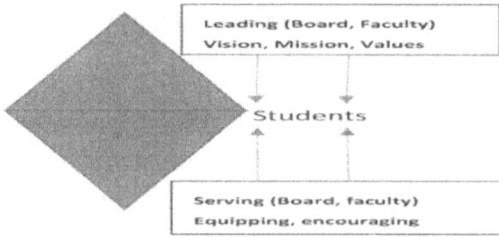

**Figure 7.1 "Dimond Model" of Servant-leadership**

Leaders are familiar with the upright triangle which has been commonly practiced in many sectors of society. Since they are responsible for the organization, their leadership moves in a downward direction to the sub-ordinates (for example, employees) who are required to be responsive to the leaders. However, it is the inverted triangle which distinguishes servant-leadership apart from other approaches to leadership. Leaders, who are at the bottom of the inverted triangle, move in an upward direction to the sub-ordinates because leadership must be responsive to needs of the employees' responsibilities. It should not be surprising that this flow of direction is not commonly practiced by leaders who devote themselves to the responsibilities described in the upright triangle. Servant-leadership moves in both downward and upward directions.

With the upright triangle, an academic institution's leadership (such as a governing board and faculty) is included at the apex and the student body is positioned at the base of the triangle. Identical to other leadership styles, servant-leaders, who are at the top of the pyramid, are responsible to lead by setting forth the vision, mission, and the core values down to the rest of the constituency. However, in this context, servant-leaders have two distinct features in contrast to authoritarian top-down style of leadership. One, the authoritarian top-down approach is avoided by adopting a participative approach for gathering information. Rather than believing they have all the answers, servant-leaders wisely seek input from the rank-and-file members for overall direction and goal setting. Kouzes and Posner state that this process is a matter of "engaging constituents in conversations about their lives, about their hopes and dreams." When people can see how their personal aspirations align with the leadership, there is a greater commitment to the organization. These leaders adopt this approach because the vision and mission exist not for their benefit but for those whom they serve, their constituency. The vision and mission become "ours," owned by everyone in the organization. Research by Kouzes and Posner unfortunately indicates that this is an area of leadership which is not commonly applied within organizations.

Also, servant-leaders are willing to share their power with others in the area of decision-making. This collaborative approach is a sharp contrast to authoritarian leaders who do not consult others. Kouzes and Posner state leaders must "strengthen" others, but "leaders have a choice: they can use their power in the service of others, or they can use it for purely selfish ends." Servant-leaders recognize when they share their decision-making power with trusted individuals, the organization benefits.

With the second triangle which is inverted, servant-leadership is positioned at the base while the rest of the organization's constituency is at the top of this triangle. The leaders (board and faculty) are now responsible to serve in an upward direction by equipping or enabling the people (such as the students) to fulfill the mission, and by encouraging them in the pursuit of the mission of the school. These leaders serve by investing their time, energy, and resources into others so that the constituency may thrive. With a genuine interest in their people, servant-leaders create and foster a caring community. With their personal interest in the well-being of the individuals, servant-leaders have greater assurance to see their organization do well. Thus, those in leadership positions, have the mandate to lead and serve those they are responsible for in their organization.

Becoming a servant-leader does not come naturally to us because this leadership approach requires a changed heart. Blanchard points out, "We have found that leadership improves when there is first a change on the inside; leadership is primarily a heart issue. We believe that if we don't get our hearts right, we simply won't ever lead like Jesus." Unfortunately, as McNeal (who works with church leaders) states, "Only in rare instances, it seems, do we run across spiritual leaders who genuinely understand that their leadership is ultimately a matter of the heart." When servant-leaders recognize the importance of paying attention to their interior lives, they have a greater desire to exalt God and his purposes which is expressed in personal humility, rather than operating out of pride and fear. In practical terms, a servant-leader's character shapes the personal core values which are constant, and deeply held beliefs which guide one's life, including leadership. When a person's core value includes servant-leadership, this approach is modelled before others. When this occurs, people "pay more attention to the values we actually use (the values-in-use) than to those we say we believe in (the espoused values)."

With this dynamic relationship between leading and serving people with a heart and life aligned to God and his purposes, we can now turn our attention to Charles Spurgeon's servant-leadership role at the College. Keeping in mind that servant-leadership is analogous to the two sides of a coin, we will first examine Spurgeon's leadership (the upright triangle), and then the ways he served the College's community (the inverted triangle).

## The Ways Spurgeon Led the Pastors' College

At the very outset when the College began, Spurgeon was willing to share the decision-making power, in part because of his many responsibilities. In the search for an "able minister" who could train aspiring pastors, Spurgeon met George Rogers. Recognizing his personal qualities and beliefs, Spurgeon empowered Rogers to be the principal of the College. While some might be tempted to hold on to the control of the College, Spurgeon was willing to share his authority believing that his meeting with Rogers was "preordained" by God. Rogers continued to be a trusted friend and invaluable colleague of Spurgeon's ministry team throughout the coming years.

Since vision sets the overall direction of an organization, one of a servant-leader's primary responsibilities involves articulating and communicating the vision to those within and outside of the constituency. John Stott defined vision as "a deep dissatisfaction with what is and a clear grasp of what could be. It begins with indignation over the status quo, and it grows into the earnest quest for an alternative." This definition aptly describes Spurgeon's passionate vision for the formation of the College. When one man, Thomas Medhurst, entered into a personal relationship with Jesus Christ through a friendship with Spurgeon, Medhurst shortly after wanted to preach the Gospel. Realizing this new convert required adequate preparation, Spurgeon met this need by personally teaching and training Medhurst. Spurgeon took the time to do this because he was dissatisfied with London's existing ministerial training colleges which quenched students' love for God and ministry. In addition, these colleges were expensive and most of the students who would come to the College were relatively poor. On the other hand, reflecting his own deeply held ministerial values, he envisioned students, called by God, who would be biblically trained in Calvinistic theology and homiletics, to be powerful preachers of the Gospel. Those who graduated would go out as pastors to renew and strengthen churches, and as evangelists who would invite people to come to Christ. Rather than acquiesce with the sad spiritual condition of many British churches, Spurgeon clearly grasped what God could do through the College which he viewed as a "seed garden for the church and the world." As the graduates were placed in churches in the United Kingdom and abroad, revitalized and new churches emerged. The history of the College illustrates that vision may arise based on a circumstance, social and cultural conditions, and personal values.

In order for this vision to become a reality, the College had to identify how it would reach the vision. The "how" is the mission which focuses on what it uniquely does to fulfill the vision. In order to be properly prepared as pastors and evangelists, Peter Morden identifies the College's three key areas of development. First, the men had to grow in their knowledge of the Bible, Christian doctrine, history and other subjects. This knowledge had to "inform" and inflame their hearts for God and people. Second, the students' gifts had to be developed in the areas of preaching and teaching, pastoral care, and evangelism. Third, the students had to grow in godliness. Without godly character, the prospective ministers would be a "disaster." Ministry flows out of who a person is.

These three areas would be accomplished through an effective strategy during the students' two years at the College. Like a "three-legged stool," the school's leadership adopted three specific approaches. First, under the tutelage of excellent teachers, training took place in the classroom. As busy as he was with his pastoral duties, Spurgeon would teach at the College on Fridays. Second, a student's gifting would be developed by participating in a local church. Many of the students came from the Metropolitan Tabernacle where Spurgeon preached. Some of the students lived in the homes of church leaders or other key members. Chang asserts that this close relationship between the College and the church was "in many ways, what set the College apart from all other colleges." Third, Spurgeon spent time with the students. He and his wife, Susannah, often invited the students to their home for dinner and fellowship. Chang states, "At the start of every semester, students were also invited to spend the day at Spurgeon home in Westwood [London], where they were able to explore the grounds, play lawn games, visit his study, and meet with Spurgeon." Chang continues to say that the students would gather with Spurgeon, and they could "ask him any question at all. As Spurgeon was accessible to his congregation, even more so, he made himself accessible to his students."

In these different settings, Spurgeon exercised leadership by influencing the students through modelling the College's vision and mission. In the classroom, he brought a pile of a wide variety of books which he had read from his library and then recommended them to his students. He was modeling lifelong learning beyond the classroom. On Sundays, as well as other days, Spurgeon showed his students how to preach from God's Word. In this home, he showed genuine pastoral care for his students. Spurgeon was following Jesus who set an example for others by his preaching, praying, and caring for people. Leading by example is the evidence of "what people look for and admire in leaders—people whose direction they willingly follow."

By setting an example of an organization's vision and mission, the leader is expressing one's core values. Although Charles Spurgeon's core values were not stated on a nicely framed wall-hanging, on the basis of his comments and actions we can suggest a list of core values for the College and its students. They would include: God's calling to ministry accompanied by godly character, competence in ministry, evangelism, and sacrificial service. This list does not represent aspirational or hoped-for values, but realized values which were lived out as a driving force in Spurgeon's life.

Effective leaders verbally communicate and articulate an organization's vision and mission. They also live out core values which both shapes the direction of the organization, and then models its vision and mission. Spurgeon's leadership demonstrated an integration between the vision/mission, the core values, and modelling them among the College's constituency.

Since its inauguration in the early 1980's, ITS has sought to train students from the Majority World to be effective Christian leaders. In their various roles at ITS, Tong and Loucks have wholeheartedly embraced and enthusiastically promoted this vision throughout the years. To fulfill the mission of the seminary, these two men also applied a three-prong strategic approach by personally influencing men and women in the classroom, encouraging the students to become involved in local churches, and by inviting students into their homes to build closer mentoring relationships.

## The Ways Spurgeon Served the Pastors' College

Keeping in mind the inverted triangle of the "diamond model," the leader serves the organization by two primary means— equipping and encouraging or caring for others. The serving side of servant-leadership is commonly overlooked, and thus, instances from Spurgeon's servant-leadership sheds light on this important area.

Spurgeon served others by equipping others so that they may be empowered to minister more capably. He followed the Apostle Paul's exhortation to pastor leaders to equip or prepare others for ministry (Eph 4:12). For example, he spent "several hours" each week teaching his recent convert and friend, Medhurst, who was previously mentioned. This investment of time is more remarkable considering Spurgeon's many pastoral responsibilities during the week. He also equipped his students at the College. As previously mentioned, Spurgeon would teach homiletics on Fridays. His teaching, preserved in Lectures to My Students, has been an immeasurable help to pastors since then. Finally, he empowered his congregation by having them involved with the College students. In addition to providing accommodations for students, their "association with a great and active church provided a wealth of instruction and a power of inspiration found nowhere else." Spurgeon was willing to share his influence with the congregants so that the students would benefit from them. The congregation was the "context for pastoral training."

In addition to serving the College and its students by equipping people, Spurgeon also served by caring for others. With several thousand people attending his church, it is remarkable that he could take the time to care, in numerous ways, for those in need. For the first five years of the College's existence, he covered all the students' educational (tuition and books) and living expenses (such as room and board, clothing and pocket money) with funds which came from the sale of his books and sermons. All of this came at a great cost to him and his wife who had to be very frugal with the remaining income. In time, he began fund-raising which was a great burden to him because he had to raise finances for many other significant ongoing ministries he had begun. Nettles notes that Spurgeon spoke of the "demands," the "strain," and the "painful depression" to meet all the financial obligations.

Spurgeon also expressed warm care for two former slaves and their wives who came from the United States in order to study under Spurgeon. When Thomas Johnson and Calvin Richardson arrived in London, Johnson wrote that Spurgeon had shown kindness to him like a "dear loving friend." On the eve of their departure to begin their ministries in Cameroon, they met in Spurgeon's home. There they shared painful memories of the past and the hopes for the future. Charles and Susannah encouraged them in the new work they would begin in West Africa. These two American couples represent the many who served around the globe and thereby fulfilling Spurgeon's vision of the College have an international influence.

Spurgeon continued to care for those who completed their training at the College and entered pastoral ministry. Since many of the College's alumni remained poor in their churches, Spurgeon raised funds to provide books, to pay for unexpected emergencies, and to assist in the pastors' retirement years. He served these pastors by caring for them in practical ways. Many former students also sought comfort and encouragement from Spurgeon who would take the time to listen to their burdens. After Medhurst left the College to his first church, Spurgeon continued to show the same care as he did when his first student entered the school. When Medhurst went through various trials, including the deaths of his daughter and then his wife, Spurgeon frequently wrote consoling letters to him.

It is no wonder that Spurgeon's love, expressed in tangible ways, created a warm, vibrant community at the College. In his classes, he did not teach in a "formal or dictatorial" manner but with a "fraternal" spirit. His lectures were far from boring. His teaching, mixed with humor and lively demonstrations of good and poor preaching, evoked lots of laughter. It is no wonder that the students clapped and cheered when the "Guv'nor" would come to the class. As previously noted, he further fostered this community spirit by having the students in his home for meals and conversation. For the alumni, Spurgeon started the Annual Conference of the Pastors' College. By inviting these pastors every year to attend the Conference, they would be encouraged by the "Guv'nor" who would give his Presidential Address (for twenty-seven years). In addition, this gathering was designed to "provide a permanent bond of union" between the students and Spurgeon. Finally, Spurgeon developed a strong community among his colleagues, such as Rogers and a dozen others, who worked closely with him over a span of twenty years. Unlike authoritarian leaders who strike fear among their peers, Spurgeon cultivated esprit de corps which made effective teamwork possible at the College. He was not a solo act.

Drs. Loucks and Tong have both equipped and empowered people at ITS. They have done this by spending countless hours with their students teaching numerous courses. These two men have deeply cared for these students who have sacrificed so much to study at ITS. Loucks and Tong have served as advocates for the students knowing their financial and family burdens. Their care has extended to visiting students in their home countries in Africa and Asia. In addition to the students, these two men have empowered some graduate students to teach and assume administrative responsibilities. I am very thankful for the opportunity Dr. Loucks gave me to become a resident faculty member and then who gave me the privilege to serve as the Dean of Students and work with him in this role for several years.

## Conclusion

Based on the servant-leadership model and a brief survey of Spurgeon's involvement at the College, Michael asserts, "With certainty, one may state that that designation [servant-leadership],

more than any other, describes Spurgeon's style of leadership. He was not interested in power and control over people." Then Michael quotes Spurgeon who told his students, "I would sooner be the leader of six free men, whose enthusiastic love is my only power over them, than play the dictator to a score of enslaved nations." Spurgeon's leadership demonstrates he served the faculty and students because he set an example of modelling the mission and core values in order for the College's vision to become a reality. He also served by unstintingly giving his time to equip pastors and evangelists empowering them to serve local churches around the world. He served by caring for his students in ways which would help them in their present and future ministries. Spurgeon's servant-
leadership enabled the College to start strongly and continue to thrive in the following years.

This brief essay reveals that International Theological Seminary has several commonalities to the Pastors' College. They include: a vison and mission to train ministers to impact the world, presidents who exemplify leading sacrificially with a commitment to the Seminary's global vison accompanied by serving in order to equip and care for students, presidents' who contribute to building community, and the churches' varied expressions of involvement with students.

However, some may object to the notion that servant-leadership applies to today's twenty-first century academic institutions. Wong and Davey state, "In the tough and tumble business world, even the term "servant leader" sounds like an oxymoron. Many CEOs are afraid that they would be perceived as weak and indecisive, if they think and behave like a humble servant."[2] While most Christian leaders give assent to servant-leadership because Jesus taught and modelled it in his life, they struggle to practice servant-leadership. In a survey, numerous Christian pastors, educators and other leaders were asked, "What is missing in Christian leadership today?" In response, more than half of those surveyed mentioned that servant-leadership was not practiced in their circles. Page

---

[2] Paul T. P. Wong, and Dean Davey, "Best Practices in Servant Leadership." Paper presented to the Servant Leadership Research Roundtable, Regent University, (July 2007), 4.

states that "few leaders actually practiced this because they did not really understand what it meant to lead like Jesus."

Wong and Page suggest two further primary barriers facing Christian leaders of academic institutions. One, if a leader works within an authoritarian hierarchy, servant-leadership cannot exist. In order for servant-leadership to function, Wong and Page claim, "The organizational structure needs to be changed from hierarchical to horizontal and participatory in order to accommodate SL [servant-leadership]." Two, in a Western culture of individualism and competitiveness, leaders can be driven by egotistic pride which is further fed by others who put them on a "pedestal." When "there are no checks and balances, self-serving leaders are free to elevate themselves and expand their territory of influence. Such egotistical leaders can be found mostly in hierarchical religious organizations." This research is humbling and reminds us that we cannot assume servant-leadership is a given in Christian academic institutions.

Practicing servant-leadership requires intentional, hard work at the organizational and personal levels. Our task is to follow the example of Jesus. Wong and Page challenge us with these words, "Jesus is equally at home with the exercise of power and the humility of servanthood. Since we are called to follow his steps, we need to find out both theoretically and practically how servanthood and leadership co-exist and how humility and power interact with each other." Fortunately, Christian academic institutions can apply the principles of servant-leadership, with encouraging effects. Research reveals the positive impact servant-leadership has on higher education. In one study, the authors conclude, "It is important to consider the transformative essence of servant-leadership in higher education as a new concept to further explain human relationships and its impact on performance."

Based on "diamond model" of servant leadership, the following offers two modest applications for academic institutions of higher education. One, existing structures can be modified in order to enhance an increase in multi-leveled participation for information gathering and decision-making. In addition to the encouraging examples of servant-leadership in today's best corporations, Page provides several examples servant-leadership positively influencing one Christian university emanating from the president to the faculty and staff. Since this university's vision is to prepare godly leaders, it is the students who benefit from servant-leadership.

Two, by including the inverted triangle of the diamond model, a shift on student learning can occur. Sharon Drury believes that servant-leadership is the best approach for faculty teaching in the classroom. Since servant-leaders seek the good of those who led over their own self-interest, professors will consider what is best for the students. She states, "Therefore, servant leaders reach their goals by first focusing on the person who will perform the task. In the classroom, teachers work with students whose task is learning in the content area. For learning to be most effective and long-lasting, teachers also function as leaders who assist students to learn how to learn." This is possible when professors who are servant-leaders, function as a "leader of learning" or "first among equals" which encourages collaborative inquiry with the students. Drury's research indicates professors who are servant-leaders "focus attention more on the students and how they learn and develop intellectually" which includes building faculty-student interpersonal relationships. Both relational and task leader behaviors are employed in servant leadership. As the ITS leadership, including the faculty, model servant-leadership, they will be influencing the students to be servant-leaders in their ministries around the globe.

In conclusion, we honor two men, Joseph Tong and Mel Loucks who have devoted much of their lives leading and serving International Theological Seminary. As presidents, board members, and professors, they have embraced and modelled the vision, mission, and values of ITS. They have sacrificially served by using their gifting to equip and encourage students in and outside of the classroom. They have also unstintingly given their time, energy and other resources to travel to many countries in Africa and Asia in order to encourage the ITS alumni in their ministries. As a by-product, they have influenced many men and women to study at ITS. The fruit of their legacy is seen in the lives of countless hundreds of graduates who are making godly disciples around the globe.

When we read about these two honored men, we might assume that we could not possibly have an equal impact on people's lives. Believing that we do not hold important roles and titles, we fail to realize that the real genius of servant-leadership rests in having a heart that is shaped by Jesus who is the ultimate servant-leader. When God transforms our hearts, then we will have a greater desire to embrace his mission for our individual lives. Using our gifting and relying on the Holy Spirt, there is no telling how God might use us as his servant-leaders.

David J. McKinley is Associate Professor of Practical Theology at International Theological Seminary, West Covina, California. He is the author of *The Psalms for Everyday Living: A Year of Daily Devotions with Charles Spurgeon's Treasury of David (2021)* and *Growing in Holiness through the Psalms: Insights from Charles Spurgeon's Treasury of David* (2023).

# Bibliography

Alshammari, Iqbal, Florentina Halimi, Cathy Daniel, Meshari Thaher Alhusaini. "Servant-Leadership In Higher Education A Look Through Students' Eyes." International Journal of Servant-Leadership 13, no. 1 (2019): 257–285.

Blanchard, Ken. "Servant-Leadership Revisited," in *Insights on Leadership: Service, Stewardship, Spirit, and Servant Leadership*, edited by Larry C. Spears, 25-26. (New York: John Wiley & Sons, 1998.

Blanchard, Ken, Phil Hodges, and Phyllis Hendry. *Lead Like Jesus Revisited: Lessons from the Greatest Leadership Role Model of All Time*. Nashville: W. Publishing Group, 2016.

Chang, Geoffrey. *Spurgeon the Pastor: Recovering a Biblical & Theological Vision for Ministry*. Nashville: B&H Publishing Group, 2022.

Dallimore, Arnold A. *Spurgeon: A Biography*. Carlisle, PA: Banner of Truth Trust, 2018.

Drury, Sharon. "Teacher as Servant Leader: A Faculty Model for Effectiveness with Students." Paper presented to the Servant Leadership Research Roundtable, Regent University. August 2005.

Kouzes, James M. and Barry Z. Posner. *Leadership Challenge: How to Keep Getting Extraordinary Things Done in Organizations*. San Francisco: Jossey-Bass, 1995.

Malphurs, Aubrey. *Values-Driven Leadership: Discovering and Developing Your Core Values for Ministry*. Grand Rapids: Baker Books, 1999.

McNeal, Reggie. A Work of the Heart: Understanding How God Shapes Spiritual Leaders. San Francisco: Jossey-Bass, 2000.

Michael, Larry J. *Spurgeon on Leadership: Key Insights for Christian Leaders from the Prince of Preachers*. Grand Rapids: Kregel Academic & Professional, 2010.

Morden, Peter. C.H. *Spurgeon: The People's Preacher. Surrey, UK: CWR, 2009.*

*Murray, Iain. "Introduction," in An All-round Ministry*, C.H. Spurgeon. London: The Banner of Truth Trust, 1972.

Nettles, Tom. *Living by Revealed Truth: The Life and Pastoral Theology of Charles Haddon Spurgeon*. Ross, Scotland: Mentor, 2015.

Page, Don. *Servant Empowered Leadership: A Hands-on Guide to Transforming You and Your Organization*. Langley, BC: Power to Change Ministries, 2009.

Stott, John. *Issues Facing Christians Today: A Major Appraisal of Contemporary Social and Moral Questions*. Grand Rapids: Zondervan, 2006.

Wong, Paul T. P. and Dean Davey. "Best Practices in Servant Leadership." Paper presented to the Servant Leadership Research Roundtable, Regent University, July 2007.

Wong, Paul T. P. and Don Page. "Servant Leadership: An Opponent-Process Model and the Revised Servant Leadership Profile." Paper presented to the Servant Leadership Research Roundtable, Regent University, August 2003.

# CHAPTER 8

# DIVERSITY, PROPHETIC VOICE, AND CRISIS LEADERSHIP[1]

by James S. Lee, PhD

## Introduction

We often see in the Bible that God raises people from the margin to be a prophetic voice or perform redemptive work for a people or a nation in a crisis. Amos was a prophet from the southern kingdom of Judah sent by God to preach and deliver God's message in the northern kingdom of Israel. Esther was the queen of Persia who intervened and prevented the genocide of her people in Persia. Joseph was a Hebrew prisoner in Egypt when the Pharaoh recognized Joseph's wisdom and talent and promoted him to be the nation's prime minister. Ruth was a Moabite woman, and through her faithful love (*hesed*) to Naomi, she helped raise Naomi's family and became an ancestor to King David. What is common among these figures is that they were culturally and ethnically aliens to their host nation or community. Yet, their unique identity and perspectives became instrumental in a nation or people overcoming a significant crisis. In this article, I will present the importance of diversity in organizational crisis leadership by examining figures in the Bible and argue that diversity and inclusion are critical to forming institutional culture for resilience and organizational crisis leadership, as globalization forms and impacts many institutions and organizations.

---

[1] It is my great honor and privilege to contribute this article to the book honoring Dr. Joseph Tong and Dr. Mel Loucks, who dedicated their lives to educating and equipping leaders from the majority world. As former presidents of International Theological Seminary, both embody resilient leadership in times of crises. The seminary weathered many challenges, but under their leadership the seminary not only survived but thrived to train numerous leaders and pastors who are now transformative leaders in their own community and country.

## The Unavoidable Consequences of Globalization: Crisis and Diversity

Goldin and Mariathasan define globalization as a "movement of people, goods, services, and ideas across a widening set of countries."[2] As we are more connected, we are affected by what happens in other parts of the world, and distant places and individuals become significant globally. There are different types of crises that derive from globalization. They are financial, supply chain, ecological, pandemic and health, and social.

a.  Financial Crisis: The Tom Yum Kung crisis in Thailand in 1997 was a prime example of a financial crisis caused by globalization. The crisis was named after the Thais' beloved national dish because the crisis was such a bitter and sour experience for the Thais, like the soup. The Bangkok Bank of Commerce gave billions of baht in questionable loans and accepted overvalued property as collateral. Corruption and laxity in regulation in the banking system were revealed and shook investors' confidence. The Thai economy collapsed, creating a very high level of unemployment. The economic crisis spread to Southeast Asia, South Korea (IMF crisis), and Japan.

b.  Supply Chain Crisis: Ukraine exports, on average, about 6 million tons of agricultural commodities such as wheat to the Middle East, Asia, and Africa. 52 percent of sunflower seed oil comes from Ukraine. When Russia blocked Black Sea ports during its war against Ukraine, the price of grain and cereals went up. Gas prices also went up with sanctions on Russian exports, including gas.

c.  Ecological Crisis: Recent floods in Pakistan in 2022 were caused by unusually heavy monsoon rains and melting glaciers. 33 million were displaced from their home due to the floods. In Nigeria, environmental devastation causes the migration of Fulanis from all over West Africa to the south of Nigeria, causing an intense conflict between Fulani herdsmen and Hausa farmers. The Sahara is moving southward at a rate

---

[2] Ian Goldin and Mike Mariathasan, *The Butterfly Defect: How Globalization Creates Systemic Risks, and What to Do about It* (Princeton, NJ: Princeton University, 2015), 1.

of 600 meters a year. Lake Chad is drying up. Fulani herdsmen who
relied on the lake are moving south for pasture and water. The further south you go down, the more the population becomes Christian. These are examples of ecological crises.

d.  Pandemics and Health Crisis: New potent Covid variants like Delta and Omicron all emerged from developing countries such as India and South Africa, where local populations had limited access to vaccines and the noble virus was allowed mutations over an extensive period of transmission.[3] Not only is the global economic imbalance a negative side effect of globalization, but also there is a direct correlation between local poverty and pandemics in the global era. Yet, the indigenous population who suffer the most from the pandemics are often scapegoated for the pandemics.

e.  Social Crisis: Migrants and social inequality. Elias Bongmba sees globalization as McDonalization, MTVization, and CNNization of the world through an "intensification of social relations."[4] Globalization is imperialistic because it creates unequal distribution of wealth between the developed and developing nations. According to Goldin and Mariathasan, while globalization has lifted significant population in the world out of poverty, regional life expectancy in sub-Saharan Africa and the former Soviet bloc has been decreasing. The number of people in extreme poverty in Africa has also increased significantly by over 10 million.[5] Global free market prioritizes profits and wealth accumulation over human freedom and communal interests. [6] Transnational

---

[3]  https://hub.jhu.edu/2021/12/21/global-vaccination-prevents-variants-durbin-moss/. Assessed August 2, 2023.

[4] Elias K. Bongmba, *Facing a Pandemic: The African Church and the Crisis of AIDS* (Baylor, TX: Baylor University, 2007), 133. Anthony Giddens speaks of local transformation as a part of globalization, in which local affairs are shaped by factors such as world money and commodity markets that are "at an infinite distance away from that neighborhood itself." *The Consequences of Modernity* (Malden, MA: Polity Press, 2013), 64.

[5] Ian Goldin and Mike Mariathansan, *The Butterfly Defect*, 32.

[6] Comaroffs points out a resurgence of belief in zombies and zombie masters in parts of postcolonial South Africa. Jean Comaroff and John L. Comaroff, "Alien-Nation: Zombies, Immigrants, and Millennial Capitalism," *The South Atlantic Quarterly* 101, no. 4 (2002): 779-805.

corporations like pharmaceutical companies control their products such as HIV/AIDS drugs, which results in limited access among those with HIV/AIDS in the developing world.[7] We have seen similar injustice unfolding during the COVID-19 crisis. 10 months after the first COVID-19 vaccine became available, the US and other developed nations were already giving out their booster shots, while nations like Burundi, a central African nation was yet to administer a single COVID vaccine.[8]

Globalization is an inevitable trend, which will continue to impact humanity. I agree with Goldin and Mariathansan's assessment that in this increasingly more connected and complex world, "globalization must be managed effectively."[9] Globalization holds both opportunities and risks. "Collective genius" can be unleashed by the education of untapped talents and widespread of resources and idea sharing, which in return will address and solve problems and challenges posed by globalization.[10]

## Diversity and Inclusion as an Asset to an Organization and its Leadership in Times of Crisis

### Key Aspects of Crisis Leadership

Mitroff understands crisis leadership as concerned with enduring issues that come from leading during a crisis and how leaders can prepare their organizations to better handle these situations over an extended period of time.[11] On the other hand, crisis management is often viewed as concentrating more on the distinct steps taken to respond to an individual crisis. In other

---

[7] For globalization's impact on inequality, see Ian Goldin and Mike Mariathansan, *The Butterfly Defect*, 168-197

[8] https://www.wsj.com/articles/covid-19-vaccine-gap-between-rich-and-poor-nations-keeps-widening-11632578312. Assessed August 2, 2023.

[9] Ian Goldin and Mike Mariathansan, *The Butterfly Defect*, 1.

[10] Ibid., 5-6.

[11] Ian Mitroff, "From Crisis Management to Crisis Leadership" in *Business: The Ultimate Resource* (ed. By L Law; London: A&C Black; 2011), quoted in Steve Firestone, *Biblical Principles of Crisis Leadership: The Role of Spirituality in Organizational Response* (Cham: Springer International Publishing AG, 2020), 16. Accessed July 4, 2023. ProQuest Ebook Central.

words, crisis leadership has a long-term view of an organization and thinks about creating a culture that is responsive to crises. By nature, crises are unpredictable and unforeseeable. Seeger et al. define a crisis as "a specific, unexpected, and non-routine event or series of events that create high levels of uncertainty and threat or perceived threat to an organization's high priority goals."[12] Klann argues that "traditionally, books and articles about crisis management place a great deal of emphasis on management actions to be taken in preparation for a crisis. This focus on management functions implies that you can prepare for a crisis by writing a plan and then executing it when the crisis occurs. Certainly, an effective leader is competent in such functions as planning, organizing, staffing, budgeting, controlling, and directing. But a narrow emphasis on management strategy and planning ignores the leadership necessary for putting the plan into action. That kind of approach sidesteps the human element that plays such a large role during a crisis—the needs, emotions, and behaviors of people at all levels of the organization."[13]

However, it doesn't mean that a leader cannot prepare his or her organization for a crisis. Prewitt and Weil see that "crisis has its genesis often in the values, beliefs, culture, or behavior of an organization which becomes incongruent with the milieu in which the organization operates. A leader, who is able to read the signals of looming crisis and understands how to harness the exigency brought on by the situation, can diminish the potential dangers and take full advantage of the resulting opportunities."[14] Thus, an

---

[12] M. W. Seeger, T. L. Sellnow, and R. R. Ulmer, "Communication, Organization and Crisis," in *Communication Yearbook* (Thousand Oak, CA: Sage, 1998), 233, quoted in Steve Firestone, *Biblical Principles of Crisis Leadership: The Role of Spirituality in Organizational Response* (Cham: Springer International Publishing AG, 2020), 8. Accessed July 4, 2023. ProQuest Ebook Central.

[13] G. Klann, Crisis leadership: Using military lessons, organizational experiences, and the power of influence to lessen the impact of chaos on the people you lead (1st ed; Greensboro, NC: Center for Creative Leadership, 2003), 27, quoted in Steve Firestone, Biblical Principles of Crisis Leadership: The Role of Spirituality in Organizational Response (Cham: Springer International Publishing AG, 2020), 16. Accessed July 4, 2023. ProQuest Ebook Central.

[14] J. E. Prewitt and R. Weil, "Organizational Opportunities Endemic in Crisis Leadership," *Journal of Management Policy and Practice* 15, no. 2 (2014):72,

organization that is adaptable and responsive to crises possesses resilience.

## The Importance of Resilience

Masten characterizes resilience as "the capacity of a dynamic system to withstand or recover from significant challenges that threaten its stability, viability, or development." [15] Resilience doesn't offer an organization immunity from crises, but it provides the ability to read the signs of time and allow the organization to reshape itself without losing its core identity and mission. Resilient leaders are not afraid of changes or taking risks. They thrive in a liminal time and space in which uncertainty rules. Unlike others, they view crises as opportunities for institutional creativity and transformation. Closed doors are not really closed. The doors are actually the path to a new possibility that awaits the right person. The most resilient leaders are effective at communicating their intentions to others. They are willing to help others understand a new strategy or direction.

## How Diversity Contributes to Institutional Resilience

Joniaková et al. speaks of cognitive diversity as an important leadership quality during a crisis. Cognitive diversity is a "difference in knowledge and perspective, based on professional diversity."[16] The difference in the way the members of a group see the world, think, process information, and hold as their values contribute to consideration of non-obvious choices and improve the quality of decisions. In uncertain times, the additional

---

quoted in Steve Firestone, *Biblical Principles of Crisis Leadership: The Role of Spirituality in Organizational Response* (Cham: Springer International Publishing AG, 2020), 17. Accessed July 4, 2023. ProQuest Ebook Central.

[15] A. S. Masten, "Resilience in Children Threatened by Extreme Adversity: Frameworks for Research, Practice, and Translational Synergy," *Development and Psychopathology* 23 (2011): 494, quoted in Steve Firestone, *Biblical Principles of Crisis Leadership: The Role of Spirituality in Organizational Response* (Cham: Springer International Publishing AG, 2020), 39. Accessed July 4, 2023. ProQuest Ebook Central.

[16] Z. Joniaková, N. Jankelová, J. Blštáková, and I. Némethová, "Cognitive Diversity as the Quality of Leadership in Crisis: Team Performance in Health Service during the COVID-19 Pandemic," Healthcare 11, no 9 (2021): 313, https://www.mdpi.com/2227-9032/9/3/313. Assessed August, 2, 2023.

supplementary information that derives from cognitive diversity helps the organization find new creative solutions. [17] However, cognitive diversity has its drawbacks. Cognitive diversity may contribute to an effective organization but not an efficient one.[18] Cognitive homogeneity contributes to efficiency through shared assumptions and cultures. Cultural diversity means different assumptions and cultural views, which delays decision-making through consensus. Diversity also tends to cause a high level of disagreement and conflicts within the organization.[19] Therefore, an organization with great cognitive diversity needs competent leadership that exhibits the value consistency of decisions. The leaders who lead by example promote a sense of security, engagement, cohesion, mutual support, and a sense of pride in the team members' work, even during a crisis. [20] In addition, an inclusive leader facilitates belongingness in the group while respecting individual uniqueness in their contribution to group processes and outcomes. The leader's pro-diversity beliefs, humility, and cognitive complexity lead to the group's empowerment and positive behavioral outcomes such as creativity, job performance, and low turnover.[21]

Lade et al. see a close connection between diversity and resilience in their studies. They apply pathway conceptions to resilience. Pathway is "a temporal sequence of actions taken by an agent or agents and the associated changes in the social-ecological system in which they are embedded. An agent could be an

---

[17] Ibid.

[18] According to Peter Drucker, effectiveness is doing the right things, while efficiency is doing things right. An efficient team will always prioritize progress, success, and hitting targets with machine-like dedication. effectiveness means understanding that the best outcome is a moving target. On the other hand, effectiveness requires using foresight to determine where resources should be invested for the best results. See Peter Drucker, *The Effective Executive: The Definitive Guide to Getting the Right Things Done* (New York: HarperCollins, 2017).

[19] Joniaková, "Cognitive Diversity."

[20] Ibid.

[21] Amy E. Randel, Benjamin M. Galvin, Lynn M. Shore, Karen Holcombe Ehrhart, Beth G. Chung, Michelle A. Dean, and Uma Kedharnath, "Inclusive Leadership: Realizing Positive Outcomes through Belongingness and Being Valued for Uniqueness," *Human Resource Management Review* 28, no 2 (2018): 190. https://www.sciencedirect.com/science/article/abs/pii/S1053482217300517?via%3Dihub. Assessed August 2, 2023

individual, household, community or other group." [22] Pathway diversity is "the diversity of future pathways available to an agent or agents." According to this theory, higher pathway leads to higher resilience. [23] Just as biodiversity is crucial for the resilience of ecosystems, resilience is improved when multiple entities perform the same function (functional redundancy). Resilience is even further improved if they respond differently to shocks or stresses (response diversity). [24] Likewise, pathway diversity can occur when different future pathways are available to an agent.[25] Resilience, in this case, is tantamount to "the diversity of current actions and capability to maintain or enhance the diversity of options in the future."[26]

## Four Examples of Crisis Leadership in the Bible

### Amos

Prophet Amos is one of the rare examples of a prophet active outside his or her homeland in the Bible. He was not a professional prophet but a shepherd from Tekoa, a town located 10 miles south from Jerusalem. In his encounter with Amaziah, the priest of Bethel, Amos explains that he is not a prophet, nor a prophet's son (Amos 7:14). While he was minding his own business of shepherding the sheep and tending sycamore trees, God sent him to the people of Israel, his neighboring kingdom. Soon, he found himself prophesying in Bethel, where the royal temple of Israel was located. Thus, Amos was an unusual person to be called to the ministry of prophecy. He was never trained as a prophet, nor did he receive a salary from the king to perform the duty. He was also an outsider to the kingdom of Israel, where he began his ministry. However, his previous vocation as a shepherd and distinct place of origin didn't prevent him from delivering messages filled with prophetic insights and predictions regarding the society of Israel.

---

[22] Steven Lade, Brian Walker, and Lisbeth Haider, "Resilience as Pathway Diversity: Linking Systems, Individual, and Temporal Perspectives on Resilience," *Ecology and Society* 25 (2020). https://arxiv.org/pdf/1911.02294.pdf. Assessed August 2, 2023.

[23] Ibid.

[24] Ibid.

[25] Ibid.

[26] Ibid.

The kingdom of Israel was enjoying great prosperity under the reign of Jeroboam II (789-748 BCE) when Amos was sent to Israel. Jeroboam II consolidated his power and expanded his territory. The rich in Israel enjoyed the wealth generated through international commerce and continued to accumulate it at the expense of the poor. What the people of Israel didn't and couldn't see was an impending rise of a powerful kingdom from afar—Assyria. The king of Assyria, Tiglath-Pileser III would lead military campaigns that resulted in the eventual fall of Samaria. It was a national crisis a very few were able to foresee. Amos was one of the few who had the foresight and warned Israel of the coming divine judgment and her exile (5:5, 27).

Amos didn't simply preach God's impending judgment. He sought to reform society and the mind of people by pointing out the oppression and injustice done to the poor and weak. The lives of people were treated lightly and exploited for financial gain (2:2). The rich were at ease, enjoying luxurious lives (4:1-3; 6:4-7). Religion was used to justify social evil and gave false security to those who brought sacrifices but never lived out the law. Thus, Amos challenged Israel's confidence as God's chosen people. In his eyes, no nation was special and immune from God's judgment. A sinful nation was subject to God's discipline (9:7-8).

The leaders of Israel accused Amos of conspiracy again their king and wanted to drive him away to his homeland, Judah. He defied them, prophesying God's judgment upon them as well (7:16-17). Amos couldn't prevent Israel from avoiding a crisis. His prophetic testimony didn't seem to make any difference. However, Amos's message provided the remnants of Israel who suffered destruction and loss of their nation with hope. He promised that God would be gracious to those who seek good, not evil, and establish justice in their midst (5:14-15). The Book of Amos ends with the message of hope and God's promise to restore the fortunes of Israel. This is a true example of resilience. Even the harshest pronouncement of judgment doesn't have the final say on the fate of Israel. Promise and hope are given to those who hear Amos' message and repent of their sins. Israel's resilience comes from the belief that God's ultimate plan for them is not death and destruction but the restoration of life and justice.[27]

## Esther

Esther is another leader who exhibits resilience in the midst of a crisis and leads her people to salvation. She is an unlikely leader because she never wanted to be in the role. She grew up as a Jewish orphan in the Persian kingdom, raised by her cousin, Mordecai. Both Mordecai and Esther were descendants of Jews who were taken into exile by Nebuchadnezzar. Mordecai served King Ahasuerus at the palace gate. While loyal to his king, Mordecai never lost his sense of identity as a Jew and refused to bow down or do obeisance to Haman, even though the king ordered everyone to do so (3:2). This brought Haman's wrath on all Jews in the kingdom, and Haman conspired to destroy them.

Esther was pushed to the palace by Mordecai, who seized the opportunity when Queen Vashti was sent away from the palace after standing her ground against King Ahasuerus and refusing to come before the king to be seen by his subjects. Upon Mordecai's instruction, Esther entered the selection process for a new queen but never revealed her Jewish identity. When the king chose her as the queen, Esther could've been happy and content to be the king's trophy wife as Vashti's replacement. But the crisis of her people put her at a crossroads. She had to choose between her own comfort and safety and risking her life to save her own people. While she initially hesitated and only acted at Mordecai's plea to intervene in the crisis of her people, Esther didn't shy away from using her privilege and power to influence the king. Using her authority and leadership, she asked all the Jews in Susa to pray and fast on her behalf. She and all her servants resolved to fast and wait for the right moment to appear before the king to plead on behalf of her people. Her famous declaration, "If I perish, I perish (5:16)," reveals her courage as a crisis leader.[28] She was not afraid of taking risks.

---

[27] Danijel Berković, "Crisis as the Way of Salvation in the Prophet Amos," *Biblijski Pogledi* 21 (2013).

[28] Elizabeth K. Hunt, "Esther and Mordecai: Emergent Team Leadership and Resilience in Crisis," in *Leadership Growth Through Crisis: An Investigation of*

She understood her privilege as God's given opportunity to lead her people in times of crisis. She didn't only help her people avert genocide but also spared the king from foolishly instigating a terrible crime. By refusing to remain as his submissive queen and speaking up for her people and herself, Esther disrupted the age-old Persian customs and male-dominant power structure. Esther's leadership gave voice to the voiceless and powerless and helped her kingdom become freer and safer for minorities because she herself knew what it meant to be on the margin of society and be neglected as an orphan girl from an underprivileged people.

## Joseph

Joseph was a resident alien who came to Egypt not by his choice but through his brothers' treacherous act of selling him into slavery. He had every reason to be bitter about his plight and fall into despair. He was a man familiar with crises. He went through a personal crisis of being separated from his family at a young age and living a life of a slave in Potiphar's house. He gained the trust of his master and became the chief steward of his master's household. However, he faced another crisis when Potiphar's wife accused him of sexually molesting her.

Nevertheless, he exhibited great resilience every time he faced a crisis and rose above the occasion. In prison, he showed himself to be reliable and trustworthy. The chief jailer committed the entire operation of the prison and the management of prisoners to Joseph. Joseph became a second man of the prison, just as he was at Potiphar's house. His repeated encounter with personal crises and development of resilience prepared him well for the national crises Egypt faced when Joseph became the prime minister of the nation.

Morrow outlines Joseph's model of crisis leadership into four phases: forecasting, preparation, management, and utilization. [29]

---

*Leader Development During Tumultuous Circumstances*, ed. Bruce E. Winston (Cham, Switzerland: Springer International Publishing AG, 2019):121-140. Hunt claims that Esther emerges as a leader exhibiting resilience born out of social relationships, spirituality, and the ability to work with others.

[29] Carl E. Morrow, "Examining Joseph's Four-Phase Model Crisis Leadership and His Development as a Crisis Leader," in *Leadership Growth Through Crisis: An Investigation of Leader Development During Tumultuous Circumstances*, edited by Bruce E. Winston (Cham, Switzerland: Springer International Publishing, 2019), 93.

First, Joseph was able to foresee the coming devastating famine through his interpretation of Pharaoh's dreams. His unique ability to interpret dreams was one of the key reasons to his gradual ascendence as a leader. The wisdom came from God. Divine insights and wisdom are important qualities for Christian crisis leaders. As Daniel declares in Dan 2:21b-22, God determines seasons and times—the course of history. God gives wisdom to the wise and knowledge to those who have understanding. God reveals deep and hidden things because God knows what is in the darkness, and nothing is hidden from God. For Joseph, forecasting the famine was complicated by the unusually bountiful years of harvest Egypt enjoyed prior to the famine. No one would've suspected that the seven years of famine would follow the seven years of abundant harvests. Only God's revelation provided Joseph with an understanding of the future.

Second, once God revealed God's plan to Joseph and Pharaoh gave Joseph the responsibility of governing his kingdom, Joseph didn't waste time preparing Egypt for the coming crisis. He saved 20 percent of what was produced during the bountiful years and stored them in different cities. Third, when the famine came, Egypt was ready to feed people who suffered from hunger. The famine was worldwide, affecting nations all over the ancient Near East, but there was food in Egypt thanks to Joseph's plan and preparation effort. Joseph's leadership saved not only the lives of Egyptians but also those of people from other nations, including his own family! Last, once Egypt overcame the famine through careful crisis preparation and management, it emerged as a global power with a competitive advantage. In the market world, competitive advantage denotes "a firm's ability to produce more efficient or superior products or services when compared to those produced by its competitors. When a firm possesses a competitive advantage, it can compete successfully in the marketplace. When that competitive advantage is sustainable, a firm's competitors will be less likely to neutralize the firm's advantage."[30]

It is quite astonishing to see that Joseph, who was sold into slavery in Egypt, emerged as a crisis leader for the nation. He was a foreigner and an outsider. Yet he gained intimate knowledge and foresight of Egypt's politics, economy, and agriculture over time

---

[30] Morrow, "Examining Joseph's Four-Phase," 95.

and reformed the nation to be prepared for a crisis. His leadership was God's gift to Egypt. His leadership, in turn, became God's instrument to bless other nations. He united Egyptians under Pharaoh's power and authority. Because of Joseph's sincerity and humility, Pharaoh never regarded Joseph as a threat to his power. He considered Joseph as his father (Gen 45:8).

## Ruth

Ruth is a Moabite. The Israelites' perception and attitude towards the Moabites in the Bible are quite negative. The Moabites are depicted as a people born out of an incestuous relationship (between Lot and his daughter). Deuteronomy 23:3 names Ammonites and Moabites specifically as people forbidden to join the Israelites in worship because of their hostility to Israel. Moses prohibits Israel from seeking Moab's welfare (shalom) and prosperity (Deut 23:2). Considering this background, it is quite surprising to see the positive portrayal of Ruth, who is the main character of the book. In the book of Ruth, the land of Moab is a place of total loss and grief for Naomi and her family. While Naomi leaves Bethlehem with her husband and sons to seek economic opportunities and prosperity in Moab, she finds herself in a tragic plight. Her husband passes away in a foreign land. Her sons marry Moabite women, but they, too, die without any offspring. As Naomi decides to return to Bethlehem, she is a different person from the time when she left her hometown. Her youth is gone (as her name means "beauty" or "delight"). She is bitter and empty. In Naomi's crisis and hopelessness, Ruth emerges as her faithful friend and companion. Ruth could have easily jumped ship and sought out a new life for herself when Naomi gave her two daughters-in-law permission to return to their mother's house.[31] But at a point when obedience to Naomi could have been an easy and convenient route, Ruth is resolute in her decision to remain with Naomi and follow her to Bethlehem. In our cultural context, Ruth's decision may not show much leadership. However, in her cultural context, it is a significant move that reveals her character and leadership. By

---

[31] Naomi's blessing to her two daughters-in-law signifies "cultural permission to leave her and an assurance that this will extend into the remainder of their lives." Rodney A. Werline, "Prayer, Politics, and Power in the Hebrew Bible," *Interpretation* 68 (2014), 10.

claiming her belonging to Naomi and her people, Ruth asserts her new path and identity. When she lived in her homeland, Ruth never had to struggle with her identity, although she was married to an Israelite man. Now that she chooses to leave her homeland and family behind, she begins to experience a conflicted identity. Nevertheless, she makes a clear decision and never turns back. Thus, her leadership consists of not shying away from the risk and challenges and embracing them courageously. Ruth chooses to remain faithful and loyal to Naomi regardless of what the consequences of her decision might be.[32]

Ruth's consistency of decisions is described as *hesed* and praised by Boaz (Ruth 3:10). I view her *hesed* as an inherent crisis leadership quality. According to Glueck, *hesed* is not random or spontaneous kindness. It is a "conduct based on relationships involving rights and duties of a family or a tribal community."[33] It is a communal bonding a community or organization in crisis needs in order to navigate crises and avoid potential fragmentation and eventual collapse of a community or organization. Ruth fosters *hesed* in her family and community, and her *hesed* is later on reciprocated by that of Boaz, who claims the role of the kinsman redeemer for Naomi's family. When Naomi is about to give up the future of her family, Ruth doesn't give up and clings to Naomi to sustain her family. Ruth plays a crucial role in bringing together Naomi and Boaz, two people who are related but are unlikely to be associated with each other, and helping form a new family. It takes a foreign woman—a Moabite at that—to help Naomi's family overcome their crisis and become reborn into a new, thriving family that eventually produces Israel's greatest king, David. Ruth truly exemplifies a woman of strength and resilience in crisis.[34]

---

[32] While Naomi sees the future as utterly hopeless and the continuation of infertility, Ruth's action communicates hope. Robin Branch, "Handling a crisis via a combination of human initiative and godly direction: Insights from the Book of Ruth," *In die Skriflig* 46 (2012), 4.

[33] Nelson Glueck, *Hesed in the Bible* (Eugene, OR: Wipf & Stock, 2011), 38. The New Revised Standard Version translates the word in Ruth 3:10 as "loyalty." I would translate it as "covenantal love."

[34] Boaz calls Ruth a woman of strength (אשת חיל) in 3:11.

## Conclusion

As we can see in four different characters in the Bible, crisis leadership does not fit in one particular mold. It takes different forms depending on the context a leader is in and the type of challenge his or her organization faces. Nevertheless, common characteristics emerge from the careful study. Their leadership sets them apart from others through their insights, courage, humility, and ability to lead others. Their difference in identity, background, and gender doesn't hamper their leadership but becomes their asset to help their organization become more resilient and adaptable to crises. The hardships they faced, which can be characterized as personal crises, become a source of resilience for them. As they serve as leaders, their diverse and unique experiences, insights, and wisdom serve as a rich well from which their organization draws strength, strength, purpose, and direction to prepare for and respond to a crisis.

## Bibliography

Berković, Danijel. "Crisis as the Way of Salvation in the Prophet Amos." *Biblijski Pogledi* 21 (2013).

Bongmba, Elias K. *Facing a Pandemic: The African Church and the Crisis of AIDS*. Baylor, TX: Baylor University, 2007.

Branch, Robin. "Handling a crisis via a combination of human initiative and godly direction: Insights from the Book of Ruth." *In die Skriflig* 46 (2012): 1-11.

Comaroff, Jean C., and Comaroff, John L. "Alien-Nation: Zombies, Immigrants, and Millennial Capitalism." *The South Atlantic Quarterly* 101 (2002): 779-805.

Drucker, Peter. *The Effective Executive: The Definitive Guide to Getting the Right Things Done*. New York: HarperCollins, 2017.

Firestone, Steve. *Biblical Principles of Crisis Leadership: The Role of Spirituality in Organizational Response*. Cham: Springer International Publishing AG, 2020.

Giddens, Anthony. *The Consequences of Modernity*. Malden, MA: Polity Press, 2013.

Glueck, Nelson. *Hesed in the Bible*. Eugene, OR: Wipf & Stock Publishers, 2011.

Goldin, Ian, and Mariathasan, Mike. *The Butterfly Defect: How Globalization Creates Systemic Risks, and What to Do about It.* Princeton, NJ: Princeton University, 2015.

Hunt, Elizabeth K. "Esther and Mordecai: Emergent Team Leadership and Resilience in Crisis." Pages 121-140 in *Leadership Growth Through Crisis: An Investigation of Leader Development During Tumultuous Circumstances.* Edited by Bruce E. Winston. Cham, Switzerland: Springer International Publishing AG, 2019.

Joniaková, Z., Jankelová, N., Blštáková, J., and Némethová, I. "Cognitive Diversity as the Quality of Leadership in Crisis: Team Performance in Health Service during the COVID-19 Pandemic." *Healthcare* 11 (2021): 313. https://www.mdpi.com/2227-9032/9/3/313. Assessed August 2, 2023.

Klann, Gene. *Crisis Leadership: Using Military Lessons, Organizational Experiences, and the Power of Influence to Lessen the Impact of Chaos on the People You Lead.* Greensboro, NC: Center for Creative Leadership, 2003.

Lade, Steven, Walker, Brian, and Haider, Lisbeth. "Resilience as Pathway Diversity: Linking Systems, Individual, and Temporal Perspectives on Resilience." *Ecology and Society* 25 (2020). https://arxiv.org/pdf/1911.02294.pdf. Assessed August 2, 2023.

Masten, A. S. "Resilience in Children Threatened by Extreme Adversity: Frameworks for Research, Practice, and Translational Synergy." *Development and Psychopathology* 23 (2011): 493-506.

Mitroff, Ian. "From Crisis Management to Crisis Leadership." Pages 293-294 in *Business: The Ultimate Resource.* Edited By L. Law. London: A&C Black, 2011.

Morrow, Carl E. "Examining Joseph's Four-Phase Model Crisis Leadership and His Development as a Crisis Leader." Pages 89-100 in *Leadership Growth Through Crisis: An Investigation of Leader Development During Tumultuous Circumstances.* Edited by Bruce E. Winston (Cham, Switzerland: Springer International Publishing, 2019).

Prewitt, J. E. and Weil, R. "Organizational Opportunities Endemic in Crisis Leadership." *Journal of Management Policy and Practice* 15 (2014): 72-87.

Randel, Amy E., Galvin, Benjamin M., Shore, Lynn M., Ehrhart, Karen Holcombe, Chung, Beth G., Dean, Michelle A., and Kedharnath, Uma. "Inclusive Leadership: Realizing Positive Outcomes through Belongingness and Being Valued for Uniqueness." *Human Resource Management Review* 28 (2018): 190-203. https://www.sciencedirect.com/science/article/abs/pii/S105 3482217300517?via%3Dihub. Assessed August 2, 2023

Seeger, M. W., Sellnow, T. L., and Ulmer, R. R. "Communication, Organization and Crisis." Pages 231-276 in *Communication Yearbook*. Thousand Oak, CA: Sage, 1998).

Werline, R. A. (2014). Prayer, Politics, and Power in the Hebrew Bible. *Interpretation* 68 (2014): 5–16. https://doi.org/10.1177/0020964313508738. Assessed August 2, 2023.

https://hub.jhu.edu/2021/12/21/global-vaccination-prevents-variants-durbin-moss/. Assessed August 2, 2023.

https://www.wsj.com/articles/covid-19-vaccine-gap-between-rich-and-poor-nations-keeps-widening-11632578312. Assessed August 2, 2023.

# CHAPTER 9

## SOME NOTES ON GOD'S ROLE IN INTERCESSION

by Rev. Dr. Michael Woodcock, DPhil

## The intercession of priests, prophets, kings, and the people.

The OT describes persons "advocating before the powerful on someone's behalf,"[1] appealing for some favorable course of action, urging against an unfavorable course of action. Abraham appeals to the Hittites to intercede with Ephron to allow Abraham to buy the cave at Machpelah as a burial place for Sarah (Gen. 23:8-9). Jonathan appeals to Saul not to kill David (1 Sam. 19:4-5). Abigail comes before David to speak on behalf of her husband Nabal, to spare his life (1 Samuel 25:18).[2] These acts of entreaty between human persons may be termed intercession; appeal is being made to someone in a position of power on behalf of a person or community (cf. Esther 7:1-3).

But this chapter is about intercession directed to God, seeking God's help or favor for others in a situation of crisis. Numbers 11:2 is a concise description of the essential act of intercession—*"And the people cried out to Moses, and Moses prayed to Yahweh, and the fire died out."* A poignant, pointed example of intercession is David's plea to Yahweh on behalf of his child, who is desperately ill—

> "And David sought God on behalf of the boy, and David fasted a fast, and he entered and spent the night and lay down with his face to the ground. And the elders of his house arose to him to

---

[1] See "Intercession," pp. 850-851 in Tremper Longman III, et al., eds. *The Baker Illustrated Bible Dictionary* (Baker, 2014). The present chapter draws on that article, which it was my privilege to contribute to the dictionary.

[2] In Jeremiah 36:25, Elnathan, Delaiah, and Gemariah urge Jehoiakim not to burn the scroll of Jeremiah's prophecies. While their appeal to the king is on behalf of Jeremiah, or in the interest of his welfare, this is not stated explicitly, as it is in other texts that use a preposition to specify the indirect object, the one for whom intercession is being made—בעד (as in Gen. 20:7; Num. 21:7; Deut. 9:26; 1 Sam. 2:23, 7:5; Jer. 29:7), -ל (1 Sam. 2:25), or על (2 Chron. 30:18; Job 42:8).

raise him from the ground, and he was not willing, and he did not eat food with them" (2 Sam. 12:16).[3]

It goes without saying that prayers of intercession are a fixed feature in the life of God's people as portrayed in the OT.[4] This is reflected in accounts of Israel's leaders—priests, prophets, and kings.

Intercession accompanies sacrifice as an important part of the priests' mediatorial role (Ezra 6:9-10; cf. Mal. 1:9). Samuel functions as a priest, assisting with priestly duties at the tabernacle at Shiloh (1 Samuel 3:1), and later offering and overseeing sacrifices at other sites (1 Samuel 10:8, 11:14-15, 16:2-5). Intercession is essential work that Samuel correlates closely with his (priestly) responsibilities of sacrifice (7:5-10) and instructing the people (1 Sam. 12:23-24).[5]

The figure of Samuel bridges priestly and prophetic roles. [6] Samuel is identified explicitly as a prophet (3:20-4:1a), and his prophetic role is portrayed vividly, by word and sign, in conjunction with his interceding for the nation (12:16-18). [7] Samuel's story presents intercession as an important work of prophets, and this is true also for Abraham (Gen. 20:7, 17), Moses (Exod. 32:7-14 [cf. Deut. 9:20, 27]; Num. 14:10-20), Elijah (1 Kings 17:17-23), Elisha (2

---

[3] These and other OT citations are my (somewhat wooden) translation.

[4] In the NT as well: see, for example, the community's prayer for the imprisoned Peter (Acts 12:5); recurring community prayer exhortations (Eph. 6:18; 1 Tim. 2:1; James 5:16); churches' prayers for Paul's fruitful ministry and deliverance from prison and death (Rom. 15:31-32; Phil. 1:19; 2 Thess. 3:2-3); and Paul's passionate intercession on behalf of his fellow Israelites, that they may be saved (Rom. 9:1-3, 10:1-4). This accords with the portrayal of Jesus in the Gospels—interceding for his disciples (Luke 22:31-32; John ch. 17), and for his crucifers (Luke 23:34), and (perhaps) his exhortation to persistence in prayer for God to bring justice in the earth (Luke 18:1-8, although here primarily prayer for oneself; and in this connection we could also note the portrayal of the prayers of the saints in heaven in Rev. 6:9-10; cf. 8:3, 16:7 ). To these examples may be added NT accounts of the heavenly intercession of the risen, ascended and reigning Christ on behalf of the church (Romans 8:34-39; Hebrews 7:25; 1 John 2:1-2). See Longman et al., eds., 851.

[5] Intercession is not highlighted in conjunction with Samuel's (arguably priestly) actions of anointing kings (1 Sam. 9:14-10:1, 16:1-13).

[6] In addition to being a priest and a prophet, Samuel is judge over Israel (1 Sam. 7:15-17); but intercession is tied especially to his priestly and prophetic roles.

[7] P. Kyle McCarter, *1 Samuel: A New Translation with Text, Notes, and Commentary* (AB; Doubleday & Company, 1980), 20, 216-218.

Kings 4:32-35; cf. 6:15-20), and Amos (Amos 7:1-6).[8] Remarkable in the portrayal of Jeremiah's ministry is Yahweh's direction *not* to intercede for the people (Jer. 7:16; 11:14; 14:11).[9] Prophets are Yahweh's servants (Amos 3:7), but at times the "servant of Yahweh" refers to a figure whose special role seems to exceed that of other prophets, as in Num. 12:4-13 and Isa. 53:12, and in these texts intercession is central to the servant's work.[10]

To the central place of intercession in the work of priests and prophets, we may observe that the intercession of kings David (2 Sam. 24:17, 25//1 Chron. 21:17) and Hezekiah (2 Kings 19:14-19; 2 Chron. 32:20; cf. Jer. 26:19) secure divine favor to avert disaster for the people.[11] Kings, prophets, and priests engage in significant acts of intercession, setting a model for Israel and underscoring hope for divine deliverance.

It is to be expected that people will request intercession for themselves
(1 Sam. 12:19; 1 Kings 13:6; cf. Acts 8:24). At the same time, God desires and seeks human acts of intercession—*"And I sought from them a man building a wall and standing in the breach before me on behalf of the land so that I not destroy it, and did not find"* (Ezek.

---

[8] Victor P. Hamilton, *Handbook on the Pentateuch*. 2nd ed. (Grand Rapids, MI: Baker Academic, 2005), 96. The intercession of prophets is a recurring feature of the Torah and the Deuteronomistic history.

[9] Christopher J. H. Wright, *The Message of Jeremiah* (InterVarsity Press, 2014), 114. Divine refusal of prophetic intercession (and thus its prohibition) intensifies the message of impending judgment in the prose sermon of Jer. 7:16. and in the poetic oracles of 11:14; 14:11; 15:1. Leslie C. Allen, *Jeremiah* (OTL; Westminster John Knox, 2008), 98. This refusal/prohibition draws attention to Yahweh's role in intercession. See also the discussion of Mari Joerstad, "'As for you, do not pray on behalf of this people': Intercession, deception and shalom in the book of Jeremiah," *Theology* 119 (5) 2016, 348–355.

[10] Isaiah 53:12 features one of the key words for intercession, פגע (also in 59:16; Gen. 23:8-9; Jer. 7:16, 27:18; Job 21:15). Another word for intercession is פלל ("pray," as in Gen. 20:7; Num. 21:7; Deut. 9:26; 1 Sam. 2:25, 7:5, 12:23; 2 Chron. 30:18; Job 42:8; Jer. 29:7, 42:4 ). A third, frequent, term is חלה (conveying the idea of mollifying, appeasing, entreating the favor of; Exod. 32:11; 1 Sam 13:12; 1 Kings 13:6; 2 Kings 13:4; Jer. 26:19; 2 Chron. 33:12; Psalm 119:58; Dan. 9:13; Zech. 7:2, 8:21-22; Mal. 1:9). But note that other texts denote intercession not with special vocabulary but simply with the common word דבר, "speak," (Gen. 18:16-33; Num. 14:13, 16:2; 21 Sam. 19:4-5, 25:18; Amos 7:2, 7).

[11] David also conducts sacrifices, like a priest, in conjunction with his intercession in 2 Sam. 24 // 1 Chron.17.

22:30). God wants to incorporate human intercession as a factor that somehow shapes the way he carries out his rule in the world. Several OT texts highlight God's prompting, inviting, instigating the act of intercession. Moreover, God's character features prominently in the content of the intercession. These observations about God's role in intercession are not new, but together they make an important contribution to biblical theology, including our account of God's ways and God's rule, and our understanding of how we participate in these. [12] Thus it is worthwhile to revisit some instances of God's prominent role in acts of intercession, here by way of a fairly close reading of Genesis 18, with more summary treatment of several other OT texts that similarly portray God's role.

## God's role in Abraham's intercession (Genesis 18:16 - 33).

Intercession is modeled in the exchange between Abraham and Yahweh in Gen.18:16-33. [13] Preparatory is a theophany account centering on Abraham's hospitality to three visitors, one of whom turns out to be Yahweh, and the conversation Yahweh has with both

---

[12] A biblical understanding of God's rule embraces the dynamic of divine/human dialogue, even though the intertwined roles of both parties have been conceptualized in various ways. See the discussion in Philip Clements-Jewery, *Intercessory Prayer: Modern Theology, Biblical Teaching and Philosophical Thought* (Routledge, 2016), 91-113, 137-138. See also Michael Widmer's comprehensive treatment of OT texts related to intercession, *Standing in the Breach: An Old Testament Theology and Spirituality of Intercessory Prayer* (Winona Lake, IN: Eisenbrauns, 2015), 48-56, 506-523, *et passim*. We might add, "Reflecting God's own deliberative process (Gen. 1:26-27, 2:18), our creation in God's image implies and makes possible our genuine conversation, participation and even disputation with God." Longman, et al., 850. The act of intercession accords with our human vocation and agency as God's image-bearers.

[13] That is the contention of this study. Speiser, 135, is among those who would characterize the passage differently; he suggests it is "a philosophical aside" on the theme of "the relation of the individual and society" and the role of "the meritorious individual" to avert judgment for a society. Robert Eisen sees the movement of the passage as morally educative for Abraham. Eisen, "The Education of Abraham; The Encounter between Abraham and God over the Fate of Sodom and Gomorrah," *Jewish Bible Quarterly* 28 (2) Apr - Jun 2000, 80-86. Goldingay, *Genesis*, 312-313, notes various approaches to the conversation between Abraham and Yahweh.

Abraham and Sarah (Gen. 18:1-15).[14] Yahweh addresses Abraham, promising to return the next year at a crucial point, כָּעֵת חַיָּה,[15] and Sarah will have a son (vv. 10, 14). The announcement of divine initiative seeks a response of assent and faith. Although Sarah, in the tent, overhears these words, and balks, laughing to herself (v. 12), Yahweh takes note of her response and addresses her concerns by insisting on his capacity for working a wonder, and by reiterating the promise (v. 14).

This promise of a son, integral to 18:1-15 (and, of course, to the whole narrative of Abraham's life), was articulated three times in ch. 17, at verses 16, 19, and 21 (which includes the temporal notice, *"in the year following"*).[16] The two restatements of the promise here in 18:10, 14 are not mere repetition but put an even finer point on the wondrous nature of the event by re-emphasizing its projected timing in the coming year.[17] The wondrous nature of this promised son's birth is heightened further in 18:11 by the narrator's note that Abram and Sarah are at an advanced age and that אֹרַח כַּנָּשִׁים, *"the way according to women (menstruation),"* has *"ceased"* (חָדַל) for Sarah, and in v. 12 by Sarah's musing on her life factors that make conception and child bearing impossible: *"after I am worn out, I will have pleasure again—and my lord is old!?"* Against these extreme limitations of body and imagination, Yahweh's rhetorical question in v. 14 throws into sharp relief his vast ability: *"is a matter too difficult (wonderful,* מִן + פלא *) for Yahweh?"* Yahweh has heard Sarah's unspoken words and knows her thoughts (vv. 12-14), and

---

[14] Judy Fentress-Williams, "Abraham and the Multiverse," *Interpretation* 77:1 (2023), 37.

[15] Lit., *"at the time living/reviving."* This may connote the season of spring (so BDB, 312). Speiser, 130, renders it *"when life would be due,"* referring to the end of a term of pregnancy. Goldingay, *Genesis*, 287 n. 7, 288, has *"at the time when there is life."* In these examples, attending closely to MT produces dynamic readings preferable to NIV, CEB *"(at) about this time."* (Arguably, NRSV *"in due season"* reflects the sense of the Hebrew a bit more closely than NIV, CEB.)

[16] Hartley, 178.

[17] The significance of this coming divine visitation and its effects is underscored in v. 14 by the addition of מֹועֵד *"appointed time,"* which echoes its use in 17:21 in the phrase מֹועֵד הַזֶּה .

by v. 15 Yahweh moves beyond addressing Abraham in Sarah's overhearing to speak to her directly.[18]

The arrival of three visitors prompts Abraham's hospitality in vv. 1-15, and turns out to be an "appearance" (v. 1) of Yahweh. The theophany-hospitality account becomes revelatory of Yahweh's power, not by an outward miraculous sign in the moment, but by what Yahweh says, hears, and knows. Yahweh's words have the effect of drawing both Abraham and Sarah into conversation. [19] Then verse 16 marks a transition as two of the visitors get up to journey toward Sodom, and Abraham walks with them to see them on their way. Then Yahweh speaks words of disclosure in vv.17-19 and 20-22 that set the stage for, and effectively prompt, a response in v. 23a: *And Abraham approached* (נגשׁ) [20] in order to engage Yahweh with a series of pointed questions and proposals that model intercession (vv. 23b-32). In these ways the first half of Ch. 18, the theophany-hospitality account, prepares for the second half of the chapter, Abraham's intercession. The second half closes with Yahweh, having finished talking with Abraham, going on his way, and Abraham returning to his place (v. 33).

Yahweh's "soliloquy"[21] in 18:17-19 is introduced in a striking manner, with the subject, Yahweh, coming before the verb, and first in the sentence, conveying emphasis. [22] Musing (aloud,

---

[18] Yahweh's rhetorical question in v. 14, while spoken to Abraham, is "directed to Sarah's imagination," in service of her faith, and Fentress-Williams, 39, suggests we might see this passage as "the call of Sarah."

[19] Fentress-Williams, 34, observes that "Sarah is pulled from the margins into the role of recipient of God's promise." and she contends, 39, that the theophany in Gen. 18:1-15 has the function of drawing both Sarah and Abraham toward deeper faith response and new integration of faith and imagination, and that this helps explain why Abraham is able to "bargain "confidently with God in vv. 16-33.

[20] It may be worth noting that in numerous texts, the verb נגשׁ ("draw near") denotes a "priestly approach to Yahweh." *BDB*, 620. Widmer, 39, maintains, "Abraham understood that God implicitly invites him to participate in the decision-making process and *draws near* to God as one who has something urgent to say" (emphasis mine).

[21] So Speiser, 135.

[22] Goldingay, *Genesis,* 288. n. 12, writes, "The placing of the subject before the verb indicates that a new theme is being introduced here." I consider also the emphatic placement of יהוה before the verb אמר, and first in the sentence, draws attention to Yahweh, and this accords with the proposal that Yahweh here unfolds his intention to spur Abraham's response.

apparently),[23] Yahweh speaks either to himself or to the other two men who came with him to Abraham's tent—

*17 "Am I the one hiding from Abraham what I am about to do?"*

The question implies it would be out of character for Yahweh not to disclose to Abraham what Yahweh is about to do.[24] Here the divine disclosure starts with information Abraham already knows:

*18 "And Abraham will surely become a nation great and numerous, and all the nations of the earth will bless themselves in him."*

This concise summary picks up earlier statements in Genesis about Yahweh's purpose in calling Abraham, stressing the creation of a people descended from Abraham (Gen. 12:2; 13:16;15:5; 17:6, 16; cf. subsequent notices in 22:17a; 26:4, 24; 28:14a; 35:11), and through him/them, the extension of blessing to the nations (Gen.12:2-3; cf. 22:18; 26:2-5; 27:29b; 28:14b).[25] Now Yahweh gives what perhaps is a new detail, or a spelling-out of a tacit assumption of the earlier promises: an insight into how Abraham and his descendants can function to make that blessing accessible to the nations:

*19 For I have known him in order that he will command his sons and his house after him and they will keep the way of Yahweh to do righteousness and justice, in order that Yahweh will cause to come upon Abraham what he spoke concerning him."*

---

[23] Hartley, 180. suggests it is not clear whether Yahweh's words in v.17 are spoken to himself or to the two messengers who are starting out on their way to Sodom, but the framing of his words in vv. 18-19 imply that Abraham has (over)heard Yahweh. Cf. Goldingay, *Genesis,* 294, 298, 300; Widmer, 35.

[24] Reuven Kimelman is among those who connect the intimacy connoted by Yahweh's question with Amos 3:7— *"For the Lord Yahweh does not do a thing if he has not revealed his secret counsel (סוד) to his servants the prophets."* As a prophet, Abraham has access to the divine council. Kimelman, "Prophecy as Arguing with God and the Ideal of Justice," *Interpretation* 68:1 (2014), 18.

[25] Another familiar, key component of Yahweh's promise and purpose, stated earlier in Genesis but not here, is that Abraham's descendants will possess the land of Canaan (12:1, 7; 13:14-17; 15:18-20; 17:8; also later in Genesis, 22:17b; 24:7; 26:3; 28:13; 35:12).

Abraham's descendants will facilitate the blessing of the nations as, and to the extent that שָׁמְרוּ דֶּרֶךְ יהוה, *"they keep the way of Yahweh."* The blessing of the nations is an outcome achieved only with the ethical and spiritual formation and embodied participation of Abraham's descendants.[26] This affords a glimpse of a pervasive pattern in the OT, that of Yahweh's rule engaging humans and incorporating their response in the carrying out of that rule.

Ch. 18 is linked with ch. 17 by Yahweh's calling and purpose for Abraham (and Sarah) and the (promised) descendants.[27] In 17:1-22, Yahweh announces the substance of this project as בְּרִית עוֹלָם, *"an enduring (everlasting) covenant"* that will bind Abraham and his descendants to Yahweh as their God (v. 7).[28] The import of Yahweh's speech in 18:17-19 coheres with and overlaps Yahweh's explication of covenant in ch. 17, although terminology and details are different.

While the noun בְּרִית, so central to ch. 17, is not used in 18:17-19, the verb יָדַע, *"know,"* (v. 19) conveys arguably a "covenantal" sense (as it does in Amos 3:2), denoting Yahweh's choice of Abraham to fulfill Yahweh's purposes in the world. Divine covenant initiative summons our human response, and here Abraham's response

---

[26] Ellen F. Davis observes that in vv. 17-19, Yahweh "evokes Abraham's role as a channel of blessing" to the nations. Davis, *Opening Israel's Scriptures* (Oxford, 2019), 30. Widmer, 34, makes explicit an implication of the passage: "Abraham's intercession for the two cities is among other things an expression of this blessing for the nations."

[27] As is no doubt obvious, the present study involves a consensual reading of the received form of the text as a coherent literary whole; indeed, as holy scripture. My observations bracket important questions about sources and models of composition. On this passage Fentress-Williams, 38, observes, "A literary reading, such as a dialogic approach, sees a pattern in the final form of the text."

[28] While 17:9-14 identifies this covenant with the act of circumcision, the covenant relationship itself is primary, and cashes out for Abraham not only as circumcision but as: (a) Yahweh greatly increasing Abram's numbers (v. 2), to become the father of many nations, signified by a name change from Abram to Abraham (vv. 4-5), specified further as Abraham becoming the source of many nations, and of kings (v. 6; cf. vv. 19-20; 35:11); (b) Yahweh giving the whole land of Canaan to Abraham and his descendants as their possession (v. 8); (c) Yahweh blessing Abraham's wife by giving Abraham a son through her and blessing her to be the mother of nations, and the source of kings, signified by her name change from Sarai to Sarah (vv.15-16); and (d) Yahweh establishing his covenant with Abraham's promised son, whom Abraham is to name Isaac, as an everlasting covenant for Isaac's descendants (v. 19; cf. v. 7).

involves commanding his descendants to a course of action. In both ch. 17 and ch. 18, Abraham's descendants feature prominently, although each chapter emphasizes different aspects of their role. In ch. 17 they will be Yahweh's covenant partners for successive generations, marked by circumcision, and numerous offspring, as noted above. Here, in ch. 18, they will be *"a nation great and numerous"* that Abraham has become, involved in the nations blessing themselves in Abraham (v. 18), similar to their role in ch. 17. But going beyond what ch. 17 says, Abraham will teach them to walk in the way of Yahweh, doing *"righteousness and justice."* [29] Abraham's doing so, and their doing so, will be key to Abraham's participation in what Yahweh has said concerning him, and key to Yahweh making real that word of promise (v. 19).[30]

At this point Yahweh pivots from self-musing to begin what is apparently a direct address to Abraham:

*20 "And Yahweh said, "The outcry against Sodom and Gomorrah—because it is great—and their sin—because it is burdensome exceedingly—"*

Yahweh's stark words add to the narrator's earlier note in 13:13 (*"the people of Sodom were wicked before Yahweh exceedingly"*) the detail that Yahweh is aware of זַעֲקַת סְדֹם וַעֲמֹרָה, *"the outcry of (against) Sodom and Gomorrah."* That outcry concerns the effects of their sin, characterized here as כָּבְדָה מְאֹד, *"burdensome exceedingly."* Yahweh is acting in accord with his character when he responds to the outcry, [31] and when he tells Abraham what he's

---

[29] Goldingay, *Genesis*, 288, renders the hendiadys צְדָקָה וּמִשְׁפָּט (*"righteousness and justice"*) as "faithfulness in the exercise of authority," and adds, 299, "The two words suggest a commitment to faithful relationships before God and in the community that find expression in the way one makes decisions." A family, a people, a nation marked by צְדָקָה וּמִשְׁפָּט has an enhanced capacity for societal flourishing at all levels, and for exercising a positive influence with other nations.

[30] Widmer, 34, makes explicit an implication of the passage: "Abraham's intercession for the two cities [that follows in vv. 23-32] is among other things an expression of this blessing for the nations."

[31] Ee Kon Kim explores the OT "outcry of distress," which is "the language of the afflicted" and serves "as an immediate and underlying motive by which Yahweh's mighty acts . . . are provoked in Israel's history of salvation." Kim "'Outcry': Its Context in Biblical Theology," *Interpretation* 42:3 (Jul 1988), 230. Kim

about to do. Responding to the outcry, Yahweh will exercise his divine prerogative to perform a site visit and make a critical assessment:

> 21 *"I will go down, now, and I will see: have they done completely according*
> *to its outcry that has come to me? And if not, I will know."*

This framing of the divine task suggests that Yahweh is likely to find the situation on the ground to be every bit as bad as reported in the outcry. If so, the crimes occasioning the outcry must be dealt with; the cities must be punished. On the other hand, if to any sufficient degree the people of the cities have done less thoroughly wickedly than the outcry claims, Yahweh will know—and will know not to destroy the cities. Yahweh's word here is all the more ominous for leaving the anticipated judgment an unstated implication.[32] Also unstated, but palpable, is the expectation of a response from Abraham. The next verse prepares for it:

> 22 *And the men turned their face from there and they went toward Sodom. And Abraham still stood before Yahweh.*

This transitional verse introduces new dramatic tension in the narrative: Abraham remains there, with Yahweh, after the men leave, and presumably he has heard Yahweh's speech. How will Abraham respond? In this moment of Abraham's stillness, with Yahweh's words hanging in the air, so to speak, Abraham is poised to make a move. In the next verses he does so:

> 23 *And Abraham approached and he said, "Will you really sweep away righteous with wicked? 24 What if there are fifty righteous*

---

helpfully identifies a recurring basic rhetorical pattern "outcry -> salvation," and traces it across many OT texts; I am not sure I agree, however, with Kim's contention, 233, that the "outcry" over Sodom and Gomorrah in Gen. 18:20-21 "caused Yahweh to 'remember' Abraham and to rescue Lot from the destruction" in Gen 19:29. Rather, the outcry leads ultimately to Yahweh's destruction of the cities, after the conditions of Abraham's intercession have been exhausted.

[32] Yet by 19:13 the two men tell Lot about the people and the city that, *"great is their outcry before Yahweh, and Yahweh sent us to destroy it."* Edward Bridge observes, "Yahweh's intention to investigate Sodom and Gomorrah should be thought of as an implied statement that Yahweh intends to destroy the cities." Bridge, "An Audacious Request: Abraham's Dialogue with God in Genesis 18," *JSOT* 40:3 (2016), 288.

*in the midst of the city? Will you really sweep away and not forgive the place on account of the fifty righteous who are in its midst? 25 Far be it from you from doing this thing – to kill righteous with wicked, and it was as the righteous so the wicked! Far be it from you! The judge of all the earth – will he not do justice?"*

Abraham's questions beginning in v. 23b respond to Yahweh's word in vv. 20-21 about the outcry against the cities. [33] With Yahweh moving toward them to hold them accountable, Abraham puts on the table the critical requirement that Yahweh do justice. As it was characteristic of Yahweh to disclose his project to Abraham above, it is also characteristic of Yahweh to distinguish between צַדִּיק, *"righteous"* (who are innocent, undeserving of judgment), and רָשָׁע, *"wicked"* (who are due for judgment).[34] Now in this hour of the cities' crisis, Abraham implies that there is a factor that would make it consistent for Yahweh to *"forgive the place"*—thinking of the city population as a whole. Its wickedness may be pervasive and egregious, and to that extent deserving of punishment. But if a city's destruction were to engulf any righteous persons who may be there, would that not be a scandalous misdeed on Yahweh's part; would not Yahweh have acted unjustly?[35] Abraham proposes that *"fifty righteous in the midst of the city"* would require Yahweh to stay its destruction; that would be justice. Yahweh accedes to the proposal:

*26 And Yahweh said, "If I find in Sodom fifty righteous in the midst of the city and I will forgive the whole place for the sake of them."*

The absence of a counterproposal from Yahweh here and in the following verses is remarkable. Abraham's conversation with Yahweh has been described as bargaining, even as market-place-style haggling.[36] But unlike the negotiations of buyers and sellers,

---

[33] John Goldingay, *Old Testament Theology, Volume Three: Israel's Life* ( Downers Grove, IL: InterVarsity Press, 2009), 267-268.

[34] Kimelman, 18-19.

[35] John Goldingay, *Old Testament Theology, Volume One: Israel's Gospel* (Downers Grove, IL: InterVarsity Press, 2003), 219.

[36] About this passage, Ellen F. Davis writes, "Abraham is a good bargainer and gets God all the way down to ten innocent Sodomites . . . ." Davis, *Opening Israel's Scriptures* (Oxford, 2019), 29. Eisen, 82, takes a different view: In v. 23, "Abraham

Yahweh simply accepts Abraham's proposal. Echoing Abraham's use of נשא, "forgive," Yahweh affirms that he will forgive the whole place if Abraham's stated condition is met. And as the conversation proceeds, Abraham will make a series of five more proposals, each based on a smaller number of righteous persons, and each time Yahweh agrees readily.

> *27 And Abraham answered and said, "Behold now I have undertaken to speak to my Lord, and I am dust and ashes. 28 What if the fifty righteous lack five? Will you destroy with the five the whole city?" And he said, "I will not destroy it if I find forty and five."*

Abraham had first raised the specter of disastrous punishment by using the term ספה, *"sweep away,"* in his opening pitch (vv. 23-24). Now in his second proposal, Abraham introduces (v. 28a), and Yahweh echoes (v. 28b), the term שחת, *"destroy."* After this point, for the remaining proposals (vv. 29-32), Abraham simply asks, *"What if are found there forty ... thirty ... twenty ... ten?"* but leaves the punishment unstated:

> *29 And he added again to speak to him and he said, "What if are found there forty?" And he said, "I will not do on account of the forty."*
> *30 And he said, "May you not, please, my Lord, be angry, and I will speak: What if are found there thirty?" And he said, "I will not do if I find there thirty."*
> *31 And he said, "Behold now I have undertaken to speak to my Lord: What if there are twenty?" And he said, "I will not destroy on account of the twenty."*
> *32 And he said, "May you not, please, my Lord, be angry, and I will speak only this once: What if are found there ten?" And he said, "I will not destroy on account of the ten."*

---

then responds to God's announcement of His decision as God would want him to, with the expected question(s) that will lead him to a better understanding of God's ways, and a critical step in his own moral education." Eisen suggests God intentionally generates Abraham's questions, but doesn't characterize the conversation as intercession (or as bargaining).

Abraham's questions, using מצא, "find," evidently are prompted by and respond to Yahweh's disclosure in v. 21 about going down to see and assess the city. Wickedness in the cities has stirred an outcry, presumably from those suffering under the conditions there; and Yahweh's disclosure of the cities' impending doom now stirs Abraham to raise a protest and to press his series of passionate pleas.[37] Yahweh's disclosures in vv. 17-22 engage Abraham and have the effect of drawing him deeper into response. John Goldingay puts it succinctly: the conversation of vv. 23-32 is "one that Yahweh wanted to initiate (17-19)."[38]

In addition, Yahweh features prominently in and as the content of Abraham's intercession, which is grounded in Yahweh's character, in the exercise of מִשְׁפָּט, *"justice"* (v. 25).[39] Abraham doesn't dispute the allegations of the cities' wickedness heard in the outcry, but he introduces the possibility that the picture may be more complicated, that there may be righteous persons there, whose presence ought to influence Yahweh's decision. Abraham leverages his appeal for cancellation of the judgment by placing in the foreground the requirement that Yahweh act in accord with his divine character: *"The judge of all the earth – will he not do justice?"*[40]

Genesis 18:16-33 establishes God's role in generating the human act of intercession. The divine initiative is seen not only in the fact

---

[37] Bridge, 292, notes that Abraham's language makes use of "politeness strategies," his conversation with Yahweh is one of emotional intensity.

[38] Goldingay, *Genesis,* 302.

[39] On the meaning of justice, consider the observation of Leonard P. Maré that "in Old Testament times judgment . . . involved the fact that everything that is currently in a state of disorder and dissonance, suffering from injustice and violence, would be set right." God intervenes "to protect the rightful claims of the weak who are powerless to make their own claim or defend themselves (cf Isaiah 1:16–17; Psalm 82:2– 4, 8; 72:1–4). Judgment thus means to set old wrongs right, to establish new power structures and values, to create a new social order characterised by Yahweh's righteousness." Maré, "Israel's praise as enactment of the gospel: Psalm 96 in missiological context," *Missionalia* 34:2/3 (Aug/Nov 2006), 405.

[40] Longman, et al., eds., 850. Goldingay, *Genesis*, 286-287, sees the entire narrative 18:1-19:38 as implicitly answering the underlying question of Yahweh's fairness to Sodom. Perhaps a detail in favor of Yahweh's fairness is that when the disaster falls, Lot and his family have fled and are no longer בְּתֹךְ הָעִיר , *"in the midst of the city,"* (vv. 24, 26); the resulting implication is that no righteous persons remain (Gen. 19:29). R. N. Whybray, "The Immorality of God: Reflections on Some Passages in Genesis, Job, Exodus, and Numbers," *JSOT* 72 (1996), 101.

that Yahweh's disclosure is sequentially prior, but also in the fact that Abraham's intercession is crafted as a direct response to it. By accepting all of Abraham's conditions without limitation, Yahweh demonstrates divine willingness, even desire, to extend forgiveness, a capacity that is not rendered invalid by the necessity of divine judgment for the accumulated egregious wickedness that occasioned the outcry, absent any mitigating factors such as those Abraham introduces. In the event, the conditions proposed by Abraham are not met—there are not even ten righteous in the city! —but Yahweh has welcomed his intercession in the process of exercising his rule.[41]

**Similar instances of God's role in intercession.** Several other OT texts that portray God's role in intercession in ways comparable to Gen. 18 may be considered briefly. In two notable examples, Exod. 32:7-14 and Num. 14:11-29, a disclosure by Yahweh leads to an act of intercession by Moses.[42] In both of these texts, that disclosure is the announcement of Yahweh's decision to destroy Israel. Moses responds immediately by interceding for Israel to be spared destruction, and in both texts Moses bases his appeal on Yahweh's character and saving work on Israel's behalf. These features of the accounts of Moses' intercession offer suggestive parallels, formally at least, to the model of God's role in Abraham's intercession.

It is worth noting, however, significant differences in how God's character grounds the intercession. Abraham doesn't dispute the wickedness of the cities, but raises the concern that righteous persons who may live there ought not to be swept away with the wicked. Abraham is drawing out one aspect of the question of Yahweh's justice. Moses agrees with Yahweh about Israel's guilt but does not raise the issue of an innocent faction being destroyed undeservedly. Rather, Moses makes the bold request that Yahweh take a different course of action than the destruction just announced, *"relent concerning the disaster for your people"* (Exod.

---

[41] Widmer, 34, writes, "God incorporates the prayers of His appointed intercessors in the outworking of His judgment"—an assertion that claims, correctly in my view, to summarize implications of Gen. 18 and other OT texts considered in this study—and that in these texts God's judgment is "characterized by grace and justice."

[42] Michael J. Chan and Joshua C. Miller, "Prayer that Prevails," *Word and World* 35:1 (2015), 32-33.

32:12; cf. Num. 14:19, *"please forgive the iniquity of this people"*). Moses asks this on the grounds that Yahweh delivered Israel, and destroying the people now in the wilderness gives Egypt reason to misconstrue Yahweh's saving purpose (Exod. 32:11-13; cf. Num. 14:13-16). Moses is drawing out other aspects of the question of justice than Abraham does, namely, the victory of Yahweh's saving purpose, Yahweh's faithfulness to that purpose, and the integrity of Yahweh's reputation in the world.[43]

The following table compares features of the intercessions of Abraham and Moses:

| | Genesis 18:16-33 (Abraham) | Exodus 32:7-14 (Moses) | Numbers 14:11-29 (-38) (Moses) |
|---|---|---|---|
| Disclosure of sin calling for divine action | great outcry against and egregious sin of Sodom and Gomorrah (18:21) | the people have become corrupt; quickly turned away from Yahweh; made and worshiped an idol, a stiff-necked people (32:7-9) | the people treat Yahweh with contempt; refuse to believe in him (14:11-12) (rebellion and fear, 9) |
| Disclosure of Yahweh's intention | "I will go down and see . . . And if not, I will know" (22) | "leave me alone that my anger may burn"; destroy the people and start over with Moses (10) | strike with plague and destroy them; make Moses into greater nation than they (12) |
| Core request of intercession | not sweep away righteous with wicked; be just (24-25) | turn from heat of anger; relent concerning the disaster (12) | forgive (19) |
| Theological basis for intercession | Yahweh's justice; esp.in distinguishing righteous from wicked (23-25) | Yahweh brought them out of Egypt with power (11) Egypt's misconstrual (12) Yahweh's promise - large people, inherit land (13) | Yahweh seen as impotent by Egypt and nations (13-16); Yahweh's declaration of divine "strength," i.e., capacity for forgiveness and punishment (17-18; cites Exod. 34:6-7) Yahweh's unfailing love and pardon (19) |
| Outcome | Yahweh accedes to six proposals to account for righteous persons in the city (23b-31) the cities are destroyed; Lot and his family are spared (19:15-26) | Yahweh relents (14) | Yahweh forgives; but faithless generation will not enter the land (20-29; cf. 30-35); men who spread bad report die from plague; Joshua and Caleb spared (36-38) |

**Figure 9.1 Comparing Features of the Intercessions of Abraham and Moses**

Worth noting also is the account of Job's intercession for his friends (Job 42:7-10). Yahweh explicitly directs the entire procedure, going beyond prompting the intercessor indirectly with

---

[43] Yahweh's purpose for Abraham and his descendants functions arguably as the background of Abraham's intercession, since it is stated by Yahweh in Gen. 18:17-19, but Abraham does not refer to it in vv. 23-32.

a disclosure of judgment, to state explicitly that Job will intercede for his friends. Yahweh (not Job, the intercessor) makes Yahweh's own vindication the central issue: speaking directly to Eliphaz, Yahweh says that Eliphaz and friends have not said *"what is right"* (נְכוֹנָה) of Yahweh, as Job had (Job 42:7). Thus, the formal arrangement differs from the accounts of Abraham and Moses, in that Yahweh speaks directly to those liable for punishment.

For their various similarities and differences, the OT narratives considered portray God's prominent role in intercession. God's words have the effect of spurring acts of intercession by Abraham and Moses, with the clear implication that God intends to instigate these intercessions. And God's character, seen in his promises and his saving work, features prominently in the content of their intercessions, as the basis for them. The vocabulary of God's character differs from Moses' intercession in Exodus 32 and Abraham's in Genesis 18. But there is arguably a conceptual overlap between all four of these texts, especially in Yahweh taking the initiative to see that acts of intercession are made.

***New Testament connections and beyond.*** How may this theme of God's initiating role in intercession be reflected in the NT? A brief summary is given in the *Baker Illustrated Bible Dictionary* article referenced earlier:

> Christ's heavenly intercession implements the saving purposes of God made real in the cross. Moreover, the work of Christ as Prophet, Priest and King implies the central role of intercession, since intercession is a function of each of these offices. ... God's initiative in intercession is intensified in the NT: God's self-giving through Christ is the foundation of an ongoing heavenly intercession that in turn gives the church increased confidence to intercede boldly. Further, God's Spirit helps us in our weakness by interceding for us in accord with God's will, even if we experience that intercession as "groans that words cannot express" (Rom. 8:26-28).[44]

---

[44] Excerpt from *The Baker Illustrated Bible Dictionary* by Tremper Longman III, copyright © 2013 by Baker Publishing Group. Used by permission of Baker Books, a division of Baker Publishing Group. Cited above in n. 1. See also the overview of NT intercession in n. 4 above.

If these suggestions of the theme in the NT are granted, then divine initiative in generating acts of intercession is integral to the biblical portrayal of God's rule. How then may this be correlated with our theological formulations? An observation by Samuel E Balentine in reference to Exodus 32 is pertinent:

> When Moses steps into the breach of brokenness and implores God to change, he risks believing that God prefers the partnership of honest dialogue to the proprietary isolation of making decisions by divine fiat."[45]

By speaking of "the partnership of honest dialogue," Balentine is touching on personal relationship as crucial context for how we may understand the exchange between Yahweh and Moses. If it is essential to the nature of genuine relationship that one person may influence another, then it would seem worthwhile to keep the dynamics of personal relationship in view when talking about intercession.

The genuineness of the divine-human interchange, with the corollary possibility that we as humans, bearing God's image, may influence or shape divine action, can serve as a valuable safeguard of the genuineness of personhood, human and divine. At the same time, as suggested earlier, Reformed and other theological systems provide frameworks for understanding divine sovereignty, including God's response to our human advocacy. [46] Clements-Jewery has explored how we may correlate the interpersonal divine-human give-and-take of the biblical accounts with our classic theological frameworks that tend toward tight systemization, and he points a promising way forward:

> It is in the context of *personal relationship* that the traditional divine attributes of omnipotence, omniscience and perfect goodness can be reinterpreted, without having to reduce prayer to the level of therapeutic meditation or rendering it unnecessary altogether (on the grounds that God as traditionally

---

[45] Balentine, "Turn, O Lord! How Long?" *Review and Expositor* 100 (Summer 2003), 471 (italics mine). It is a remarkable move for Moses to make, since Yahweh has just said to him, *"And now, leave me alone, and my anger will burn against them and I will destroy them"* (v. 10).

[46] See, for example, the discussion of divine and human agency in prayer in Lutheran theology in Chan and Miller, 34-39.

understood might be expected to give what is needed without being asked). Certain things may be granted to people who pray only when God is asked for them. This asking is the necessary condition for God to respond by giving what is needed. It expresses the personal nature of the relationship between God and the one who prays and is also a means of strengthening that relationship. The requirement that God is to be asked before intervening in human lives is a safeguard against either spoiling or dominating the person who stands in a personal relationship with God. It could also be seen as a diminishment of personhood if God intervened on all occasions without being asked.[47]

Our theological formulations about divine sovereignty need to include some account of God's openness to taking seriously our human prayers of intercession. That openness may be considered possible or potential, but it is still an openness to direct divine action in accord with and in response to human advocacy.[48] The OT passages considered herein provide a start, in the glimpses they afford of God's role in intercession.

---

I am honored to share with others in paying tribute to Dr. Joseph Tong and Dr. Mel Loucks, in thanking them for their constant faithfulness, love and wisdom, and in giving thanks to God for their fruitful ministry—here, especially, their godly and strategic leadership of International Theological Seminary.

## Bibliography

Allen, Leslie C. *Jeremiah: A Commentary*. OTL. Louisville, KY: Westminster John Knox, 2008.

---

[47] Clements-Jewery,138

[48] As Balentine, 470, puts it: "Moses [in Exod. 32] bets on the possibility that God's decision to punish Israel is not irrevocable, that God is still open to consider other possibilities, that God will welcome and respond to suggestions from ordinary mortals like Moses. Moses dares to believe that in the moment of decision, when God assesses Israel's failures and how to respond to them, God does not want to be left alone."

Balentine, Samuel E. "Turn, O Lord! How Long?" *Review and Expositor* 100 (Summer 2003), 465-481.

Bridge, Edward. "An Audacious Request: Abraham's Dialogue with God in Genesis 18," *Journal for the Study of the Old Testament* 40:3 (2016), 281-296.

Chan, Michael J., and Joshua C. Miller. "Prayer that Prevails," *Word and World* 35:1 (2015), 31-39.

Clements-Jewery, Philip. *Intercessory Prayer: Modern Theology, Biblical Teaching and Philosophical Thought*, New York, NY: Routledge, 2016.

Davis, Ellen F. *Opening Israel's Scriptures.* New York: Oxford University Press, 2019.

Eisen, Robert. "The Education of Abraham; The Encounter between Abraham and God over the Fate of Sodom and Gomorrah," *Jewish Bible Quarterly* 28:1 (Apr - Jun 2000), 80-86.

Fentress-Williams, Judy, "Abraham and the Multiverse" *Interpretation* 77:1 (2023), 33-39.

Goldingay, John. *Genesis.* Baker Commentary on the Old Testament; Bill T. Arnold, ed. Grand Rapids, MI: Baker Academic, 2020.

_____. *Old Testament Theology. Volume One: Israel's Gospel.* Downers Grove, IL: InterVarsity Press, 2003.

_____. *Old Testament Theology. Volume Three: Israel's Life.* Downers Grove, IL: InterVarsity Press, 2009.

Hamilton, Victor P. *Handbook on the Pentateuch.* 2nd ed. Grand Rapids, MI: Baker Academic, 2005.

Hartley, John E. *Genesis.* New International Bible Commentary; Robert L. Hubbard Jr. and Robert K. Johnston, eds. Peabody, MA: Hendrickson Publishers, 2000.

Joerstad, Mari. "'As for you, do not pray on behalf of this people': Intercession, deception and shalom in the book of Jeremiah," *Theology* 119:5 (2016), 348–355.

Kim, Ee Kon. "'Outcry': Its Context in Biblical Theology," *Interpretation* 42:3 (Jul 1988), 229-239.

Kimelman, Reuven. "Prophecy as Arguing with God and the Ideal of Justice," *Interpretation* 68:1 (2014), 17–27.

Longman, Tremper III, et. al., eds. "Intercession," pp. 850-851 in *The Baker Illustrated Bible Dictionary.* Grand Rapids, MI: Baker Books, 2014.

Maré, Leonard P., "Israel's praise as enactment of the gospel: Psalm 96 in missiological context," *Missionalia* 34:2/3 (Aug/Nov 2006), 395-407.

McCarter, P. Kyle, Jr.. *1 Samuel: A New Translation with Introduction, Notes, and Commentary.* The Anchor Bible, Vol,. 8; William Foxwell Albright and David Noel Freedman, eds. Garden City, NY: Doubleday & Company, Inc., 1980.

Speiser, E. A. *Genesis: Introduction, Translation, and Notes.* The Anchor Bible, Vol. 1; William Foxwell Albright and David Noel Freedman, eds. Garden City, NY: Doubleday & Company, Inc., 1964.

Whybray, R. N. "The Immorality of God: Reflections on Some Passages in Genesis, Job, Exodus, and Numbers," *Journal for the Study of the Old Testament* 72 (1996) 89-120.

Widmer, Michael. *Standing in the Breach: An Old Testament Theology and Spirituality of Intercessory Prayer.* Winona Lake, IN: Eisenbrauns, 2015.

Wright, Christopher J. H. *The Message of Jeremiah.* The Bible Speaks Today; Alec Motyer, et. al., eds. Downers Grove, IL: InterVarsity Press, 2014.

# PART IV

# INTERVIEW OF HONOREES

# GRACE THROUGH GOD'S WILL AND CALLING - INSPIRATIONS FROM DR. JOSEPH TONG'S LIFE STORY

by Susan Liu

Dr. Joseph Tong has lived an admirable life for eighty-one years. He is chosen by God and was born to serve Him. For almost three decades, God called on him to serve at ITS, and it's God's will that his life is blessed with ups and downs. Dr. Tong has graduated over 500 students at ITS and at least 4,500 more overseas. He is a great teacher and often gives his students candid advice like a good friend. It's an honor to interview Dr. Tong and to learn about God's grace through his fascinating life events.

## Made to do God's work

Dr. Tong was the youngest son in his family. He was born in Xiamen, China in 1942 but moved to Indonesia when he was very young. He graduated from high school and studied in a seminary at the age of seventeen. Not only was he the youngest student there, but also he was an excellent student. Beside being smart, he was exceptionally diligent in reading books, studying the Bible and praying out loud. Most importantly, Dr. Tong also gave credit to his Christian mother in raising him and his nine other siblings all by herself as a young widow. Prayers are the most powerful tool she used to raise her children as God's servants.

After college, Dr. Tong became a senior pastor at the age of twenty-three, and he had preached over 2,000 messages in Indonesia. In need of a graduate degree, Dr. Tong came to the United States in 1975 to study in MDiv and ThM programs at Calvin

Theological Seminary. Dr. John H. Kromminga, the second ITS President who later invited him to teach at ITS, had been his guidance throughout his ThM program. In 1978, Dr. Tong attended the University of Southern California and received his PhD degree in Education Psychology in just two and a half years.

## Invested and Served with Fervor

After getting his PhD at the age of thirty-seven, Dr. Tong went into the real estate business for five to seven years while serving at a church. At the highest point of his business, his real estate company managed to make close to 60 million dollars. At the lowest point, however, his company went into bankruptcy. Worse, he was deceived when signing a contract and ended up being in $700,000 debt. Though it had taken him almost seven years to pay off the amount, it was God's will that the failure enabled him to gain experience to help build up ITS financially.

Shortly after Dr. Tong joined the ITS faculty in the early nineties, he generously invested $20,000 in the seminary and convinced two members of his church to each match the amount. Besides teaching, Dr. Tong also wrote a self-study report on ITS and developed a five-year strategic plan to build up the seminary. He said ITS gave him a great amount of freedom to self-start his projects, and along with his fervor, he appointed himself to be the Director of Advancement at ITS.

During his presidency from 1995 to 2008, Dr. Tong achieved many great accomplishments at ITS. The seminary was already issuing I-20s to international students in 1984, but under his leadership, the number of students started to grow, first from thirty to seventy, and then to 100. Moreover, Dr. Tong had also led ITS to attain accreditations from the Bureau for Private and Post-Secondary Education (BPPE), Asia Theological Association (ATA) and Association of Theological Schools (ATS). Furthermore, ITS and Calvin Theological Seminary started a joint program to help ThM students finish their last year of the degree program. Last, but not least, Dr. Tong had set a goal to have ITS offer 100 scholarships, at least two for each country, to train church leaders around the world. And it is by God's grace that the goal has already been reached at ITS.

## Grateful for Things Done or Not

Dr. Tong never regrets choosing ITS for his career. He had been offered to teach as a professor at Calvin Theological Seminary, but he turned it down. God had a bigger plan for Dr. Tong in a much smaller and struggling reformed seminary. Though his expertise is in Philosophy and Systematic Theology, Dr. Tong was called to engage in theological education. He might have retired from ITS in 2008, but he continues to teach as a Professor Emeritus to this day; his heart will always have a place to serve at ITS.

However, he did mention one regret. After selling the Wilshire campus, ITS spent 2 million dollars on a 100-acre land in Azusa, CA. Dr. Tong had hoped to build a resident campus there, but the building permit was not granted. Looking back, Dr. Tong has learned from all mistakes and achievements and is grateful for all things that "have or have not" and "done or not done".

## Singing Softly for God's Mercy

Dr. Tong was also humbled by a near-death situation about twenty-years ago. Mrs. Joy Tong, his beloved wife, was very sick, and he was informed after finishing a class at ITS that she would rest in Jesus' arms at any minute. On the way to the hospital, Dr. Tong suddenly collided head-on with a car. He became unconscious but was pulled out of his car by a patrolling police woman before it exploded and went into flames. His arms were broken, his head was covered in blood and was transported to a hospital by a helicopter. Though unconscious, Dr. Tong remembered a hymn *Love the Lord Deeper*; it's about letting go of worldly pleasures, pleading for God's mercy and loving God more. He was told later that he was actually singing the hymn softly while everybody was crying around him. On the other hand, Mrs. Tong was calling out his name while being half conscious in another hospital. When Dr. Tong fully awoke more than 12 hours later, he asked God, "Lord you spared my life.What can I do for you?"

God faithfully and graciously healed both Dr. Tong and Mrs. Tong. In only three weeks, they shared their testimony together at Chinese Evangelical Free Church by standing before a full house of 600 attendees. He led the whole congregation to sing the same hymn again with teary eyes. During the testimony, he said when he faced death, one thought that came to his mind was the regret of not loving God enough and serving Him more. Therefore, he urged Christians to do more for the Lord when they are still alive and able. They should let go of worldly things and thoughts, take up their own cross and follow Him. Let God be more, and they become less.

## Always on a Mission

Besides serving at ITS, Dr. Tong has also a heart and a burden for mission. In fact, he was a missionary of Overseas Missionary Fellowship (OMF) before coming to the US. As a preacher, he has been invited to speak at churches in North America, Central America, South America and throughout Asia. As a professor, he has taught at other seminaries in the US, Korea, Indonesia, etc. As a president, Dr. Tong led ITS to collaborate with Calvin Theological Seminary and Reformed Theological Seminary (RTS) in Mississippi in 1990 to offer special training and research opportunities to seminary students in Indonesia. He offered thousands of dollars of funding to provide twenty scholarships to seminaries there. Dr. Tong also started four seminaries in Indonesia and a program to send Indonesian students to study in the US in 1995.

Now in his eighties, Dr. Tong's pace might have slowed down, but he still walks 2,000 steps every morning and afternoon, a habit he developed three years ago. In addition to sleeping early, praying extendedly and preparing for lecture notes, Dr. Tong has also been recording his preaching messages to be distributed in Taiwan and Indonesia.

In February 2020, Mrs. Joy Tong went home to be with the Lord. His former students and ITS alumni, including Dr. Monica Kao, Fan Cuimei and Luo Zhucheng, have taken up the task to care for him. God faithfully makes sure he is well taken care of as he took good care of so many ITS students in the past. Dr. Tong and Mrs Tong have a daughter named Elizabeth and three grandchildren Ezra, Serena and Elijah.

## Conclusion

Dr. Tong served the longest tenure at ITS as a president. Under his leadership, not only was ITS registered, accredited and growing, but the scholarship program has also become the greatest asset and blessing for both ITS and the students. As a person, Dr. Tong showed us that a brilliant mind with diligence and fervor can achieve great results. On the other hand, it's God's will that the major obstacles and failures in his professional and personal life have humbled him but made him a wiser and more resilient servant. God is also gracious to all the mistakes he made. Dr. Tong's advice for his students is to stay humble and grateful while self-searching. This interview showed us that though ITS and many other seminaries are struggling these days, the bigger the challenge is, the more glory God will display in His divine work. Rest assured that God knows and He is always in control.

# THE INSPIRING JOURNEY OF DR. LOUCKS

by Ei Meren Gusto

## Introduction

Dr. Melvin Louck's remarkable journey in ministry is a testament to the profound impact one person can make through dedication, faith, and unwavering support. From the very beginning, Dr. Loucks understood the importance of family and the sacrifices they would make to help him fulfill his calling. He humbly explains, "All the ministries I do would have been impossible if not for the unwavering support of my family, especially my wife Linda, who has been my constant companion in supporting me every step of the way." Throughout his career, he embraced teaching, leadership, and a steadfast commitment to the Word of God. This biography chronicles the life of Dr. Loucks, highlighting his experiences, achievements, and the enduring legacy he's made at ITS.

## Early Life and Marriage

Dr. Loucks' met his wife Linda, while he was a seminary student at Trinity Seminary and she was attending Trinity College. As they began to discuss marriage, Dr. Loucks revealed his calling to the ministry, a path that often comes with financial challenges. Undeterred, Linda committed herself wholeheartedly to supporting Dr. Loucks in his endeavors. She has since devoted over three decades of her career to teaching in primary schools, exemplifying the couple's shared commitment to education and service.

## Ministry at ITS

Dr. Loucks' professional career at International Theological Seminary (ITS), primarily surrounded his role as an associate professor for many years. His dedication to teaching was unparalleled, and he garnered the support and admiration of both faculty and staff at ITS. Through his mentorship, countless students received guidance and inspiration, enabling them to make significant contributions within their communities. Dr. Loucks' impact extended beyond the classroom, as he had the privilege of visiting alumni around the world, witnessing firsthand the transformative effects of their education. Their entrepreneurial ventures, schools, church plants, and other initiatives stand as testaments to the quality education and guidance they received at ITS.

## Presidency and Transformation at ITS

Dr. Loucks accepted the role of President during a period of uncertainty at ITS. His tenure lasted 4 years and marked a significant period of transition for the seminary. Dr. Loucks prioritized establishing order within the administrative offices, appointing more Vice Presidents, and creating the Administrative Council to facilitate collaborative decision-making within leadership. By fostering transparency and faculty involvement, he transformed the seminary into a more inclusive institution. Dr. Loucks' determination to diversify the board led to the appointment of the first African board member and the inclusion of ITS graduates, further enriching the seminary's leadership by representing a more holistic demographic of the student body to its key stakeholders.

## A Heart for Students and Guiding Principles

While Dr. Loucks had other offers to teach elsewhere, he explains his primary motivation to stay at ITS has always been the students. He derives immense joy from witnessing the profound impact these students have on their communities following graduation. Whether starting businesses, planting churches, or initiating educational projects, these students' endeavors exemplify the valuable education and guidance they received at ITS. Dr. Loucks' offers three pieces of advice to his students.

1. Keep God first. Dr. Loucks notes, "God is still on His throne no matter what circumstances arise in your ministry and life. Our God is a god of providence and sovereignty. Nothing occurs outside of his providence."
2. Commit to servant leadership. "We are called to be servants to the people God has called us to minister to. We're not called to be their overlords or masters. By exemplifying servant leadership, you can become an example of Christian servanthood to those whom you are ministering to."
3. Strive to be a lifetime learner of God's Word. Dr. Loucks encourages students not to just rely on past knowledge or past sermons but rather always be intentional about sermon preparations. "I am completely committed to the complete authority and truth of God's Word. When we preach and teach, we need to maintain that commitment to the Word of God. Follow Paul's command to preach the word, not just pick a theme and find passages in the bible to fit the theme, but to meditate on the scriptures themselves and ask what the scriptures can teach us about life, truth, and Christian living." Dr. Loucks firmly believes in the importance of continuous learning and preparing for each teaching or preaching opportunity. His unwavering commitment to the authority and truth of God's Word shines through in his teachings, inspiring others to follow in his footsteps.

Even in retirement, Dr. Loucks continues to invest his time, teaching online courses and remaining actively engaged in ministries such as Global Teaching Network and his local church Emmanual Evangelical Free Church.

## Hope for the Future and a Word of Caution

Looking ahead, Dr. Loucks hopes that ITS will continue to increase as an institution and impact the world at large. He prays that ITS will maintain its unwavering commitment to the inherent, sufficient, and infallible Word of God.

"Seminaries in recent years are making adjustments to their programs to attract more students. To do so, they've had to significantly simplify their programs and course offerings. Language courses are no longer required to be taught, and more emphasis is being placed on practical theology. Important foundational courses are being minimized in order to relate better to individuals in a post-modern age that cares more about how we feel about faith than what the bible actually teaches about faith. Many seminaries have weakened their views on the place of scripture in the lives of the students. **We at ITS need to be very careful about drifting away from our strong biblical foundation**." ITS can have something to offer if it continues to stress the importance of a strong, biblically-based curriculum and a curriculum that teaches not only how to do practical ministry but also how to do that practical ministry without minimizing the Word of God." He believes that ITS has a valuable contribution to make by emphasizing a strong, biblically-based curriculum that prepares students for practical ministry without compromising the importance of Scripture. "After all, all we're seeing in our post-modern era, will eventually fade, but the truth of God's Word will remain."

## Conclusion

Dr. Loucks' life journey as a minister, educator, and leader has left an indelible mark on the hearts and minds of countless individuals. Through his unwavering dedication to family, teaching, and the Word of God, Dr. Loucks has influenced generations of students, empowered communities, and transformed the landscape of ITS. His story stands as a testament to the power of faith, perseverance, and servant leadership, reminding us all to remain steadfast in our own callings and to embrace the transformative potential of a life committed to ministry.

# PART V

# TRIBUTES TO HONOREES

# TRIBUTES TO DR. TONG

## 对唐老师感言 - Monica Lau

有一种情感不能够相守却能天长地久，有一种付出不求回报却没有尽头，有一种坚持不离不弃却永不放手。唐老师，谢谢您多年来用心关爱和教导。願神继续看顧你、圣灵继续運行、见证主恩,直到再见神的面。

Dr. Tong, Chen,Huayang, Mrs. Tong and Monica Lau (From left to right)

There is a kind of emotion that cannot stay together but can last forever; there is a kind of giving that does not ask for return but does not end, and there is a kind of persistence that never gives up but never lets go. Dr. Tong, thank you for your care and teaching over the years. May God continue to watch over you, the Holy Spirit will continue to touch you, to testify to the grace of the Lord, until you meet God again.

## 给唐老师的感谢辞 - 顾莉华 (LiHua Gu)

第一次见到唐老师是他在我家的房顶上。室友告诉我,他是我们神学院的校长。我当时非常吃惊：神学院的校长还帮学生爬上房顶装电话线?! 后来我信了主，2003 年也进 ITS 学习。记得那时唐老师一边上课，一边要在厨房煮午饭给学生们吃。他一看见当天的学生来的比较多，就在菜里多加一把盐。20 年后，唐老师在身体非常软弱的时候，还做我教牧学博士论文的指导老师，细心地为我修改论文，直到论文完成。我很感恩做唐老师的学生。他是一位神学教育家，又是有牧者心肠的牧者。唐老师是我效法的榜样。

顾莉华 (Li Hua Gu) 2003-2008, MDiv and ThM 毕业 2023, DMin 毕业

The first time I met Dr. Tong was on the roof of my apartment. My roommate told me he was the president of our seminary. I was surprised: The president of the seminary also helped students climb the roof to install telephone lines?! Later I became a Christian and entered ITS to study in 2003. I remember when Dr. Tong was teaching in class, he was also cooking lunch for the students in the kitchen. When he saw that there were more students coming that day, he added a pinch of salt to the dish. Twenty years later, when Dr. Tong was very weak, he was still the supervisor of my doctoral dissertation in pastoral care, carefully revising the dissertation for me until it was completed. I am very grateful to be a student of Dr. Tong. He is a theological educator and a pastor with a pastoral heart. Dr. Tong is a role model for me to learn from.

Li Hua Gu 2003-2008, M.Div and Th.M., 2023, D.Min graduate

## 致唐老師 - 曹淼 (Miao Cao)

在美国五年，在唐老师家里住了三年多，心里对唐老师充满了感恩之情！非常感谢恩师唐老师打开了我神学视野上的广度与深度，也感谢唐老师在各方面对我与我的妻子的照顾与指导！更感谢唐老师用他活生生为主摆上一切地殉道精神深深地影响着我们的服事！愿我们接续这种生命影响生命的服事，也能够传递这种为主牺牲一切地殉道精神给下一代！愿主记念唐老师所付出的一切！愿主继续透过他的生命赐福给更多的人！

学生: 曹淼 敬上

Being in the United States for five years, I have lived in Dr. Tong's house for more than three years, and I am full of gratitude to him! I am very grateful to my mentor, Dr. Tong, for opening up the breadth and depth of my theological vision, and also thank him for caring and guiding me and my wife in all aspects! I am even more grateful to Dr. Tong for using his spirit of martyrdom to sacrifice everything for the Lord, which deeply influences our service! May we continue this life-affecting service, and pass on this martyrdom spirit of sacrificing everything for the Lord to the next generation! May the Lord remember everything Dr. Tong has done! May the Lord continue to bless more people through his life!

Sincerely,
Student Cao Miao

---

## 致唐老師 - 李愛蓉 (Airong Li)

唐山故里出人傑。
崇尚倍仰走天路，
怀抱信念走天涯，
愛里忍耐扶弱者，
主恩充滿人生旅，
侍主育人做榜樣。

榮耀主名、赞美主!

李愛蓉寫於
夏威夷

(李愛蓉於 2011 年來 ITS 讀道學碩士，2015 年毕業。現在夏威夷定居。)

Outstanding person from the hometown of Mount Tong,
Advocating faith while treading on the road to heaven,
Walking around the earth with faith embraced,
Helping the weak with patience and love,
Lord's grace fills his life journey,
Serving the Lord with teachings and setting an example.
Glory to the name of the Lord, praise the Lord!

Written by Li Airong in Hawaii

(Li Airong attended ITS from 2011 to 2015, graduated with a master's degree in Taoism. She now lives in Hawaii)

---

## 致唐老师感谢辞 - 李明星 (James Mingxing Li)

早在 2006 年就认识唐老师，刚开始被他上课所带出来的信息所着迷；后常在课堂上听他的见证: 诗 68:5 "神在他的圣所作孤儿的父，作寡妇的伸冤者。" 他常用他的经历来鼓励我们:1、在天上的阿爸，父成全了他; 所以，他也尽力成全了别人。2、成为学生们的遮盖，如牧羊人细心看顾他的羊群。3、回应神恩，有教无类。唐老师在中国各处所创办的真道学苑，在毕业前都有一个多月的真道题库的考试，我看到许多在小学、初中就已辍学在外打工的同学，不住地背诵，我们有的人根本不知道那里面所表达的意思(如,哲理神学)......唐老师早已桃李满天下，但还是"尽心、尽性、尽力、尽意爱主、事奉主；又要爱学生如同自己。(路 10:27)"
在 ITS40 周年之际，祝母校成为更多人的祝福，也跟随唐老师的脚　　踪　　，　　砥　　砺　　前　　行　　！

学生 李明星 2023 年父亲节 于柔似蜜

I first met Dr. Tong in 2006 and was first fascinated by the messages he brought about in class; he often shared his testimony and encouraged us with Psalm 68:5 (NIV)"A father to the fatherless, a defender of widows, is God in his holy dwelling." 1. Abba the Father in heaven, has perfected Dr. Tong; he often tried his best to perfect others. 2. Dr. Tong being the students' refuge is like a shepherd watching over his flock. 3. Responding to the grace of God, Dr. Tong has offered education to all. Dr. Tong also founded The Zhendao Academy in various places in China. I remember there was an examination from the Zhendao question bank more than a month before graduation, I saw many students who had dropped out of primary and junior high schools kept reciting the answers while holding down day jobs; some of us didn't even know the meaning expressed in those questions (for example, philosophy Theology)... Dr. Tong has already trained graduates all over the world, but he still "'Love the Lord your God with all your heart and with all your soul and with all your strength and with all your mind' and, 'Love your 'students' as yourself. (Luke 10:27 NIV)" On the occasion of the 40th anniversary of ITS, I wish my alma mater a blessing for more people to follow Dr. Tong's footsteps and forge ahead!

Written in 2023 by student James Li Mingxing on Father's Day in the City of Rosemead

## 唐老师祝辞 - 肖爱克 (Aike Xiao)

感谢唐牧师给了我系统神学思维，从本体论出发，以神本和人本对比分析来阐述和处理问题。

2002 届入学，2005 届 M.Div 毕业，肖爱克敬上！

Thanks to Pastor Tong for giving me systematic theological thinking, starting from ontology, and explaining and dealing with problems with a comparative analysis of God-centered and Human-centered.

Aike Xiao, enrolled in 2002 and graduated from M.Div in 2005

## 寫給唐老師的話 - 陳華揚 (Huayang Chen)

非常感恩能夠成為唐老師的學生。在他全球眾多的學生弟子中，我雖只是那最不起眼的一位，但他生命的所活出來的愛神愛人的品格卻成為激勵我一生的榜樣。非常榮幸，2016-2017 兩年的時間里，我住在唐老師家。跟唐老師和唐師母朝夕相處，更是看到一位性情中的唐老師，無論是身教還是言教都彰顯出他美好的人格魅力。雖然他生氣時我們大氣不敢出一聲，但更多時候，老人家卻如老頑童般可愛可親。很多有趣好玩的事情永遠存留在記憶中。

記得有一次唐老師、師母、我們在餐桌上照常用餐，愉悅情致中他就在師母臉上貼近親吻，完全不管我在旁邊打心眼裡的"嫉

Dr. Tong and Mrs. Tong

妒"，我也直言道："唐老師，你們也太酸了吧!"那一刻真從內心為兩位老人家這般感情喝彩，這就是唐老師。唐老師年級大了，經常東西隨手放，忘了找不到，特別有三樣東西是他每天必要找的。車鑰匙 錢包、眼鏡，因為我喜歡收拾東西規整，只要他東西找不到，老人家總是一句話："華揚，我的眼鏡你給我放在那裡的。"其實很多時候是他自己隨手放在那裡了。大多數時間還真可以給他找到，因為也知道他會放在那裡或忘在那裡的。也有暫時找不到的時候，他就會生氣地說："就是你又收到那裡去了"。還不能辯解，因為他急了會更生氣。但是我從來不以為然，而且還樂此不疲，因為連他生氣也透出老小孩的可愛可親。

唐老師是用生命踐行著信仰，雖然也有聽到有個別人說他的不是，但是我依然被這位敬愛的老師深深感動和激勵。願上帝繼續恩待、看顧、保守唐老師!

2017 屆 陳華揚 2023.05.22

To Dr. Tong:

I am very grateful to be a student of Dr. Tong. Among his many students and disciples around the world, I am only the most inconspicuous one, but his character of loving God and loving others in his life has become an example that inspires me throughout my life.

It is a great honor to stay at Dr. Tong's house for two years from 2016 to 2017. Getting along with Dr. Tong and Mrs. Tong day and night, I saw a Mr. Tong with a good temperament, whether it was doing by example or teaching, he had shown his beautiful personality charm. Although we dared not speak loudly when he was angry, the old man was as cute and amiable as an old urchin most of the time. Many of his interesting and funny things will remain in my memory forever. I remember once Dr. Tong, Mrs. Tong, and we were eating at the table as usual. In his joyful mood, he kissed Mrs Tong on her face, completely ignoring the "jealousy" in my heart, and so I said bluntly: "Dr. Tong, you too are simply unbelievable!" At that moment, I really applauded the feelings of the two old people from the bottom of my heart, this is Dr. Tong. Dr. Tong was getting older, and he often put things away and forgot where to find them. In particular, there were three things that he needed to look for every day. Car keys, wallet, glasses. Because I like to keep things tidy, as long as he couldn't find anything, the old man would always say: "Huayang, where did you put my glasses?." Most of the time, he could actually find it, because he knew he would put it there or forget it there. Sometimes when he couldn't find it for a while, he would say angrily, "That's where you hide it again." I couldn't defend myself because he would get angrier if he was in a hurry. But I never took it seriously and was never tired of it. Even when he was angry, he revealed the cuteness of an old child.

Dr. Tong practiced his faith throughout his life. Although I heard some people say something negative about him, I was still deeply moved and inspired by this beloved teacher. May God continue to be gracious, watch over and protect Dr. Tong!

Class of 2017 Huayang Chen 2023.05.22

---

## 致唐老師 - 宮景耀牧师 (Rev. Daniel Gong)

我是宫景耀牧师 (Rev. Daniel Gong)，2003 年开始在 ITS 的学习，到 2008 年毕业离开加州的。

下面是 ITS 四十周年庆中写给唐院上的感谢辞:

崇真道继古启今，

怀圣爱育徒若子;

师千载超然教义，

父心显忠仆典范。

宫景耀牧师为真华人基督教会 2023 年五月 29 日于里士满维吉尼亚州

I am Rev. Daniel Gong started studying at ITS in 2003 and graduated in 2008 and left California.

The following is the thank you letter to the Dr. Tong during the 40th anniversary of ITS:

Upholds the truth inherits the past and inspires the present,
Conceives holy love and raise disciples like sons,
Master the transcendental teachings for thousands of years,
A father's heart and a model of a loyal servant.

By Rev. Daniel Gong of Aletheia Chinese Christian Church on May 29th, 2023 in Richmond, Virginia

## 感谢唐老师 - 邴荣全 (Stephen Rongquan Bing)

敬爱的唐老师平安！

感谢主！二十一年前我在新加坡教会听唐崇怀牧师讲道，真理明确，逻辑清晰，声情并茂，引经据典，娓娓道来，深感！有醍醐灌顶之功，茅塞顿开之效，活泼的生命之道直抵人心，那语重心长提出挑战信徒意志关乎生命和生活的问题至今仍回响在耳畔：你所从事的是工作？是事业？还
是事奉？

感谢主！赐我有机会在唐老师门下受教学习五年其间获益良多，更有幸听您讲述个人的见证和心得。。。。。。

在工作上：
唐老师曾经在大起大落之时没有怨神尤人，而是谦卑顺服与主更加亲近！如今在大落大起之际也没有喜出望外而是荣辱不惊向主更加热爱和更深的敬拜！在生活中出现乌云密布，惊涛骇浪，跌
宕起伏，百感交集之日总是藏身主怀信心仰望，靠主的真理和应许乘风破浪安然航行！在这一切
过后发出掷地有声地宣告：一切都是神的恩典！

在生命上：
活出所信的基督！靠主的恩典和真理行公义，好怜悯,存谦卑的心，与神同行，并用生命建立生
命。

在服侍上：

如今唐老师已是耄耋之年却越发笃信恩主基督，肩负使命，奔跑天路,生命丰盛，精神矍铄，思绪飞扬，笔耕不辍，教书育人，诲人不倦，桃李天下，高举基督，传道救人，主名得荣!

愿主赐福唐老师日子如何，力量也必如何! 继续成为教会的祝福和多人的祝福!

愿平安，健康，喜乐归于唐老师!

愿荣耀颂赞归于神!

学生邴荣全敬上 6-20-2023

Peace to dear and respected Dr. Tong!

Thank God! Twenty-one years ago, I listened to Pastor Joseph Tong''s sermon in a church in Singapore. His truth was explicit, the logic was clear, and the voice and emotion were plentiful. His power of enlightenment, his lively way of life reaching people's hearts, and the earnest question challenging the believer's will and life still echoed in my ears: What do you do for a living? Do you take it as a job, a career or to serve?

Thank God, I have been given the opportunity to study under Dr. Tong for five years, and I have benefited a lot during those years. I am even more honored to listen to his personal testimony and experience. . .

At work: Dr. Tong did not blame God and others during ups and downs, but humbled and obeyed to get closer to the Lord! Now through my own ups and downs, I learned not to overjoy, not to be surprised either by honor or disgrace; I simply love and worship the Lord more deeply! When there are dark clouds, turbulent waves, and ups and downs in life, I always hide in the Lord and look up with confidence even on the day of mixed feelings as well as relying on the Lord's truth and promises to sail safely through the storms! After all this, I made a loud and clear declaration: everything is God's grace!

In life: Live out the Christ you believe in! Act righteously by the grace and truth of the Lord, love mercifully, be humble, walk with God, and build life with life.

In terms of service: Though Dr. Tong is now an octogenarian, he believes in Christ more and more. He still shoulders the mission, runs the road of heaven, lives life to the fullest, never stops writing, advising, teaching, preaching and saving people, let the name of the Lord be glorified! May the Lord bless Dr. Tong, what his life is, so will his strength! Continue to be a blessing to the church and a blessing to many!

May peace, health and joy belong to Dr. Tong!

Glory and praise be to God!

From student Stephen Rongquan Bing, 6-20-2023

---

## 唐崇怀院长给我留下的生命烙印 - 赵保罗牧师 (Rev. Qiusheng Zhao)

2002 年 9 月，感谢神的带领，我来到国际神学院就读 Th.M，从那个时候我认识了唐牧师。唐牧师非常独特：他比大多数教授更像牧师，比大多数牧师更像教授。他在课堂上用一个又一个问题来挑战我们更深地思考和理解信仰。

多年过去了，唐牧师在课堂上传授的知识记得不是那么清楚了。但是我们却非常清晰地记得：他一下飞机就跑来上课，下了课就去厨房给大家做饭。这个时候他不像是老师，而像是一位父亲。

唐牧师教给我们两个字"成全"。尽量给他人创造机会，尽量帮助他人成功，尽量 成全他人。唐牧师是这样待我的，我们今天也如此去待他人。

谢谢唐牧师!我们好爱你!

赵保罗牧师(Qiusheng Zhao) 刘惠敏师母(Huimin Liu)
俄罗斯圣彼得堡华人基督教会

In September 2002, thanks to God's guidance, I came to the International Theological
Seminary to study Th.M. From then on, I got to know Dr. Tong. Dr. Tong is quite unique: he is more a pastor than most professors, more a professor than most pastors. He used question after question in class to challenge us to think deeper and understand faith.

Years have passed, the knowledge Dr. Tong taught in class has become not so clear. But we remember very clearly: he came to class as soon as he got off the plane, and went to the kitchen to cook for everyone after class. At this time, he was not like a teacher, but like a father.

Dr. Tong taught us the word "fulfill". He tried to create opportunities for others, try to help
others succeed, and try to fulfill others. Dr. Tong treated me this way, and we should treat others
like this today!

Thank you, Dr. Tong! We love you so much!

Rev. Qiusheng Zhao & Huimin Liu
Chinese Christian Church in St. Petersburg, Russia

## 寫給唐老師的話 - 陳永盛 (Yong Sheng Chen)

唐老師愛神愛人，把學生都當成自己的孩子，有教無類，只想幫助別人，為神國培養更多基督的門徒。自己節省，對需要的人傾囊相助。博覽群書，講課寓知識於有趣的故事，使人在愉快中接受真理。唐老師理論和實踐並存，不只是講課滔滔不絕，修理汽車，修建房子，煮大鍋飯樣樣拿手。感謝神差遣唐老師教導我，改變了我的生命和人生。唐老師是我生命的祝福，我也求神使我成為別人的祝福。

學生: 陳永盛 2009 年畢業

Dr. Tong loves God and loves people, and treats students as his own children. He teaches without discrimination, and only wants to help others and cultivate more disciples of Christ for the Kingdom of God. Frugal himself but gives freely to those in need. He reads a lot of books, and often combines knowledge with interesting stories during lectures so that people can accept the truth in a happy way. Dr. Tong's theory and practice coexist; not only are his lectures plentiful, he is also good at repairing cars, building houses, and cooking big pots. Thank you God for sending Dr. Tong to teach me, which changed my life and the way I live. Dr. Tong is a blessing in my life, and I also ask God to make me a blessing to others.

Student: Yongsheng Chen, graduated in 2009

---

## 致唐老師 - 祝浩明 (Hao Ming Zhu)

敬爱的唐老师: 主内平安

您是一位为父为母的老师，您也是学富五车、通情达理、尽心侍奉的老师，您更是可爱悲悯常
发小皮气的老师! 哈哈哈。

祝浩明 (M.Div, 2022)

Dear Dr. Tong,

You are a teacher who is a father and a mother. You are also a teacher who is knowledgeable, reasonable, and dedicated to serving God. You are also a teacher who is lovely, compassionate and sometimes loses a little temper! Hahaha.

Zhu, Hao Ming (M.Div, 2022)

---

## 致唐老師 - 閆海萍 (Sammi Haiping Yan)

感謝唐老師:

世人奮勇當強人，距今 1800 百多年前的政治家，軍事家及詩人的曹操作詩: 老驥伏櫪，志在千里，烈士暮年，壯心不已。他的帝國祇維繫四十幾年就土崩瓦解。

強人竭力作超人，有被世人山呼萬歲的皇帝，也有被捧殺一句頂一萬句的獨裁者，這些假神都已經灰飛煙滅。

人人皆能成義人，神在《聖經》中應許:「你們得救是本乎恩，也因著信。這並不是出於自己，乃是神所賜的(以弗所書 2:8)。」

感謝神，賜我信主於中國，生命健康成長於國際神學院唐老師門下的恩典。五年間我看到的唐老師是一位和藹可親的牧師，睿智博學的教授，更是一位慈愛的父親! 神在《聖經》中教導:「你們學基督的，師傅雖有一萬，為父的卻是不多，因我在基督耶穌裡用福音生了你們(林前 4:15)。」

如今唐老師已到耄耋之年，但他仍然靠主的恩典和真理信心滿滿,熱心似火，撒種收割,累累碩果!

願神賜福唐老師健康喜樂!

願神幫助唐老師作工有力!

Thank you, Dr. Tong,

People in the world are brave to be strong. Cao Cao, a Chinese statesman, military strategist and poet more than 1800 years ago, wrote a poem, "An old man with aspirations for a thousand miles, a martyr in his old age, with a strong heart". His empire lasted only forty years before falling apart.

The strongman tried his best to be a superman. There were emperors who were called "long lived" by the world, and there were also emperors who were highly exalted and tyrants who claimed his one sentence was worth 10,000 sentences. These false gods have all been wiped out.

Everyone can be justified. God promised in the Bible, "It is by grace you have been saved through faith. This is not of yourselves but is given by God (Ephesians 2:8). "

Thank God for granting me the grace to believe in the Lord in China and grow up healthily under the discipleship of Dr. Tong from the International Theological Seminary. During the five years, Dr. Tong I had seen was an amiable pastor, a wise and knowledgeable professor, and even a loving father! God taught in the Bible, "Although you have ten thousand teachers of Christ, you have not many fathers; for I have begotten you in Christ Jesus by the gospel (1 Corinthians 4:15)."

Now Dr. Tong has reached an octogenarian age, but he is still full of confidence in the Lord's grace and truth, with enthusiasm, sowing seeds and reaping, bearing fruitful fruits!

May God bless Dr Tong to be healthy and happy!
May God help Dr. Tong to work effectively!

Student: Yan Haiping, Date 6-21-2023

---

## 感谢唐老师的话语 - 侯榕坪 (Rongping Hou)

唐老师，您好!

我是 2019 届的毕业生侯榕坪，我虽然不是您最好的学生，但你是我最好的老师，用这条短信送祝福，每一个字都带有我深深的关怀，绵绵的问候，款款的相思，殷殷的惦念。值此母校 40 年校庆之际，我奉上衷心的祝福和诚挚的感谢，感谢学校培养出一批批优秀的传道人，为基督教的传播贡献应有的力量，祝唐老师身体健康，一切荣耀归于主。

Hello, Dr. Tong!

I am Hou Rongping, a graduate of the class of 2019. Although I am not your best student, you are my best teacher. I send blessings to you through this text message; every word contains my deep care, lingering greetings, lots of love and earnest concern. On the occasion of the 40th anniversary of my alma mater, I would like to extend my heartfelt blessings and sincere thanks. I would like to thank ITS for cultivating many outstanding preachers who have contributed their due strength in spreading the Christianity. I wish Dr. Tong good health and all the glory to the Lord.

---

## 写给唐老师的话 - 田布 (Pu Tian)

我是 2013 年到 2016 年在读的学生，田布。感谢唐老师三年的培养和关怀! 在 ITS 成立 40 周年之际，我想对老师说：“谢谢您,老师!”

学生:田布

I am Pu Tian, a student from 2013 to 2016 at ITS. Thanks to Dr. Tong for his three years of training and care! On the occasion of the 40th anniversary of ITS, I would like to say this to you, "Thank you, teacher!"

Student: Pu Tian

---

## 感謝唐老師 - 楊征基 (Cheng-Chi Yang)

唐老師的教育立場是有教無類，只求以基督的真理、話語帶來人們生命的更新變化。不在乎人外表的顯赫、體面，而著重內在的良善與公義。

有人玩笑說老師教導教會的厚黑學; 我認為他是希望同學們不要太天真、單方面的角度看待教會內的多面性人際關係，而能夠智慧、靈巧的警惕、考慮事情。

個人生活儉樸，待人儒雅、包容，留顏面，正如他常說的: 真理具有涵包性。故雖著重真理，卻不至於咄咄逼人，不給人壓力，易於相處; 可謂良師益友也!

感謝唐老師!

楊征基 Cheng-Chi Yang。2012-2015。神學碩士班。

Dr. Tong's educational stance is that there is no discrimination for learners; instead, he only seeks to bring about renewal and changes in people's lives with the truth and words of Christ. He cares little about the magnificence and decency of a person's appearance but focuses on inner goodness and righteousness.

Some people joked about his teaching of boldness and toughness; I think he hopes that students will not look at the multi-faceted interpersonal relationships in church from an assuming and one-sided perspective but be able to be vigilant and consider things wisely and dexterously.
Personally, Dr. Tong is a frugal, polite, tolerant, and kind individual, as he often says, "truth is inclusive".
Although he focuses on the truth, he is not aggressive, does not pressure people, and is easy to get along with. He can rightfully be called a good teacher and a helpful friend!

Thank you, Dr. Tong!
Cheng-Chi Yang, 2012-2015, ThM.

## 与唐牧師不解之緣 - 宿濤 (Tao Su)

唐老師，二十年前我与您在 ITS 首次相見,自此結下不解之緣。

您既有讓學生可畏之時，更有令學生可敬、效法之處:

　　"崇懷" 者，名如其人。您敬神愛人，沒有虛假。心懷崇高，名副其實。在對包括我在內的眾多學生關愛、幫助有加;

　　拼命加捨命。對從事的神學教育您盡心盡力，如今 80 加一，他仍然講道、教學，培育學生不輟，猶如摩西在神的家中那樣盡職盡忠，鞠躬盡瘁，死而後已。見證了為主的道 "犧牲生命的，必得着生命" 的真理。您在傳授知識的同時傳遞、影響着生命;

　　信仰歸元、博學專長。您對東西文化融會貫通，語言、哲學運用自如，但這些工具的運用都是始於一，歸於一(弗 1:10)，為了一。

　　在感念您的教誨與栽培的同時我也不曾忘記師母對您獻身神學教育的全力支持。在我們家臨別去德州事奉前夕師母贈送的純棉棉伴隨我們轉展北美，珍藏至今。

　　日月如梭，回望 1998 年在澳洲作訪問學者期間，我曾謝拒了神學院的錄取。儘管有神的應許，但我當時不明白個中緣由，直到五年後的 2003 年我從夏威夷專程去 LA，在 ITS 見到您才開始意識到這次旅程是五年前神應許的實現。(林前 2:9-10) ......

"十年樹木，百年樹人"。願受您栽培的學生中有更多人像您那樣在神的家中作忠心有見識的僕人，"不要人誇顏色好,只留清氣滿乾坤"。

您的學生: 宿濤 (ITS MA, 2005)

Dr. Tong, I met you for the first time at ITS 20 years ago, and we have been connected since then.

Though you are tough on your students, you also are a role model and respectful figure to them:

You stay true to his Chinese first name, "Chonghuai". You genuinely worship God and love people. Your noble heart is worthy of your name, caring and helping so many students including me.

You desperately devote your life to students. You have devoted yourself to theological education. Now 81, You still preach, teach, and train students unceasingly, just like Moses in God's house, who was devoted until the end. You witness the truth of the Lord's word, "whoever
sacrifices his life will find it". You've influenced so many while teaching and imparting knowledge.

Your faith returns to unity and erudition. You are well-versed in Eastern and Western cultures and master language and philosophy freely. They start from one, return to one (Ephesians 1:10), and are for one.

While I am grateful for your teaching and cultivation, I have never forgotten Mrs. Tong's full support for your dedication to theological education. On the eve of our family leaving to serve in Texas, a gift made with pure cotton given by Mrs. Tong accompanied us to North America and has been treasured to this day.

Time flies, looking back at the time when I was a visiting scholar in Australia in 1998, I
declined admission to the seminary. Although there was God's promise, I was unable to understand. It wasn't until five years later, in 2003, that I made a special trip from Hawaii to LA. When I met you at ITS, I realized that this journey was the fulfillment of God's promise five years ago. (1 Corinthians 2:9-10) ...

"It takes ten years to cultivate a tree, but a hundred years to cultivate a person". May more students trained by you are faithful and insightful servants in God's family like you. "Don't let people boast about your good looks, leave only clean air to fill the heaven and earth."

Your student: Su Tao (ITS MA 2005)

---

## 记念 ITS 成立 40 周年写给唐崇怀老师的感谢词 - 邓秋英 (Qiuying Deng)

在 ITS 学校学习的三年时间里，是我这一生收获最大的地方，我看到了唐老师一生辛勤劳苦的工作，他犹如父亲一般的慈爱倾倒在他的学生中，他风趣幽默的教学风格深深的影响着我们，他是我一生敬仰的老牧者。

邓秋英 2012-2015, M.Div

The three years of studying at ITS is the time when I gained the most in my life. I have seen the life-long hard work of Dr. Tong; he poured out the fatherly love on his students with a humorous teaching style that deeply influenced us. He is an aged shepherd whom I admire all my life.

Deng, Qiuying 2012-2015, M.Div

---

## By Dr. Premkumar Dharmaraj

I Praise God for Dr. Joseph Tong, the stalwart of International Theological Seminary who has been associated with the seminary from the early years of its history (1984-Present). He has contributed much to the institutional leadership and direction as the President of the seminary for thirteen years (1995-2008).

I do appreciate Dr. Tong's unwavering commitment to Reformed Theology and his openness to other theological perspectives. He is a great theologian, teacher, and preacher. His depth of understanding in Philosophical and Systematic Theology is commendable. He has been a "Father" figure to the ITS family over the past decade as he continued to teach and serve the seminary community despite his challenging health conditions. It exhibits his explicit love for the school and devotion to its mission.

May God continue to strengthen him to be a source of inspiration and blessing to ITS community.

Dr. Premkumar Dharmaraj

---

## By Dr. Joy Palmer

"Be faithful unto death ...." Rev. 2:10 (KJV)

Dr Tong's life is an example of how it is to follow Jesus Christ. In health and in sickness, he faithfully loved and served his Savior and Lord. I asked him several times, "Dr. Tong, when are you going to retire?" He would answer me, "I am re-retired!" Dr Tong demands faithfulness to God from others. He has high expectations from ITS staff, professors, and students alike. He would say what he meant and meant what he said.

I met Dr. Tong in 2008 (Winter Quarter). I did not understand why he was quite harsh on me until two years before I left ITS in 2018. I realized that his desire for me is to excel and to be faithful in the work as Academic Dean and professor. He challenged me, admonished me, and taught me that contributed to who I am today. He provided me opportunities to teach in Asia through the ITS partnership program.

When I think of Dr Tong, I cannot help but to thank God for his endurance and faithfulness to God. I thank him for his loving admonition to me to set higher standards on myself and for the encouragement to remain "faithful unto death" to my Savior and Lord Jesus Christ.

Tribute from Jaretha Joy Jimena-Palmer, Ph.D., VP of Academic Affairs, 2010-2018

# TRIBUTES TO DR. LOUCKS

## By Dr. David McKinley

After my first year of teaching at ITS, Dr. Mel Loucks encouraged me to consider becoming a resident faculty member. I will always be thankful for his personal encouragement which prompted me to do so. Later, in his role as President, he asked me to consider assuming the Dean of Students' position. Serving in this capacity gave me an opportunity to work closely with him for a few years. During this time, I observed his commitment to ITS, his concern for the students, and his desire for a team of people to work around him. Although the role as President demanded much from Dr. Loucks, he unstintingly gave of his time and energy while drawing from his vast academic experience to capably lead ITS. Thank you for your service to ITS!

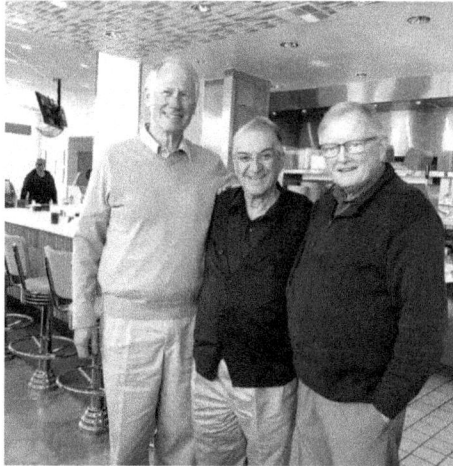

Photo:Dr. David McKinley, Dr. Peter Hintzoglou and Dr. Mel Loucks (From left to right)

---

## By Eddie A Rigdon

In 1986, my wife Joan and I decided to join the Emmanuel Evangelical Free Church in Burbank. We had been told by a friend that the church was mission minded. That's where we first met Dr. Mel Loucks, who was serving as their Mission Pastor. It was apparent to us how much the church loved him, and the love Dr. Loucks had for missions.

In the late '80s, Dr. Loucks announced they would take a mission team to Cebu Island in the Philippines. Joan and I applied to join the team, and we were accepted. The rest is history. As a result of that first trip and the influence Dr. Loucks has had on our lives for over 35 years, we have had the joy and blessing of ministering with him worldwide through the Global Teaching Network. Dr. Loucks was one of the founders.

After receiving his Ph.D. from Fuller, Dr. Loucks received two job offers, one from Biola University, a prestigious private Christian college, and the other from the International Theological Seminary (ITS), newly established and focused explicitly on developing and training leaders from the majority world to fulfill the Great Commission. He chose ITS. Dr. Loucks, 40 years later, with great passion and a deep love for the ITS students, continues to be faithful. He is one of the most beloved faculty members at the school.

Since the age of 18, Dr. Loucks has kept track of every book he's ever read and is a prolific reader with a wide range of knowledge. In addition, he has journaled every day since then. And I'm proud to be a part of some of those journals, as he is my dear friend and a mentor in God's Word. He's one of the humblest men I know. And his greatest love is that of the Lord Jesus Christ as his Lord and Savior. He has truly made a worldwide impact on people's lives for eternity.

---

## By Tony Rondinella

Mel is one of my best friends, even though I didn't have him as a professor he has had a great impact on my life. It is kind of awesome that a good friend could really change the course of your life. Mel's love for the lost and his ability to mobilize people, has made all the difference in me. He has sent me all over the world, both near and far. It has been my honor to share the gospel with over 10,000 people and to be a part of hundreds coming to Christ. I am so thankful for his challenging and encouraging me.

Tony Rondinella

---

## By Carey McLeod

I have been a close friend of Mel Loucks for seventy years, having attended Emmanuel Church in Burbank together since 1952. While I pursued a career in the business world, Mel pursued a career in full-time Christian service with a passion for world missions. Mel has been committed to Biblical teaching at ITS, as well as teaching abroad, having co-founded Global Teaching Network (GTN) to take the classroom to underprivileged pastors that don't have access to an accredited seminary. Mel knows the Bible and Mel knows world history. He can really bring the two together. He is a people person who cares for and maintains contact with just about everyone that he ever met. I've never had a better friend!

Carey McLeod

---

## By Arlene Larson

Mel Locks has played a very special role in my life. I have had the privilege of knowing him and working with him on staff as a ministry assistant and office manager at Emmanuel Evangelical Free Church. Ministering and working with him for some 28 years has provided life-changing experiences for me.

Pastor Mel knew that I had a passion for teaching and ministering to women and in March of 2009 he asked me if I would be interested in taking some extensive training in the "Pathway to Purpose for Women" program and share it with women around the world by becoming part of the Global Teaching Network (GTN). I was humbled and I thank God that Pastor Mel saw something in me that he felt could be developed and used to bring glory to our Lord Jesus Christ. I have now had the privilege of teaching pastor's wives and women leaders for over 12 years.

Thank you, Pastor Mel, for continuing to support and encourage me and for being a Godly role model.

---

### By Dr. Premkumar Dharmaraj

I have great appreciation for Dr. Mel Loucks commitment to the mission of the global church even as he served locally as Missions Pastor of his church. He is an erudite Professor and has been teaching Systematic Theology at ITS for the past forty years (1983-Present). However, Dr. Loucks has been involved in global mission by visiting several countries in Asia and Africa and training the pastors and leaders of the church. I applaud his passion, interest, and involvement in equipping people in those countries.

Dr. Loucks is a great leader, and he has contributed to the leadership of International Theological Seminary since its beginnings and particularly as the President of the Seminary from 2010 to 2013. It has been my privilege to work with him in mentoring the students through the process of writing their thesis and dissertation. He is such a great team member to work with since he has a real heart to help the students in a substantial way.

May God bless him and make him a blessing to the church at large.

Dr. Premkumar Dharmaraj

---

### By Pastor Stathis Tanatzis (MA, 2018-2020), Greece

"Dr Mel Loucks has been an inspiration for me and my wife since we first met him back in 2018. His passion for the ministry, his deep knowledge of God's word and his easy-to-approach character were some of the virtues that really touched and blessed us. He is one of the main reasons that, after finishing my MA programme in 2020, I saw a real change in me and my ministry. God bless you, Dr. Mel Loucks, and may He continue to bless and educate people in ministry through you and your life."

---

### By Rev. Alemekezeke Kenneth Phiri (MA, 2016-2018 ), Malawi

"Dr. Melvin Loucks is an astute theologian, a man of faith, and totally devoted to God. The two years I spent under his tutelage I found out that his clear explanation of Reformed Theology opened my understanding of scriptures. Dr. Loucks helped me to possess two qualities; solid biblical scholarship and a fervent heart of devotion for God."

## By Pastor Harka Khadka (MA, 2006-2008), Nepal

"Dr Mel Locks who taught me in Master in Theology. He was such a loving and dedicated lecturer. His depth of theological knowledge and lives impacted me and whole Nepali students. Nepali leaders who went through theological education in ITS are making big impact."

## By Fonjoh, Philip Kindong (ThM, 2015-2017), Cameroon

"Professor Melvin Loucks is a professor I admired and love to sit learning from him. His teachings are always focused on ministering to the whole person and are Christ centered. His love for International Students is seen in the way he interacts with them while at ITS and after graduation. I have learned from him to be focus, consistent and balance as I pursue academic and ministry."

## By Bako OM Dogari (DMin, 2018-2020), Ghana

"Dr. Mel Loucks, apparently always simplistic in superficies, is an astute academician cum theologian with a prodigious and meticulous personality, who is prolifically gifted with a rare enigma particularly in the way he handles 'Ethics and Social Issues' a Course he taught me at ITS, my Alma-Mater. His combination of wisdom and experience does not betray his copious but softly spoken explications of ethical issues as if from his memoriter, but always had a flow in making ludic conclusions on issues for which most of us as his students, found illuminating, insightful and convincing enough. Thanks Professor Loucks, for making such an impact into my life"

## By Fitsum Tsige (DMin, 2018-2020), Ethiopia

"I have never seen a theology professor who takes his call very seriously like Dr. Mel Loucks. Despite the size of the class, whether to one or many he is always well prepared and delivers his lesson so beautifully. The flow of his thought is incredibly fascinating. I was blessed to be part of this generation and to benefit from his incredible knowledge."

Dr. Mel Loucks and his wife Linda

# PART VI

# HISTORY OF ITS

# ITS HISTORY & TIMELINES

## International Theological Seminary: A Brief History

by Mya Mansoor

During the 1970s, as the Korean immigrant population in Los Angeles steadily grew, numerous churches began sprouting. As a result, many pastors and elders of these newly established Korean churches felt an increasing need to form seminary schools for their men and women of faith. "Dr. John Eui-Whan Kim, a church historian, professor, and a pastor of a fast-growing church, was one of those church leaders." While others aimed to establish seminary schools for Korean immigrants in their native language, Dr. Kim was motivated by the idea of world mission and resolved to devote a seminary for students from developing countries. Dr. Kim sought to focus on Christian ministry and leadership through spiritual formation, academic excellence, and personal transformation for people of all nations. After sharing his vision with church elders and ensuring their support, International Theological Seminary was established in 1982 as a venture of faith. Since its inception, ITS has remained faithful in its mission of preparing leaders for the global church to this day.

In its early years, the forefront of development for the International Theological Seminary was primarily physical. From generating public recognition to attract students, to securing faculty and a more permanent location, to creating its own academic library, there was much to be done. By 1983, just one year after its founding, ITS moved from its first location at William Carey University at the U.S. Center for World Missions to a new campus on S. Virgil Avenue, which was found and purchased by Dr. Tong. This move was a significant milestone for ITS, as it allowed the school to expand its program offerings and accept more students. Dr. John H. Kromminga, former president of Calvin Theological Seminary in Grand Rapids, was elected as the second president of ITS in 1984. For the next six years under Dr. Kromminga's presidency, student enrollment steadily increased. When Dr. John E.

Kim was re-established as president in 1990, ITS had already begun showing signs of outgrowing the S. Virgil campus. "When I began teaching at ITS in 1984, we had less than twenty-five students. I can remember some of our early graduation ceremonies in which as few as three or four students graduated. Now we have over eighty students and in May... over thirty students will march in our graduation ceremonies," said Dr. Mel Loucks in a 1993 edition of Network, ITS's former newsletter. That same year, ITS relocated to a new campus in El Monte, but due to continued rapid growth, the following year on October 2, 1994, ITS dedicated a new facility on Wilshire Avenue in a "service of praise and worship". This location became known as the Wilshire Campus, which included an auditorium, several individual classrooms, a student center, and an official library*, which had expanded to over 16,000 physical volumes, with an additional 5,000 books on microfilm and microfiche. "[T]he 1994/95 school year began with record enrollment," with a total of 106 students. With ITS settling into a new campus, growing its student body, and expanding its academic library, Dr. John E. Kim felt called to accept the invitation he'd received from Chong Shin University in Seoul to serve as their president in 1995.

In his stead, Dr. Joseph Tong was elected to serve as ITS's fourth president. During Dr. Tong's tenure as president, ITS underwent tremendous development because of his commitment to academic excellence and spiritual formation. Just three years after Dr. Tong was elected, ITS "...received the full accreditation by the ATA (Asia Theological Association) in 1998." This achievement highlighted ITS's commitment to meeting the highest academic standards and provided students with the assurance of receiving an education of the highest quality. By late 2003, just ten years after having moved to Wilshire, ITS began preparations to relocate to El Monte. The move to the El Monte campus was completed in early 2004. Two years later, the seminary received "full accreditation by the ATS (Association of Theological Schools in the US and Canada) in 2006." Due to this achievement, ITS grew to international renown for its mission education and variety of degree programs offered.

Dr. Tong was the longest-serving president in the school's history, from 1995- 2008. "After Dr. Tong's retirement from ITS in 2008, Dr. See Nam Kim was appointed to serve as the fifth president of ITS from June 2008- December 2009. Due to Dr. Kim's resignation, Elder Calvin Lee was appointed by the board as Interim President between January and May 2010." Dr. Mel Loucks served as ITS's sixth president from June 2010 to December 2013. Following his retirement, Dr. James Lee was appointed as the seventh and current president of ITS in January of the following year.

Under Dr. James Lee's presidency, ITS began expanding its offerings and services in order to better prepare students for ministry and leadership in a rapidly changing world. "Along with providing them an affordable theological education...students develop self-sustainable business models they can implement in their ministries when they graduate." This vocational work initiative recognizes the importance of equipping students with practical skills, which allows them to serve their communities effectively and sustainably.

Additionally, ITS moved to its current location in West Covina over the summer of 2019 and purchased its first and second homes for guest housing in late 2019 and early 2020. Both homes are located within a half-mile of the West Covina campus, which allows guests—whether alumni, missionaries, or prospective students—to be unencumbered with the challenges of finding affordable housing or transportation in the Los Angeles area.

In August of 2021, ITS also announced its offerings of online and hybrid classes to provide for students who are unable to come to the US for myriad reasons, from political unrest abroad to difficulties in obtaining work or student visas. This innovative approach of hybrid classes has provided ITS students with a more flexible and accessible means to pursue their education.

By providing training in vocational work, offering new amenities, and introducing hybrid classes, ITS prepares students to serve and lead in their communities with excellence and God's providence. "International Theological Seminary serves as a world-class training organization, equipping pastors and community leaders to transform their local communities into vibrant places of worship, mission, and justice." Combining innovative academia with a diverse campus community has allowed ITS to "graduate more than 1,000 students in all of its academic programs" over the past forty years. Since its founding in 1982, the core philosophy of ITS remains unchanged as it continues to pursue an ambitious vision for the future: preparing leaders for the global church.

Virgil Ave Campus

**1982**
International Theological Seminary is founded by ITS' first president Dr. John E. Kim. ITS begins its first class at William Carey University in Pasadena, CA

**1983**
ITS moves from William Carey University in Pasadena, CA to S. Virgil Ave Campus

**1984**
- Dr. John H. Kromminga is appointed the 2nd President of ITS (1984-1990)
- Dr. Mel Loucks begins teaching
- Less than 25 total students at ITS

**1989**
ITS Newsletter Network makes its first appearance in September

**1990**
Dr. Kim serves as the 3rd President. (1990-1995)

**1991**
ITS (purchases and) begins renovation plans for El Monte campus

**1992**
- ITS' 10th Anniversary
- Dr. Fred Cheung is invited to teach at ITS for the first time by Dr. Joseph Tong
- Dr. Tong is Executive Vice President of ITS

**1993**
- ITS' largest class to date, with more than 80 students
- ITS' largest graduation class to date, with a total of 35 students graduating on May 21, 1993. The ceremony was held at Chinese Evangelical Free Church in Monterey Park at 7:30pm
- ITS prepares to move to El Monte campus over summer. "...for many friends of ITS who have loaned us money for a period of two years (1991) in order to complete the renovations on the new campus building."
- ITS address after September 1993 is 3215-3225 N. Tyler, El Monte CA 91731

EL Monte Campus

**1994**
- ITS Choir Program gave a marvelous concert coupled with a cultural program at L.A.C.P.C. It was the first program done by ITS and was well received
- ITS announces it will move to a new campus on 1600 Wilshire Blvd in the fall of 1994. "Dr. John E. Kim, president of ITS announced that some of the people at L.A.C.P.C had negotiated and purchased a large three-story building at the corner of Union and Wilshire Blvd in Los Angeles. The structure was an office building and is now undergoing the necessary alterations to make it suitable for the ITS campus
- Dedication service for Wilshire was held on October 2, 1994. Choir from Los Angeles Korean Christian Presbyterian Church (L.A.C.P.C.) Dr. Ananda Perera conducted a song-service, Dr. John E Kim read 1 Corinthians 6:19-20, Dr. Samuel Kim translated his father's speech into English, Dr. Mel Loucks gave closing benediction

Wilshire Campus

# ITS GENERAL TIMELINE

Dr. John H. Kromminga

## 1994 (continues)

- Library is moved from El Monte to 1600 Wilshire over Thanksgiving break, thanks to assistance from student and faculty volunteers
- Mrs. Edna Perera has moved from school office position to cataloging library books in the Bib-base system. ITS Field Education program is created
- Dr. Fred Cheung is Vice President of Development and Advancement ITS
- Dr. Mel Loucks has been serving ITS for 11 years and is now joining with full faculty status and will function as Assistant Dean and Faculty Secretary
- Dr. John H. Kromminga passes away
- Dr. See Nam Kim is now joining with full faculty status and will serve as Dean of Students
- Dr. Carl Kromminga is visiting to teach for the Fall Quarter
- ITS Cultural Night, October 29th at Monterey Park Chinese Evangelical Free Church
- Record enrollment of 106 students (school year 94-95)

## 1995

- On February 1st, 1995 at the close of chapel service, pres. Dr. John E Kim and vice president Dr. Joseph Tong recognized and presented a plaque of appreciation to Mrs. Choi Young Ae and Mr. Fred Hu for their dedication and generosity to ITS for gifting each over $100,000 for endowment and scholarship funds." Mr. Fred Hu also volunteered to be the internal auditor preparing financial reports and tax forms, while Mrs. Choi Young Ae provided dinners every year for the prospective graduates
- Feb 2, 1995, Mrs. Claire Kromminga, widow of late president Dr. John Kromminga passes away
- Dr. John E. Kim leaves ITS to take post as president of Chong Shin University in Seoul, South Korea. He is appointed as Chancellor of ITS and continues his support from abroad
- Dr. Joseph Tong is elected as the 4th President. (post Feb 1995- June 2008).
- 28 ITS graduates spring 1995. Graduation ceremony held at the Los Angeles Christian Presbyterian Church
- Development of the ITS library wa s a major highlight in the first year in the new ITS building in the 1994-1995 school year with 16,000 books, with additional 5,000 on microfilm/ microfiche added
- Dr. Fred Cheung will join ITS full time in Nov 1995 and provide assistance in development and teaching
- Dr. Ananda and Mrs. Edna Perera retire from the positions of administrator and executive secretary of the seminary. The two of them primarily handled the library move/ organization
- Mrs. Lin Ai Chu is coming in as librarian starting the fall semester

Dr. John E. Kim

Wilshire Campus Library

## 1997

Dr. John E. Kim (founder) visits, gives speech at opening ceremony for spring semester

## 1998

ITS receives full ATA accreditation (Asia Theological Association)

**2000**
Dr. Tong elected Chairman of the Board. He has temporarily taken over the Chair of Practical Theology

**2003**
ITS announces official move to El Monte campus

**2004**
ITS completes move to El Monte campus in late January/early February

**2006**
ITS receives full accreditation of ATS (Association of Theological Schools in US & Canada)

**2008**
- Dr. Tong retires
- Dr. See Nam Kim is appointed the 5th President (June 2008- Dec 2009)

**2009**
Dr. See Nam Kim resigns from presidency in December

**2010**
- Dr. E Kim passes away on May 10th, 2010
- Elder Calvin Lee is appointed as Interim President (Jan-May of 2010)
- Dr. Mel Loucks is appointed as the 6th President in June 2010 (June 2010-December 2013)

**2012**
ITS celebrates 30th Anniversary

**2013**
Dr. Mel Loucks retires in December

**2014**
Dr. James S. Lee is appointed the 7th President as of January 1st

**2019**
- ITS moves to new and current campus in West Covina and purchases the first off-campus housing

West Covina Campus

**2020**
ITS purchases the second off-campus housing

**2021**
Hybrid classes are now available for '21-22 academic year, announced August 1st

**2022**
- ITS Launches Doctor of Intercultural Studies (DICS) Program, announced July 15th
- "Global Table" (Cultural Night) event, October 29th
- "ITS 40th Birthday Worship Service" event, November 6th

Global Table, October 29th 2022

# ITS PRESIDENT

## 1982 - 1984
Dr. John E. Kim

## 1984 - 1990
Dr. John H, Kromminga
(Deceased)

## 1990 - 1995
Dr. John E. Kim (Moved to Korea)

## 1995 - 2008
Dr. Joseph Tong (Retired)

## 2008 - 2009
Dr. See Ham Kim (Resigned)

## Jan. 2010 - May 2010
Elder Calvin Lee (Interim)

## Jun. 2010 - 2013
Dr. Melvin Loucks (Retired)

## 2014 - Present
Dr. James S. Lee (Current)